SOPHIE

The Sophie Tucker Story

MICHAEL FREEDLAND

THE WOBURN PRESS

First published 1978 in Great Britain by
THE WOBURN PRESS
Gainsborough House, Gainsborough Road,
London, E11 1RS, England

Copyright © 1978

ISBN 0 7130 0153 4

Phototypesetting by Saildean Limited
Printed in Great Britain by
T. J. Press (Padstow) Ltd., Padstow, Cornwall

SOPHIE

The Sophie Tucker Story

Also by Michael Freedland

AL JOLSON

IRVING BERLIN

JAMES CAGNEY

FRED ASTAIRE

As she's remembered best (1950)

For

TED SHAPIRO

who knew her for 45 years

Acknowledgments

Thanks for help in preparing this book must begin and end with Ted Shapiro, who for almost a half century was Sophie Tucker's right hand—the one on the piano keys. In a series of lengthy sessions he allowed me to dig deep into the recesses of his memory and so get beyond the Sophie Tucker legend. Thanks, too, must go to people like George Burns, Max Bygraves, Cyril Berlin and Sammy Cahn, who provided memories and comments. Valuable help was also provided by the librarians of the London Evening Standard; the British Library; and the Lincoln Centre Library in New York, custodians of everything ever written about Sophie Tucker and of her own correspondence, on which I was privileged to be able to draw heavily. I would thank too, for their help in research, Ruth Mindel and Alva Robson, and for her speedy, incredibly accurate typing, Beryl Whiteman.

MICHAEL FREEDLAND

Contents

Illustrations

Pictures from the Sophie Tucker collection, and from Ted
Shapiro.

The Last of the Red-Hot Mamas

She couldn't really sing—not in a way that would turn your muscles to jelly or have you leaving the theatre humming her big number.

When Sophie Tucker shouted "Some Of These Days", it wasn't easy to decide whether she was really sighing over an unrequited love or simply laughing at the idea of a man ever finding her the least bit enticing. Even when she first went into show business, it was only with the help of an obliging whalebone industry that she could appear to be more than just a mass of superfluous flesh.

She called herself The Last of the Red Hot Mamas and sang about her Yiddisher Mama—yet there was little that was maternal about this brash figure. How could there be when she constantly sang risqué songs about men whose bedroom performances rarely matched the billing they had given themselves?

Her whole life was a paradox, a mass of contradictory stories which, when reassembled and reassessed, make up a larger-than-life figure, whose own ambition and success was matched only by her generosity.

Most of those who worked with Sophie Tucker and knew her during a phenomenally long career speak of her with affection if not love. To others, her memory is clouded by events and experiences that even now bring shudders up and down their spines.

She was part of a generation that produced entertainers who sparkled, rather than mere stars who shone. She was part of an age in which entertainment meant vaudeville and vaudeville represented sleazy rat-infested theatres and uncomfortable "theatrical" boarding houses.

But from this came an industry which today is big business in the living rooms of homes in almost every country of the world. Sophie Tucker saw the changing face of that business—from vaudeville stage to television screen —and became part of that story. She dispensed her own brand of entertainment as though it were a life-giving elixir—and to many it was.

A king, a queen, a Prince of Wales, a collection of Presidents became devoted admirers of a woman who lacked many of the accepted social graces. Soldiers in two world wars begged her for pictures that might have had more effect at the business end of a gun than on the wall of a barrack room.

How? Why? The explanation, hopefully, will emerge from the following pages. But there is a short answer to be going on with: She was one of the greatest personalities the entertainment world has produced.

2

Some of These Days

The tale of the big star born in a hostile foreign land who finds success and glory in the New World with a new name is familiar enough. To make them credible, there are always a few essential differences which serve to separate one story from the other right from the beginning. In Sophie Tucker's particular case the differences came before the beginning.

It started, in fact, when Private Kalish of the Imperial Russian Army decided he had had enough of military life and that the time had come to desert. It was about 1887 and Kalish was a young man with responsibilities—a son of two and a wife who was only 15 years older than their child.

Now, escaping from this part of Southern Russia was tricky enough for any man in the Czar's uniform. If he were caught, a youngster could consider himself lucky to leave Siberia before he was 70. More likely, he would end up facing a firing squad or left hanging from a tree on the snow-covered outskirts of his native village—as an example to any of his fellow conscripts who might think of wanting out, too.

Kalish and his child wife were products of the "shtetl", the small village that consisted largely of enough craftsmen to keep life going and their wives and their children. And always a rabbi to guide the destiny of the poverty-stricken Jewish community who made up the bulk of the population.

3

However hard it was for a soldier to escape in those dying days of the reign of Czar Alexander Alexandrovich, it was harder still to contemplate taking his wife and baby with him. For Kalish, the problems were greater than even that—his wife was pregnant again.

He was not the first in the shtetl to think about leaving. For years words had been whispered about a new promised land which beckoned, if not with milk and honey like the one for which the men yearned in their prayers three times a day, certainly with material wealth on a scale they could not imagine in Russia. It was called America.

Over the years a pattern had emerged. The men of the family would go first—bribing their way across towns, villages and fields with a few kopeks for a policeman here, a rouble or two for a customs inspector there. When they reached America, had thrown off their old-country clothes and habits and had begun making their living—usually over a sewing machine in an airless sweatshop—they would send a few dollars back to the shtetl and with them a message to their wives: "Come".

Kalish sent his message quicker than most. Fortunately for him, his wife, now—to use the terminology of the day —heavy with child, was also quicker witted than other women of her age and background. The note was not signed in the usual way, but by . . . "Charles Abuza".

It was several weeks before the harrassed young woman heard the reason for her husband's change of identity. It seems that he had only just escaped the clutches of the Russian secret police before teaming up with a sickly Italian gentleman who was also about to start a new life in America. The Italian, however, was not to see the Statue of Liberty, that symbol standing in the mouth of the Hudson River which represented all the cherished hopes of the country's immigrants. On the journey over he died. Kalish, never certain in his own mind that the secret police would abandon hope of catching up with him, decided to take on the man's identity.

So it was an Italian who only spoke Russian and Yiddish whose name went into the card index files on Ellis Island, the first staging post for these new Americans. If the

4

newly-named Abuza's wife Jenny was not as excited as he at the story when they finally caught up with each other, there was good reason. She had had quite an adventure herself.

She and her son Philip were riding over a mud road in an old, rickety horse-drawn cart when the young woman's body suddenly was racked with pain—a pain that came for a moment, disappeared and then came back again. Each time, the pain was more severe, and came quicker than the one before. She was in labour.

A tap on the driver's shoulder and a whispered word in Yiddish brought the cart to a stop. She was helped down to the road followed first by her pathetic collection of bundles and then by little Philip.

She never knew the exact location of that spot. She wasn't even sure if she was in Russia or Poland. And the date it happened was as much a mystery as the name of the place—which partly explains why birthdays were such complicated things to arrange for Russian Jews of that time.

All that this frightened young woman did know was that she and Philip were totally alone on a deserted country road. There was, however, a farmhouse close by.

Women of her stock had an instinctive sense of pride which told them never to ask strangers for anything. This time, however, had to be an exception. She knocked on the farmhouse door and when the farmer's wife received her, the look on the girl's face and the bulge around her stomach spoke the only language that was necessary.

Mrs. Kalish, soon to become Mrs. Abuza, was gently led to a small, clean room, and laid down on a feather bed. Minutes later, the cries of a healthy baby girl announced to the world the birth of the future Sophie Tucker. For the moment she was first little "Sophela". If her mother thought of surnames at the time, Sophie Kalish.

The strange thing about the change of name to Abuza was just how quickly it was accepted. From the moment he landed in America, Sophie's father regarded himself as Mr. Abuza. To his wife, once she had acclimatised herself to her first look at this new world, he was simply "Papa". His wife he called "Mein Dolly".

For the first eight years of her life, Sophie Abuza lived

in Boston. Years later, she was to say, "I ain't learned my English at Harvard". Her syntax and her sex made the statement superfluous, but she was getting an education of sorts—seeing her mother either at the stove cooking, or on her knees scrubbing. The times were hard and left their mark on young Sophie—a mark she carried to her dying day. One day her mother was so bamboozled by crying children —a second son, Moses and a daughter Annie had been added to the family circle now—that she sat Sophie down on a red hot poker. The line made by this instrument of torture was to be branded on her backside for life.

In 1896, the Abuza clan moved house—to Hartford, Connecticut, a place that seemed to symbolise small-town America but which in later years was to become the insurance capital of the world.

Papa Abuza decided that the time was ripe to stop working for other people and to open his own restaurant. But it would be their own kind of restaurant—in a district made up of their own people. For Hartford, not a stone's throw from New York in modern travel terms, was already becoming something of an overspill town for the ghettos of the Lower East Side. And it was in the Lower East Side of Hartford, in the town's new Jewish quarter, that the Abuzas' kosher restaurant opened with a speciality of the house—no meal would cost more than 25 cents.

For that quarter there was a choice of traditional Jewish-style delicacies—from pickled herring or chopped liver through bean soup or borscht to veal, pot roast or hamburgers.

News of this value-for-money deal had spread throughout the town, and before long the Abuzas were expanding their bill of fare—with a special 50-cent dinner that boasted steak, chicken or duck, a choice of potatoes (boiled, mashed or fried), green peas, carrots or sauerkraut and deserts that ranged from noodle and carrot pudding and potato kugel to prunes and lemon meringue pie.

When Abuza had really settled down, he started offering glasses of whisky at 25 cents a nip and beer at 15 cents. For youngsters and abstemious wives, there was also soda pop.

6

Business never actually thrived, but the wolf of starvation was kept from the door—after all, how could they starve with all that food around? If they had no customers, they could always eat the stock.

As things turned out, there were always customers and before long, a particular kind of customer, too. Word of the magic Jewish culinary delights offered by the Abuzas spread along the Yiddish theatre circuit—so that Hartford became a much sought-after booking for the players who would tour one town after another. Jacob Adler, the Tomashefskys—Boris and his wife—and Madam Lipsky would make a bee line for the place after each show.

These performers spread the word in the profession, too. Before long, the touring vaudevillians would go there, too. In particular, a pair of comedian brothers called Willie and Eugene Howard.

Sophie was particularly impressed by these two men. They would carry the patter of their Broadway act to the tables at the restaurant. The people around them laughed so much that their soup got cold—a big sin in a kosher restaurant.

The young Abuza girl helped in the business. She'd scrub floors, wash dishes and wait at table. She became so expert a waitress that she could balance a tray bearing a dozen different dishes at a single time—and remember who ordered what. "I never spilt as much as a drop of cheese on anybody," she remarked a couple of years afterwards. "I was the whole cheese at our joint."

As she got older, her mother's feet began to hurt so Sophie had to spend more and more time in the kitchen. It was to have a disastrous effect on her school work.

Previously, she had been noticed as a bright pupil at the Brown School at Hartford, particularly by the principal Charles Ames who regarded her as a girl with "personality"—the meaning of which she spent weeks trying to discover.

She was popular at school, too—even if she was already being teased as the "fat girl". Friends like John Sudarsky, Minnie DeNezzo, Willie Gross and Herman Weissman looked to Sophie to help them with their homework. But

7

those days didn't last. The pressures of the Abuza restaurant
kitchen got too much and after she arrived at school she
would fall asleep at her desk—only to wake up with a start
when a teacher deliberately dropped a heavy book in front
of her and to doze off yet again minutes later and then
awaken after a thump around the ear.

At the end of a day at school, she would be back at the
restaurant, massage her mother's feet, prepare more dishes
for the customers and carry them over to their tables.

She also took it upon herself to broaden her sphere of
activities—by singing to the customers. Even with hands that
dish-washing had made as red as the beetroot used for the
restaurant borscht, she had begun to fancy herself as a girl
with talent. She was certainly an extrovert.

When the place was filled with the vaudevillians whom
she had secretly come to admire—in one evening the tiny
café could be accommodating the then magic names of Sam
Bernard, Sam Harris and Webber and Fields—she would
gently slide into one of the popular songs of the day. Her
favourite was "Oh, Mr. Greenback". The pianist from the
nearby Poli Theatre, Harry Tighe, was a regular, too, and if
the customers would shout for the "fat girl" to sing for them,
she would go into the "Mr. Greenback" number before any
other.

She was serving the Howard Brothers with their favourite dish of gefilte fish and boiled potato one Friday night,
when Willie Howard pulled her to his side. "You gotta swell
voice, kid," he told her. "You ought to go to New York."

The Howards doubtless promptly forgot the conversation, but Sophie didn't. When she sneaked out of the
restaurant for an occasional evening off, it was to the Poli or
one of the other local vaudeville houses that she went.

The oil from the footlights and the sweat from the
audience may have lent an unpleasant air to the theatre for
such a young girl, but to her it held all the joys and the
temptations that she knew it would. "One day," she told her
sister Annie, "one day I'm going to be a vaudeville star."

All her mother said when she heard the statement was
"Sophie Abuza!" She pronounced the name in such a loud
voice that the words she didn't actually say came out equally

strong and clear. The stage was going to be no place for a nice Jewish girl.

By now, Sophie had found a name for the job she did—she was a "kitchen mechanic." It meant that everything that went wrong in the kitchen fell to Sophie to sort out. Then when she left school, the kitchen mechanic went into business 18 to 19 hours a day, seven days a week.

As she scrubbed the tables and sorted out the day's cutlery, she dreamed of seeing her name on the easels outside the vaudeville theatres—electricity had not yet brought to Hartford the joy of seeing a name actually in lights. As she served plates of noodle soup to the stars, she imagined she was sitting down with them—talking shop and mentally adding up her own week's takings. At night, she calculated the number of maids who would be bringing in the flowers that arrived after each performance.

She spent two years dreaming those dreams—and sorting out the problems in the restaurant business at the same time. When her mother became ill with diabetes, she did all the cooking by herself. When Mrs. Abuza went to New York for one of the first experimental injections of insulin, she was in charge again. By the time she was 16, she was also able to use some influence on her father—who by now had become something of a soft touch for every sponger who walked the streets of Hartford. There was little Sophie could do to stop him giving away what little money he had, but her mother had found the answer—she would empty his trouser pockets at least twice a day and dole him out enough for what expenses she thought he could legitimately incur.

He wasn't just a soft touch for local spongers, but also for con men. On one occasion, he was persuaded to sell up the restaurant and take over another in New York. The day he saw the Manhattan place for the first time, it was filled to overflowing with dozens of customers. He didn't realise that every one of them had been planted there by the vendors specially for his benefit. It took another two years before he could build up his old Hartford restaurant again.

Soon after the move back to Hartford, Abuza's establishment was all but destroyed by fire. A poorly-paying business that catches alight is also likely to have an unpleasant effect on the insurance company. So it was Sophie, now weighing something like 140 lb but who was still only 16 years old, who had to sort it out with them.

"It was an honest fire," she begged the assessor and resorted to a habit that was later to pay big dividends on the stage. She burst into tears. The man's heart melted and the Abuzas were back in business—this time concentrating most of their efforts on a delicatessen counter.

But there were still floors to scrub and Sophie, people believed, was well cushioned to take on the role—despite the evident problem of once getting down on her knees, finding it difficult to get up again.

Like 30 million housewives and a few hundred thousand kitchen maids, Sophie thought of other things as she washed the floors to a shine—and sang as she did so. Not loud stage songs, but soft melodies which in those days were as easily passed from one person to another as the common cold. A name for that sort of singing had already found its way into the language—crooning.

Poli's Theatre became more and more a Mecca for Sophie. If she could persuade a friend to go with her, the Abuzas didn't mind. If she went alone, they tut-tutted about her being a nice Orthodox Jewish girl and it wasn't really right. More than anything, they were worried about her morals. The theatre girls who called in at the restaurant wore blouses that seemed to be exposing as much of their breasts as they hid, and that was the sort of blouse Sophie begged her mother to be allowed to wear.

If nice Jewish girls ever became nuns, Sophie would have been on her way to the nearest convent there and then. Fortunately for her, they never—or at least rarely—did.

Sophie also had a will as strong as her muscles and an ambition as big as her hips. She went to matinées at Poli's and once more she dreamed. Reality usually came along in the shape of Harry Tighe, who delighted in chasing her all the way home and being rewarded with a clandestine kiss.

After a time, Harry had competition—a smart young man who looked as though he were made for better things than merely driving a pair of horses for a brewery. Sophie thought so, at any rate. His name was Louis Tuck.

10

Mama and Papa Abuza did not notice anything particularly odd the day that Sophie put on her cleanest blouse and
combed her long golden hair just that little bit more
carefully than usual. As always, they were talking about
business and, no doubt, whether there was any sense in
raising the price of their 25-cent gefilte fish meals.

The Abuzas did begin to worry, however, when Sophie
failed to return home at her usual time—and she was almost
never late. For 15 minutes, Papa paced the shop floor and for
another 15 the street outside. His sigh of relief when she
eventually appeared three hours later echoed round the
restaurant.

The fact that Louis Tuck was with her didn't seem to
have any importance to begin with. Except that it was Louis
who spoke first. He could see that Sophie's parents were
about to kill him with their looks and he was a great believer
in the dictum that the best form of defence was attack.

"Listen," he said, "we were married this afternoon."
They were late getting back because the civil ceremony had
taken place at Holyoke, Mass. The Massachussets marriage
licensing laws were easier than those in Connecticut.

It had not been an easy statement for Tuck to make. It
was certainly much harder to receive. To the Jewish parents
of a girl "with prospects", marriages were not merely made
in heaven, they are also arranged in the front parlour. And
not only had Sophie married a man whom they hardly knew,
they didn't know his parents either. The worst sin of all was
that there had been no marriage broker—the "shadchan"
who with his untidy umbrella as his badge of office was
always brought into "decent" marriages.

Probably at that moment the Abuzas wished they had
stayed behind in Russia. Enduring 30 years' conscription in
the Czar's army was an honourable thing to do if you had no
alternative. But a marriage in City Hall? It was a disgrace for
any girl. For the Abuzas it represented a blight on the family
name.

As it was with all the big decisions, it was probably
Mama who spoke first. She and her husband endeavoured to
decipher the crisp marriage licence that had just been
awarded by the town of Holyoke, then they huddled together

11

and agreed after a lengthy discussion in Yiddish that mother had made up their minds.

No one, but no one, was going to know of this scandal—but, at the same time, who were the Abuzas (of borscht and blintzes fame) to fight City Hall? Legally married in the eyes of Teddy Roosevelt they were. In the eyes of God, they were not. So there had to be a new wedding —with a rabbi to read the marriage contract, a cantor to recite the blessings and a wine glass for Louis to shatter as a symbol of the break with his life as a single man.

Mama still shook her head as she thought about it. But, she must have reasoned, too, he was at least a Jewish boy.

That night, as Sophie recalled in her autobiography "Some of These Days", she scrubbed the floors singing "I'd Leave My Happy Home For You-oo-oo."

Since her mother had wisely suggested that now that she had made her bed she had to lie on it—but alone—the wedding had to be quick. It was—and with none of the trimmings missing. The family were, after all, in the catering business, so it was easier for the Abuzas than most.

Just as easily and as much according to plan, Sophie realised she was pregnant. She carried on working in the restaurant but getting down on all fours was even more difficult now than it had been before. In the first few months she felt so sick that the aromas of the restaurant were positively unbearable for her. As the nine months drew to their close, she adopted the traditional pose of "ladies in waiting" of the time and took to her bed. Louis, meanwhile, took to staying out late—he was never happy about sharing the Abuzas' flat although he had little option but to do so. He gambled and the beer smells with which he was frequently adorned didn't all come from the brewery dray that he drove.

Sophie was 17 when her baby was born—the same age that her mother had been when she herself made her very first entrance on that road to Poland. The baby was a boy whom she called Albert. But Albert immediately became Bert and, seemingly for ever, Bert was to be called simply "Son".

Bert was less than two years old when his father left

home for good. It might reasonably be thought that at such times a mother would realise her responsibility to her baby and go out to work to make enough money to feed them both.

Sophie pondered that point to herself—and then came to a rather different conclusion. She could appease her conscience by an interesting piece of self-deception—and in the end, if things went well, her "Son" would be better off than ever.

One night about this time, the Howard brothers were back in Hartford and back eating gefilte fish at Abuzas' restaurant. They repeated their suggestion to Sophie that she ought to see New York. This time, they wrote her a note—addressed to music publisher Harry von Tilzer—commending "the fat girl with the big voice". Perhaps, they thought, she could become a song plugger in Tin Pan Alley, a street of dreams that in its time had as much turned into an avenue of nightmares as had Broadway. Perhaps, she decided, she could.

She told Annie what she wanted to do and left her younger sister little alternative but to stay home and hold her baby. Sophie may have told herself that she was going to make a fortune for the family. It would be the charitable thing to say that she did. But the Abuzas would not have let either Sophie or Bert starve. She may not have admitted that the prospect of the bright lights of Broadway was too much for a 19-year-old girl to resist. But she wasn't merely leaving Hartford, she was leaving Bert. You could have said she was deserting him.

Honky-Tonk

Any legendary statements about the streets of New York being paved with gold receded far into Sophie Tuck's memory after her first day in the city on her own. Doubtless, her conscience pricked her but she would have felt better had she been able to land that job with von Tilzer.

The music publisher, as did all the others in Tin Pan Alley in 1907, depended on his office as his shop window. There was no big record industry at the time and certainly there were no radio programmes to make a tune popular. It all depended on the publisher's ability to convince a performer to use one of his numbers in an act. The big acts got Mr. von Tilzer's personal attention. The smaller ones depended on the salesmanship of an underling—possibly a piano player, frequently a girl singer. And that was the problem before Sophie could open her mouth and prove to von Tilzer that she had a way with a song.

The girls he wanted had to have hips that made men's mouths drool, waists that defied all the laws of nature and busts that looked as though they had been carved by a sculptor. Sophie, she had to admit to herself, had none of these attributes. When she sat on a piano stool in one of the publisher's booths, she overflowed the piece of furniture generously.

This lady, said the publisher, could be good behind a

delicatessen counter, but selling songs? The male entertainers would be shuffling their way out of the office before
she had a chance to sing a note. What von Tilzer said may be
best summarised in that near hallowed phrase of the
theatrical audition, "don't call us, we'll call you".

She sat around in a seedy hotel room near 42nd Street
waiting for that call, but it never came. She tried to reason to
herself why, in fact, she was spending so much time in that
hotel room which must have cost her all of 35 cents a night.
The answer was pathetically real: She had packed her one
good dress, and it was raining heavily every day. If she got
the dress wet, then where would she be?

Finding her fortune, she called it, when she first stepped
on to that train at Hartford station. Now she was beginning
to be honest with herself. She had simply run away—and
back home at Hartford the Abuzas were beside themselves
with anguish. Running away they understood—after all, that
was precisely what they had done themselves less than 20
years before. But leaving a baby behind? That they couldn't
understand—and worst of all, it was difficult to justify to the
neighbours and to the customers.

Sophie had been collecting a nest egg ready for that day
when she would go fortune-hunting. Now it was disappear-
ing before her eyes. After a couple of weeks of this, she
decided to spend money only once a day—in the evening
and on enough food to keep her well. For the first time in
her life, Sophie was beginning to lose weight, but she didn't
feel good with it.

Even so, her pride was still partially intact—intact
enough, in fact, to write a letter home, promising that things
were going to get very exciting "some of these days". The
importance of that last phrase was then as lost on the Abuzas
as it was on Sophie herself.

There was, however, a perceptible change in the air. She
was so desperate the night she spent her daily allowance at
the Café Monopol on Eighth Street, that she asked the
proprietor if he would like her to sing. "Sure," he said, "Let
me see what you can do."

For his benefit she warbled "Mr. Greenback" and he
decided he quite liked what he heard. "What's your name,

honey?" he asked. She began to write: "Sophie Tuck . . ."
But something told her it didn't look right—perhaps because
she was no longer feeling so friendly towards Mr. Tuck.
"Sophie Tucker," she wrote on and the proprietor told her to
start singing straight away.

No matter how hungry the newly-named Sophie Tucker
was, she set her sights higher than the Monopol and being
paid in left-overs. She set about seeing New York. At a dive
in Chinatown called Nigger Mike's she sang a song handed
to her by one of its singing waiters, a curly-haired youngster
called Israel Berlin—he had changed his name, too. Origin-
ally, Israel Baline, a printer had recently misspelled it as
"I. Berlin" on the cover of his first songsheet and he liked
it that way. Before very long, Israel Berlin became Irving
Berlin.

From little China she graduated to New York's German
colony and to a beer cellar—or rathskeller as it called
itself—named the German Village. Everywhere she went,
she walked—it saved money and meant that she wouldn't be
without her 50 cents for dinner in the evening.

She had been recommended to try getting a job at the
place, but she might just have never got there. On the way,
round about 40th street, she saw something that previously
she had only heard talked about in very hushed tones. Girls,
who to a country hick like Sophie seemed to be exquisitely
dressed and showing just enough bare skin to be enticing,
were leisurely pacing up and down the street. This, she
considered, might be a good way of making a not too
difficult living. Sex, she believed, could be pleasurable—if
she kept control of herself—and there would then be plenty
of money to send home for Bert.

For that moment, she confessed not very long afterwards, her mind swayed—like the handbags being carried by
the tarts. The moment turned into several minutes. She
would make up that mind, she decided, when the first
"customer" made his approach. After all, if she didn't like
him, she'd just turn on a haughty expression.

The first approach came with a tap on her shoulder. She
froze, then whizzed around like a firecracker. "Yes," she
stammered—and realised she was facing a young policeman

who looked as though he might be as new to his beat as she was to hers.

"What are you doing here?" he asked—but the smile on his face indicated that he was not about to drive her instantly into the paddy wagon. "I wanna go on the stage," she blurted, still stammering as she did so. "Well, kid," he answered, "This ain't the stage."

Sophie's next words poured out without interruption: "I know. But I'm starving. I've got nowhere to sleep."

At which point, he marched Sophie off—not into the nearest precinct house but to his own home. His wife gave her some supper, a clean nightdress and showed her to their tiny spare bedroom. The next thing she remembered was falling asleep in a flood of tears and waking up next morning to find the young cop's wife asking what she would like for breakfast.

She never forgot that couple.

From the policeman's home, she went round more restaurants and got more jobs singing above the din of meals being served and trays being dropped. She also went into the German Village itself and then to a nearby establishment that she had been told was a "night club". She had heard of such places but had never seen one. Certainly she had never seen one like this.

Only seconds after walking into the place, she made her first big mistake. Ambitious singers were expected to line up and wait to be inspected by the club's owner, a man appropriately named Mr. Jumbo.

Sophie didn't do that, however. Her feet were giving her so much trouble that when she saw an empty table, she just sat at it, sprawling her legs out in front of her as she did so. When a man in a homburg hat sat next to her, she smiled politely and hoped that he would either go away or not notice the state of her feet—which by now had been separated from their shoes.

He didn't go away and the way he stared at her heaving bosom, it was easy to see that he wasn't interested in her feet either. He leaned over towards her and the whisky fumes emanating from his mouth seemed about to explode.

"How about it dearie?" he asked. "Shall we go upstairs now?"

17

That was the moment when Sophie Tucker realised what sort of a night club this was. Nobody called it a brothel but nobody had to, either. It was as bad as the street from which she had been so mercifully parted.

After having walked her feet off for yet another night, Sophie was in no mood to think of polite ladylike language. She let out a torrent of abuse at the man the like of which she herself had not heard since an irate vaudevillian told her father his chicken soup was cold.

She then burst into tears. This was a brothel without a madam and when Mr. Jumbo came up to see what the trouble was all about, he sounded sympathetic. Did she still want a job singing?

She told him that she did.

She knew now that she shouldn't sit at a table—ever. That would simply be advertising a commodity that was not for sale, or even for rent. If she wanted to sing, she would have to sit behind the rail on the platform which encircled the whole establishment and served as a stage.

The job didn't last long; she didn't want it to. But it gave her just a few cents to spend on things other than food. She bought a couple of dresses on hire purchase—and went to the theatre. The first show she attended had as one of the supporting acts a pianist called Harry Tighe. That made her feel better. She sat next to a comfortably dressed woman who dropped a programme. "Thank you," said the woman. "Thank YOU," said Sophie. And then she realised why she said it. She wanted to be talked to.

She was never to feel quite certain that anyone really did want to talk to her for her own sake. When they did, the appreciation could be embarrassing.

She still hoped, above all, to be embarrassed by the sound of applause that brought the roof down, but it didn't happen. If it were to come to pass, she would have to work for it. It was a man called Chris Brown who helped things along—although he didn't know it.

Brown was one of the innovators of something that became a hallowed institution in American vaudeville— "amateur nights". He agreed to give Sophie a chance to show what she could do, but there was always the penalty

18

for amateurs who strayed too far from accepted professional standards: the derision of an audience.

Promoters of these evenings were getting their "stars" simply for cash prizes, yet charged for admission. So the ticket-buying public knew what a bargain they offered the theatremen. If they liked an artist, their applause could win over the loudest group of customers who ever packed these smoke-filled auditoriums. But if they didn't ... then they jeered, shouted, threw fruit and were in a mood to start a public lynching. It was then that the proprietor came to the aid of his "talent"—with either a sandbag to put him out of his misery in one fell swoop or a hook to drag him into the wings.

That was what Sophie Tucker could have faced at the 125th Street Theatre in 1908. She handed the orchestra leader an envelope containing her three favourite songs —"All I Get Is Sympathy", "Why Was I Ever Born Lazy" and "Rosie, My Duskie Georgia Rosie"—and started to perform. Above the hubbub of the customers she detected Chris Brown's voice: "She's not my idea of a good-looking girl," he said. "She's too big and ugly."

It was like a red rag to a bull (changing the metaphor to the feminine gender wouldn't be fair to Sophie—and she was far from placid by that time). She had got to the theatre especially early that evening, had put on her best make-up and sat in the wings listening to careers being smashed by the audience's hammer blows. She knew that if she could survive that first number, she not only would be on the way to a life in show business, but also to winning the first prize—which that night was $100. She had never seen that sort of money in one lump before.

Brown said that she would only stand a chance if she put on blackface—which for a man was just that, a black makeup on his face. But Sophie wore a low-cut dress. So after a bottle cork was burned by a candle, the residue was applied liberally to her face, her arms and her cleavage.

The burnt cork got wedged into her ears and stained her head to the roots of her golden hair, but she persevered, determined to show this clever man that more came out of plain wrappings than just French postcards.

19

The "fat, ugly" girl got through the first number. More listened to the second one and by the time the third was under way, you could have heard a girl dropping the hat pin she was about to stick into the behind of the man then making a pass at her.

The $100 cheque was hers. So was an introduction to a man called Joe Woods, an agent. Woods found her work on the Park vaudeville circuit—known in the trade as "strictly small-time", but which was a good training ground for acts on their way up, and a steady if poor living for those who were either standing still or sliding their way down.

She was paid $20 a week, but a dollar was deducted every week towards the $25 Woods estimated to be the value of a white satin gown he pulled out of his stockroom cupboard and which he said Sophie needed to wear.

Now, she began to think, she might be able to make the family proud of her—perhaps raise enough money to send Bert away to school. She wasn't thinking about any ordinary school for her son. Somehow, she liked the idea of the smart uniforms worn by the boys in the American military academies. She was still a teenager herself and didn't bother to think about the ravages of military life—or even that the boy's grandfather had gone to America simply to escape military service. As in many other aspects of her life, this was to prove a bee in her bonnet that was never allowed to fly away.

Her first out-of-town stop was in her own state of Connecticut, at Meriden. But she decided not to go home to Hartford—she couldn't be sure how the old folks there would greet her. The money went home regularly every week—she took out a money order to send to her mother at the same time as the one that went to Woods towards the dress and his commission—but she knew what her running away had meant to the Abuzas and her conscience was still pricking her. One prayer ran through her mind—as much to make the family respect her as bring her wealth: "God, please make me a headliner".

The Park Circuit job folded with the coming of spring. So she had to find new work. It came via three names who were before very long to revolutionise show business on the far-distant West Coast: Nicholas Schenck, Marcus Loew and Adolph Zukor.

On New York's 116th Street, the men had opened one of America's first cinemas. There was room, they told Sophie, for a talented young singer like her—if she wanted to earn $16 a week. All she had to do was sing 20 times a day in between the movies. It didn't really seem like hard work.

Sophie felt success was within her grasp. She hadn't been so happy since the day she and Louis Tuck waltzed into City Hall.

As for Louis, she now barely thought about him. She worried about Bert for a time but then when her work became so all-engrossing, she let him slip from her mind, too. The one person for whom she did feel, however, was her father. She knew how he hated having his trouser pockets robbed and she hoped more than anything else that she would before long be able to restore what she took to be his now injured dignity.

With the thought in mind of one day proving to Hartford just how fast she was going to climb to greater things, she went into her nearest Woolworth store and made two purchases. One was the kind of scrapbook children used for anything from school projects to their first love letters. The second was a ledger, into which she scribbled details of her week's bookings, how many performances she was going to have to give each day—and how much she paid in commission.

The first page showed that in the week of November 23 1907 she was at the Manhattan Theatre New York, and that she only had to give 10 daily performances—and five per-cent of her $16 to her agent. The following week she was at the Bijou in Meriden—20 daily shows again. For the week of January 6, 1908 she was back at the Manhattan Theatre. That, she emphasised in her book, was a "picture engagement". There was obviously a sense of prestige in that work for her.

But the movie houses were just peepshows that had not yet outgrown the tag of being called "Nickelodeons". People were still prepared to spend hard-earned nickels on watching a man sneeze. If they saw a railway engine coming

21

towards them on the screen, there would be wholesale panic. Sophie Tucker's role in the midst of all this was to be rather like that of a male comedian in a nude show—the audience politely listened to his stories while waiting expectantly to see next a glance of nipple or even a flash of thigh.

Sophie was tolerated, but caused little excitement.

The tour continued—wherever anyone wanted to offer work to a big fat, ugly girl and listen to her singing coon songs. She was, however, developing a complex about her appearance. Maybe it was her restaurant background, but she always found it difficult to consider cutting down on food. So she bought herself an extra tight corset and tried to pin in the waist and push out the bust. Her hips didn't matter—fashions of the day accentuated a nice wide behind and she needed no help at all in that direction.

Throughout the country she tramped, on and off trains, carrying her own luggage in all weathers, from one theatrical boarding house to another. At one of these houses she actually paid for her own mattress. As she said at the time: "Although the hearts of these theatrical landladies are soft, their mattresses are hard."

In the winter, she went round the vaudeville houses and played whatever dates she could get at the movie theatres that were beginning to mushroom throughout the South. In the summer, the lush bookings were at the state and county fairs—where not all the men reserved their hands simply for feeling the vegetable produce. Whether or not she succumbed to their advances is no longer important. She has said that at the time she was "still a completely inexperienced Hartford girl".

Certainly, she didn't tell any admirer—and there were undoubtedly those who liked their women big and cuddly—that she was a married woman or that she had a young son. She hardly remembered it herself sometimes; at others she was stricken by remorse. But she never let it stand in the way of her career prospects. Only once in two years did she go back to Hartford—to find that although Annie was doing a marvellous job for Bert and her brother Philip had married one of her own old schoolfriends, the air was distinctly electric. The family told her they understood—but

KLAW&ERLANGER
MANAGERS'EXCHANGE

MARC KLAW
A. L. ERLANGER

NEW AMSTERDAM THEATRE BUILDING, 42ND STREET, NEAR BROADWAY

Representing the Principal Theatres and Attractions in the United States

CABLE ADDRESS
"Rosmarine"

CHARLES OSGOOD
Manager Booking Dept.

NEW YORK, ... Apr. 30/09 _____

Miss Sophie Tucker,
  "Gay New York" Co.,
    % Empire Theatre,
      Albany, N. Y.

Dear Miss Tucker:-
              I received your letter yesterday, and referred
it to Mr. Florenz Ziegfeld, Jr., who is getting up a summer entertainment for the Roof of our New York Theatre.   You will
probably hear from him.
                    Very truly yours,

                      Marc Klaw

n 168

THE WESTERN UNION TELEGRAPH COMPANY.
————INCORPORATED————
24,000 OFFICES IN AMERICA.   CABLE SERVICE TO ALL THE WORLD.

This Company TRANSMITS and DELIVERS messages only on conditions limiting its liability, which have been assented to by the sender of the following message
Errors can be guarded against only by repeating a message back to the sending station for comparison, and the Company will not hold itself liable for errors or delay
in transmission or delivery of Unrepeated Messages, beyond the amount of tolls paid thereon, nor in any case where the claim is not presented in writing within sixty days
after the message is filed with the Company for transmission.
This is an UNREPEATED MESSAGE, and is delivered by request of the sender, under the conditions named above.
ROBERT C. CLOWRY, President and General Manager.

RECEIVED at

6ny at cx 20pd

        Mv New York N Y May 6-7-09

Miss Sophie Tucker

           Empire Theatre, Holyoke Mass

Please wire me ansonia apartements NewYork what hour you

appear   also what matinee will you be near NewYork next week

        F Ziegfeld, Jr   945am

      1909 The news was that Mr. Ziegfeld wanted to see her

In 1915, the name Sophie Tucker sold the music

one neighbour was heard to use a particularly unpleasant word—"whore". It didn't sound any nicer then than it does today.

She was more determined than ever not to go back to Hartford till the town was ready to hang out the flags for her. As for Bert, Annie promised to bring him to New York to see her—and she did.

All the time, Sophie was concentrating on the act. She wasn't completely sure about the blackface makeup—audiences took a lot of convincing that she wasn't really a Negress. So, she developed a way of proving it to them. At the end of her show she would do an ever-so-genteel striptease. She only peeled off her long white gloves, but whether the customers' gasps were in anticipation of what they thought might be coming off next or simply from the shock of seeing that she really was white, can't readily be substantiated.

Sophie was developing a style that she would hone and perfect in future years. Every now and again she would insert the odd word in Yiddish—which caused howls of laughter up North but derision down South. The Jewish population of the towns below the Mason-Dixon Line didn't approve at all. "The chutzpah of that nigress usin' Jewish words," summed up many of their reactions. So Sophie peeled off her gloves earlier than usual—and if that didn't make the point, she began to wash the makeup off her face in their presence.

Sophie was sensible. It was all a good apprenticeship, and even if audiences didn't always appreciate what she was doing, the people in the theatre business understood. One day, someone suggested she go and see Tony Pastor.

Pastor was to vaudeville what Barnum and Bailey were to the three-ringed American circus. He had his own theatre on 14th Street—Tin Pan Alley itself—and it was there above all other places that song pluggers would go to sell their wares. Harry von Tilzer, who had been so remiss as to fail to see the potential offered by Sophie a year or so before, had employed Irving Berlin to sing his songs from the balcony of Tony Pastor's Music Hall before he went to Nigger Mike's.

Pastor was the Italian who was giving vaudeville an

23

entirely new look, running the Music Hall as though it were a conveyor belt of exciting talent. She wrote him a letter: "I'm a damned good black-faced singer with a voice that would shoot the bulbs off your lamps." He replied that she ought to pop in and see him.

It only seemed a daunting prospect when she finally did get in to see him. This was the man who had featured Eddie Foy and who had just given a start to a sad-eyed kid called Buster Keaton.

Now it was Sophie Tucker who was going to have to kill 'em in the aisles—if she could handle the big man; although physically Pastor was as small as Sophie was large. A movie film of their meeting would have looked like something out of the Marx Brothers—with the little man's head barely coming up to Sophie's bosom as she begged him for a job.

"How much do you want?" he asked her. To a girl who thought of $20 a week as big money, it was a daunting question. She thought quickly, did some sums in her head and splattered, "$50 a week." Pastor looked up at her with an air that said: "I've been here before, but I understand." "Will you take $40?" All Sophie could do was to hold herself back from suffocating him. Her kisses must have made him feel as though he had been out in the rain.

She wasn't given a particularly good spot on the bill—but to be at Pastor's was good enough, for starters. And she was noticed. *Variety* recorded the fact that she was a "One" artist—which meant that she performed before the first of three levels of backcloths while the scenery men behind juggled with getting the next set ready; the really big stars had the whole stage to themselves.

But this was a start and Sophie Tucker in blackface makeup, but without the wig that had always made her slightly grotesque, was going to make the most of it.

Rehearsals were due to begin at 9.30 on the first Monday morning of the show's week. Sophie checked in at 8 o'clock, was given the keys to her very own dressing room and the number-one "rehearsal check". Every performer turning up to rehearsal was given a "check" with a number on it—the fact that Sophie's was number one meant that she could perform whatever song she wanted to sing and that

24

every act after Sophie's would have to defer to her if they were planning to sing one of the same tunes. So far so good. The pianist she was given to accompany her wasn't so exciting. She had only been in the theatre for an hour or so before she realised that the best acts got a bright, jazzy player called Burt Green and the poorer ones a Mr. Brody—who Sophie decided had first seen the light of day with Noah and the Flood.

Vaudeville was known laughingly as the "Two-a-Day"—two shows a day, that is. Pastor's was a continuous performance from 2 o'clock in the afternoon—and that was when Sophie went on, to the sound of clumping feet and the lifting of unoiled seats. But somehow a miracle happened. Certainly, it seemed like one to a young girl who still prayed above all else to become a headliner.

The people quietened down, and although there were no microphones in those days, there was a discernible vibration echoing through the building.

"Not bad, kid," said Pastor when she came off, staring up as he did so at the lace embroidery at the top of her dress. For the next performance, he promised she would get a better spot in the bill—and yes, she could have the other piano player to accompany her.

This time, there was quiet right from the moment the sign went up on the easel at the side of the stage: "Sophie Tucker—Coon Shouter."

Variety's critic Walt—the theatrical Bible insisted on all its contributors having a) only first names and b) short ones at that—recorded that she was on stage for all of 14 minutes.

"Enthusiasm and evident delight in her work," he went on, "a routine of songs particularly adapted to her voice and style and a most agreeable stage presence brought Miss Sophie Tucker to a substantial hit. She sang the 'Cubanola Girl', 'Southern Rose' and 'Carrie', putting something new into all of them. . . . The young woman has a way of ingratiating herself at once and possessing not alone good looks, but magnetism to back it."

Well, perhaps Walt did need a new pair of glasses—or maybe he was sitting too far back in the theatre—but Sophie's real magnetism even early in 1909 was to make people forget that she was a "big, ugly girl". Certainly she worked as though there would never be a tomorrow.

At the end of that week at Pastor's a man called Guss Hill knocked on her dressing room door. "Would you like to be in Pittsburg on Monday?" he asked—and Sophie's tongue hung out. Pastor's existed as much to feed other theatres as to entertain audiences and if she couldn't get a job out of her week there, she might as well go back to scrubbing floors at Abuza's restaurant.

She had barely said "Yes, I will," before she realised what the man was offering. "The Gaiety Theatre at 8 o'clock, Monday morning." The only trouble was that the Gaiety wasn't vaudeville—it was burlesque, known in the trade as the "old burleycue" and on occasions by other less polite names.

Burlesque, in short, was not very nice. It was the place where men went to see girls wear pink tights. There were rumours that in some of the places young ladies did unexpected things with tassles.

She would have to sing in between sketches that usually managed to feature either a doctor and a nurse who wore a low-cut dress or a parson who wasn't entirely concentrating on his Book of Common Prayer.

And as vaudeville had circuits, burlesque had the "Wheel"—with towns and cities up and down the country each having their own burlesque house that served as a spoke to that wheel.

Sophie's experience in burlesque was another good lesson. Her material got very slightly risqué, but there was nothing sexy about what she did. When she sang, however, she managed to make the chandeliers in the better theatres positively shake.

She also earned $50 a week with a guaranteed eight-month run. Often she was working in the same town as another young burlesque entertainer called Fanny Brice. They became firm friends.

Sophie was with a company called the Gay Masquer-adors and she was all set to enjoy her eight months with the firm. But a week at Holyoke, Massachusetts—the place to which she and Louis had run away to get married—put an

26

end to that. In the audience there one night was Marc Klaw—the man who with Abe Erlanger had set up the Klaw-Erlanger vaudeville circuit and who together a few years before had masterminded an organisation that was not to see its like again until Al Capone moved in on Chicago.

No one, it seemed, ever liked a Broadway mogul. These men wouldn't give the time of day to a lowly performer or a stage hand. The Shubert Brothers had been known to route a train carrying artists with whom they were in dispute into a goods yard for two days—rather than agree to their terms. Florenz Ziegfeld used to send telegrams rather than sully his voice by asking an artist to come and see him. Yet it was Abe Erlanger who was known as the bad one. He was the villain's villain.

With Klaw he had convinced the theatre industry that it needed order in its business—an organisation which would make sure that artists would have a set route when they went on tour and not have to spend a week going from east to west for a three-day booking, only to find that the theatre had double-booked the act in the first place so as not to be left high and dry—and, yes, be told that the other act got here first. On the other hand, there were also managers who would double-book theatres. So there was always someone left either without a top star or a pair of performing seals.

Erlanger said he could sort out this chaos. But what he did, in fact, was to get his Klaws into everyone's business. With Marc Klaw and a few faithful lieutenants he started an organisation called, appropriately, the Syndicate—which controlled every act booked into every theatre in America. If you wanted out of the Syndicate you could get out—but as a result you either had no bookings or you had no acts, depending on which side of the footlights you did your business. There were no heavy-handed protection rackets involved. They weren't needed. Until Congress stepped in several years later, it was all perfectly legal.

Marc Klaw was in Holyoke that night as he went about his trade of organising everybody else's life. When he could manage it, he doubled with a bit of talent-spotting. When he saw young Sophie Tucker, he wondered whether perhaps he hadn't made an interesting find.

27

Klaw was looking for an interesting new attraction for the Ziegfeld Follies—run by Florenz Ziegfeld under Syndicate management—which had only just begun to make an impact on the Broadway scene. There had only been two Follies before—in 1907 and 1908—and Ziegfeld was determined that his .1909 version would be more exciting, more glittering than anything seen before.

Ziegfeld was already getting a reputation for extravagance—girls bathed in asses' milk on stage and only the best materials had to be used in their dresses. Never was a seam allowed to be out of place. He devoted himself to a crusade—called Glorifying the American Girl. So how did Sophie Tucker fit into this? Even the Follies had to have its "characters" and Klaw felt that Miss Tucker was as close to being one of those as anyone he had ever seen.

He came round to her dressing room after the show and asked if she were interested in Broadway.

There were no promises made—contrary to Sophie's own tale of being immediately told she could have $100 a week. It was not the last time she made events fit what she took to be an interesting story.

But Klaw kept an eye on her. When Sophie was playing in a show called "Gay New York" at the Empire Theatre, Albany, she wrote asking him whether he had yet made up his mind.

He replied: "I received your letter yesterday and referred it to Mr. Florenz Ziegfeld Jr., who is getting up a summer entertainment for the Roof of our New York Theatre. You will probably hear from him."

She did. It came a week later when she was back at the Empire, Holyoke. A telegram arrived at the stage door. After she had fumbled with the envelope and opened it, she saw the magic signature: F. Ziegfeld Jr. The message said: PLEASE WIRE ME ANSONIA APARTMENTS NEW YORK WHAT HOUR YOU APPEAR ALSO WHAT MATINEE WILL YOU BE NEAR NEW YORK NEXT WEEK.

That week at the Manhattan Theatre, Ziegfeld saw Sophie Tucker for himself—and liked what he saw. He decided she might even make the Follies.

The Follies

Ziegfeld was not just the most ambitious showman on Broadway, he was already on the way to being the most successful—and, with the help of Klaw and Erlanger, the only way he was going was up.

Yet even he had to wait through months of seemingly endless rehearsals, negotiations and arguments before he could get a show on the road. He signed contracts, agreed to pay his artists a certain sum of money—and then hoped all the pieces would fit into the right slots at the right time. If they didn't, Ziegfeld was not the only sufferer. With no powerful unions to back them, the artists waited penniless until the curtain went up.

As she waited, Sophie had another worry on her hands. In her book, she says that Guss Hill didn't want to stand in her way and enforce the contract that said she owed the burlesque wheel another season's work. In truth, Hill slapped in a writ demanding $1,500 compensation. Sophie was frantic, but brother Moe, who had moved in with her while studying at college, decided the time had come for him to play lawyer—and eventually had the bill reduced to $150. She was learning the ropes about show business the hard way.

Sophie was luckier than others who had Ziegfeld contracts. Hers said she was going to get $100 a week.

Her time on the wheel was due to come to an end at Boston. For the occasion, with thoughts of her future assured stardom in the Follies uppermost in their minds, the management decided to cash in on her fame.

For the first time in her hardly meteoric career, Sophie was given important billing. The show was at the Howard Atheneum Theatre and on hoardings and billboards throughout the city was plastered the name SOPHIE TUCKER. And underneath, the legend, WORLD-RENOWNED COON SHOUTER.

Now, everybody knows that some of the most important things in life happen completely by accident. An accident that week in Boston killed in one fell swoop Sophie Tucker's career as a coon shouter.

For months, she had toned down the harsh blackface makeup produced by burning a cork. The "coon" she played—and it was theatrical convention to adopt the pose without any suggestion of racial hatemongering—was now a light-skinned one. Her makeup was known in the trade as "high yellow". At least, it was until she reached Boston.

The screams from Sophie's dressing room minutes before the matinée on that first day in Boston might almost have been heard in the kitchen of the Abuzas' restaurant. "Where is it?" she screeched. "Where is it? What am I going to do? I'm finished . . . finished. With a career with Ziegfeld, I'm going to be a laughing stock."

The problem was that her baggage had failed to come off the train at Boston station at the same time as she did and was now happily trailing off upstate. To any traveller, that is a nightmare. To a touring performer like Sophie Tucker it was roughly equivalent to an industrialist seeing his factory disappear in an earthquake. In the trunk were all her costumes. In it, too, was her makeup.

"Get out there as you are and stop your nonsense!" called the stage manager. As he slapped Sophie round the face his admonition couldn't have been more salutary. In a profession where the first commandment is that the show must go on, he was giving her the alternative of making an entrance or slipping out the backway for all time.

She chose to go on. Wearing a heavy tailored suit over

an intensely tight corset and with a single hot spotlight shining on her, Sophie, the "world-renowned coon singer" appeared on stage to a series of catcalls from people who considered they had been taken for a ride.

In "Some Of These Days", she said she told the audience: "You all can see I'm a white girl. Well, I'll tell you something more: I'm not Southern. I grew up right here in Boston, at 22 Salem Street. I'm a Jewish girl and I just learned this Southern accent doing a blackface act for two years. And now Mr. Leader, please play my song. . . ."

As usual, Sophie Tucker was not going to allow the truth to interfere with a good story. If it were good for business to ignore the fact that her most impressionable years were spent in Hartford, why mention it? By the time she had finished punching out Irving Berlin's "That Lovin' Rag," Sophie was as wet as the proverbial rag herself—and the audience were standing on their seats calling for more.

She repeated the performance and the audience repeated its enthusiastic response at the evening show. Next day, her trunk arrived at the theatre. But the manager wouldn't allow her to use anything from it for her act.

"Kinda like you without blackface," he told her—and he asked Josephine Travers, the headliner of the show, if she could lend Sophie one of her gowns. With a little persuasion and a great deal of problems with buttons, Sophie was squeezed into the long white dress—complete with train.

The elegant Miss Tucker hobbled out on to the stage —and promptly tripped over the train. What more could an audience ask of a comedienne? They assumed it was part of the act and Sophie Tucker had them eating out of the palms of her hands before she could ease herself to her feet.

It was good enough to last the week out.

When Sophie made her first entrance at the stagedoor of the New York Theatre, she still had the sound of the Boston audience's applause that night ringing in her ears. She felt a star.

A few hours in the rehearsal room at the theatre should have told Sophie that she was still nothing of the kind. Not only had Ziegfeld failed to talk to her, but everyone else was ignoring her, too. As all the other artists practised their steps and rehearsed their numbers, Sophie sat out in the wings or on a chair in the centre of the hall. No one asked her to sing a note. When she asked anyone who appeared to be in authority what she should do, she was brushed aside.

Finally, she plucked up enough courage to tap Ziegfeld himself on the back and ask him when she was going to do her piece—and what that piece would be. If she had been more sophisticated or more knowledgeable in the ways of the theatre, she would never have had the guts to do that. Ziegfeld was known to consign to oblivion anyone with the temerity to call him "Ziggy" and to fire an artist whom he caught failing to address him as "Mr" in a conversation with someone else. But there must have been something about Sophie's smile that day.

All he said was "Yes, Miss Tucker? You sing don't you?" and went about his business. He went about that business for something like another eight weeks—eight weeks in which she didn't know whether she was going to do anything in the Follies or not.

Finally, the matter was resolved—by Teddy Roosevelt returning from a hunting expedition in the African jungles. There was only a week to go till the show was going to have its try-out pre-Broadway run at Atlantic City and Ziegfeld had made up his mind—an entirely new routine was needed. The theme would be the jungle with new staging, new scenery and new songs. When Ziegfeld decided, his minions had to implement those decisions.

A stage director was employed for this scene alone. A songwriter was brought in to write a new number. A designer was at work on the costumes and another on the set. But who was going to perform the "Jungle" number?

"Try Miss Tucker," said Ziegfeld.

The number was written, the stage prepared and Sophie was ready to rehearse it—when she discovered she couldn't sing a note. Her voice had completely left her. The director, far from collapsing in a heap as he might have been expected to do at that stage, told her not to worry and to walk through the role as though she were singing. She did.

The director decided that it was all going to be all right on the night and told her she could have another spot, too—before the finale, a "stage wait" while the scenery movers were preparing the set. Sophie Tucker felt that she had arrived.

When opening night came at Atlantic City on June 17 1909, Sophie had sung "It's Moving Day Way Down in Jungle Town" to herself so many times that she must have felt like a chimpanzee—or an elephant.

Irving Berlin had written two numbers for her final spot, "The Yiddisher Rag"—Jewish dialect numbers were in their heyday, and who better than Sophie to exploit them?—and, appropriately enough to give the evening an ecumenical flavour, "The Right Church, but the Wrong Pew".

As the opening hour drew near, Sophie was in a state of near-panic. Atlantic City was New York with sea around it. The place was so near Broadway that not only did the Manhattan socialites go to the Atlantic City openings, but so did the critics—the celebrated Butchers of Broadway. Sophie felt this was make-or-break for her career and she was determined it would be make.

There were more than Ziegfeld and Klaw and Erlinger to impress. In that audience were Diamond Jim Brady and his girlfriend Lillian Russell; the queen of Broadway chanteuses Fay Templeton, and the most important performer of the era, George M. Cohan. Charles Dillingham, one of Ziegfeld's main rivals, was there too, and so was Irving Berlin. She was more scared now than she had been at any other time in her life but when she went out on the stage singing the jungle number, the impression she made was startling. She was loud—important in an age when there were no microphones—she was tuneful and she was funny. She had persuaded the audience not only to laugh with her and cheer her, but to forget the beautiful Lilliane Lorraine—Flo Ziegfeld's current flame for whom he had only just cut Anna Held out of his life.

Annabelle Whitford, who was acclaimed as the Nell Brinkley Girl of 1909, Mae Murray and Vera Maxwell were among the other Ziegfeld girls on parade. But while Sophie Tucker sang, their importance declined.

The real star of the show was Nora Bayes; a tough spitfire of a performer who gossips had once said was a lady of easy virtue, but who had adopted the airs—if not always the graces—of a lady of society. There were whispers about her being not entirely happy with Sophie's performance. Were the people out front just that little bit too enthusiastic about her routine? She hoped so, but was frightened to find out. After all, why all that fuss about a jungle full of natives fleeting up a clump of trees—with Sophie as a leopard—just because President Roosevelt had returned?

When Ziegfeld saw Sophie in her leopard costume he did what he was seen to do only rarely inside a theatre—he burst into laughter. W. C. Fields, Will Rogers and Eddie Cantor, they were to go down into history as Ziegfeld's greatest comedians. Yet the showman always insisted he couldn't see anything funny in any of them and was afraid they were all taking him to the cleaners.

But Sophie, he could see, had something. When she did her solo number, gowned in a magnificent creation, just before the finale, he was absolutely convinced.

The set for that very last number in the show was every bit the pièce de résistance it was intended to be. There were more lights than had been seen on a stage before. Fountains played and on the staircases and roundabouts were the stars—each one looking more glamorous, more enticing than the one before. It was rumoured to have cost $40,000 to stage that number alone.

It was not only a costly set to stage—it was also a time-consuming one. The set erectors had worked out that they needed seven or eight minutes at least to stage it. They were so worried about time that they asked Sophie to take as long as she could to do her three numbers—the third was "The Cubanola Glide" by Harry von Tilzer.

After the thrill of the jungle number, Sophie was not only able to oblige, but the adrenalin was pumping so hard through her system now that the very idea of having the spotlight to herself for so long was nourishment to her. She brought the house down. The audience made so much noise cheering her that when she had finished the curtain had to stay down for much longer than planned—to allow the public's enthusiasm to cool sufficiently for them to gasp in admiration at the setting of the finale.

34

Sophie Tucker walked off the stage that night in Atlantic City convinced that Ziegfeld was already ordering a new Number One dressing room for her at his New York Theatre the following week. As she walked off, however, she could hear screams from Nora Bayes's room. "I'll not work while that woman is on," she shouted at the top of her voice as Ziegfeld tried to cool the atmosphere. Minutes later, he was knocking on Sophie's door: "Sorry kid," he told her. "You'll have to give up your solo spot."

Nora Bayes had given Ziegfeld the alternative of either having her as his star or featuring the still unknown Sophie Tucker. Either Sophie went or she did—and in 1909, Nora Bayes was the name he wanted to draw in the crowds. Poor Sophie. She dropped her chin into her lap—and howled.

Years later, she said: "There was, I suppose, no real interest in a big fat girl. Nora Bayes was right. I was too good. She was the star. When you are a star, you must let nothing interfere with your success."

As far as Sophie was concerned, from that day on Nora Bayes never existed—although she was to partially relent in time.

In the words of a later age, that was show business. It was also show business to pretend it had never happened and go back to working in the jungle number as though that were the most important in the show.

Salt was put in her wounds, however, when, the next night, Ziegfeld personally announced from the stage that Miss Tucker would no longer be performing her solo. Sophie burst into tears again.

Nora Bayes wasn't really happy with the Follies—and not just with Sophie. The show reached New York and there was constant friction between her and Ziegfeld.

The reviews of the show were great. One even found room to mention "Miss Sophie Tucker, whom you could hear as far away as Harlem."

But tempers back stage continued to be fraught—none of them helped by the weather. It was the hottest night New York had known in a generation—and any summer's day in America's biggest city could be calculated to drive sane men mad and tee-totallers to drink. In those days before the

35

introduction of air-conditioning, standing on a theatre stage in heavy costume with makeup cracking all over your face could be an unbearable experience. It was on such a night, six weeks after the opening at the Jardin de Paris at the top of the New York Theatre, that Nora Bayes cracked up—and announced she was leaving.

The only person in the whole company who was excited by this new development was Sophie Tucker. Perhaps now, she thought, she could have her solo back? Ziegfeld was completely non-committal about the idea. A few days later, he brought in a replacement for Miss Bayes—Eva Tanguay, who was known as the "I Don't Care Girl", a name calculated to bring in as many customers as her predecessor. She was on stage only once when she, too, issued an ultimatum to Ziegfeld: "Either I have the jungle number or I leave." Sophie was left with nothing—except memories of a brief Ziegfeld Follies career and a friendship with a coloured maid called Mollie.

Mollie had been in show business herself—as part of a black dancing act. In the Follies, she was dresser to Lillian Lorraine. Night after night when neither she nor Sophie had much with which to occupy themselves, they talked—with Mollie offering sound words of advice about not letting disappointments get her down. After all, she herself had never made the sort of grade she had expected to achieve.

When Sophie left the Follies—without a dollar's compensation—Mollie left with her. She said that when Miss Tucker earned enough money to pay for a maid she would like to be it—a promise Sophie was going to keep.

Now, however, she was unemployed—and feeling more than ever like the nickname her coloured friend had given her, "Patsy". She also had domestic problems. Louis Tuck and she had not seen each other for more than a year and although neither had yet contemplated legally separating and eventually going to the divorce courts, both had found themselves other loves.

For a time, Sophie was having an affair with her second cousin, an undertaker called John Ellsmere, who revelled in the title, "the best-dressed man on Third Avenue". He loved telling his friends: "Sophie's just crazy about me. But I don't care anything for her." The trouble was that once he said it to another man who had been secretly dating Sophie, Marty Corrigan.

Corrigan rolled his hand into a fist, thrust it at Ellsmere's jaw and said: "That's what you'll get if you say to anyone again that she's crazy about you."

It did seem, however, that Sophie was developing a passion for Ellsmere. She would find excuses to go and see him—either at his Bronx apartment or even at his funeral parlour. More and more, however, she saw him in the company of another young woman—a pretty schoolteacher called Emeline Wasseau.

It was a case of hate at first sight.

Finally, the schoolteacher won. She and Ellsmere were married and Sophie was invited to the wedding. She decided against her better judgement to accept the invitation and that meant she had to buy them a present. But it would be a way, she thought, of getting her own back. While they were still rivals in love, she had heard Emeline say that she hated anything made of brass. So that was what she bought them for a wedding present—a brass-legged table with an onyx top surrounded by more brass. Emeline let her know how much she appreciated the gift. "That old maid did it on purpose," she told her new husband. The existence of Louis Tuck was by that time practically unknown—and certainly no one was told about Bert.

The story of Emeline and her coffee table didn't end with the presentation of the gift. It lay dormant for the next two years when it was to erupt again. In the meantime, Sophie was more concerned with getting her career back on to the rails, and her responsibilities had grown by this time, too—because Moe was studying law at Yale and she promised to put him through college.

It was at the offices of Irving Berlin's publishing firm, Waterson, Berlin and Snyder, that her next break came—and now it seemed that nothing was going to be allowed to hold back the career of Miss Sophie Tucker. She met an old vaudevillian called Harry Cooper—a customer of Abuzas' restaurant. He suggested that she introduce herself to a certain Mr. William Morris.

37

Nobody's Fool

As Sophie Tucker, Ziegfeld-star-who-never-was, contemplated her future, she had one paradoxical consolation. Even if Eva Tanguay had smothered her in roses and insisted that she take over the lead spot in the show, she could never have managed it. Just as her career seemed to be in ribbons around her ankles, so her voice gave out. And this time, it seemed that nothing could save it.

For six months, Sophie tried to sing, and for six months nothing at all came out of her mouth. Her nervous reaction to the Ziegfeld collapse had been to suffer from what appeared to be permanent laryngitis.

Then, suddenly, while making her usual attempt to sing—she found that she could produce notes after all. Brother Moe had now moved into her New York apartment and the day she discovered her voice had returned, she swung him round and round in her arms.

And she capped that instant burst of enthusiasm with a note to William Morris—mentioning Harry Cooper, Abuza's restaurant and her sensational appearances with Mr. Ziegfeld.

Morris at the time was running his own vaudeville circuit. It was the Big Time, with some of the finest names in the two-a-day vying with each other for top billing—people like Sir Harry Lauder, Charlie Chaplin and the leading female impersonator of the day, Julian Eltinge.

Sophie in 1917

Ted Shapiro right after World War I. Wellington Cross is in the middle.
The fleet-footed one on the left? Fred Astaire.

Arrived London 7.30 P.M. '14. Mr & Mrs. William Morris and Jr. and Harry Foster met us at Waterloo Station.

Can you imagine a Taxi loading 10 trunks + baggage and passengers and hauling us all over to the hotel? fare 1/6 25cen and 2 shillings — 44 cents tip for all?

Registered at Piccadilly Hotel.

Beautiful, big spacious rooms & bath £1·6 a day ($5·12)

No steam heat charged 2/0 a day for a fire (47 cents)

Everything smacked of the ancient days, plumbing of the 1492 vintage.

Very courteous servants, pages boys, and all the bells.

Dined with the Morris family, Joe, Lou & Jane Harry + etc at the Piccadilly grill. Very nice but O. for an American band. English bands know only one kind of music "Classic" and that lets them out.

Mon. apr 3. We lunched at the Savoy, lots of americans there, Irene Franklin, Burton green, met Jack Hascall, Paul Murray lots of friends. did enjoy my coffee, English people cannot make good coffee. Cream with coffee priceless.

Went to the Colliseum matinee. Worst vaudeville show I've ever seen. So slow. such stage waits English artists dirty looking. majority old nose comedy no class. very

He saw Sophie dressed—with the help of Mollie—in all her finery, heard her sing "Wild Cherry Rag", and decided to take a chance. She could, he said, make $40 a week if she were any good on his American Music Hall circuit. "Right," Sophie told him. "I'll prove to you how good I am."

A week after her first booking at the American in Manhattan Morris called Sophie into his office. "If you sing like that, you can have $75 a week." Just what the young girl did when she heard that isn't on record, but it isn't stretching the imagination too far to think that she smothered Morris in kisses while soaking his collar with her tears.

In 1909 she arrived for the first time in Chicago—a city that was to become a second home to her in the not too distant future—and found a warm welcome from *The Chicago Examiner* even if the paper did make it clear that she wasn't exactly the sort of girl you would lose in a crowd. "And speaking of elephants and ladies," recorded the *Examiner*, "there is Sophie Tucker. If life were as large as Sophie Tucker, there would be room for all of us. I don't mind saying at once that Sophie Tucker is MY kind of headliner, even if the American management does employ a different position for her."

"Headliner". That was the one word Sophie wanted to read about herself more than any other. She promptly cut out the notice and with pride of place stuck it on the front page of her very first scrapbook.

That scrapbook was beginning to be as important to her as her bank statement. When she did things now, she did them with the scrapbook in view. No one had taught her the art of being a publicist, but she was now developing a nose for news that was as sharp as that of any budding young reporter on the threshold of a career in journalism. When she heard about the troubles of another act on the bill at the Chicago American, it was nothing less than a gift from heaven.

The act in question was Consul the Great—a chimpanzee. Consul was considered so important by the American management that they booked him into an hotel suite at the Auditorium Hotel annexe—but the hotel was not so considerate. It double-booked the suite and Sophie arrived there first. So what should she do? Stay where she was—or give in to a chimpanzee? She thought quickly, remembered a reporter she had got to know on the *Chicago Examiner* and gave the chimp the room.

"A knock at the door, a brief conversation and Miss Tucker shook her shapely head in assent," the paper reported, delighted that they had found so co-operative a contact. "The porter called and took out her trunks. Miss Tucker is a very beautiful women [which shows just how friendly she had become with the newspaperman] and she is welcome in any hotel. So she moved to one of the other fashionable hostelries and Consul, when he arrives tonight, will occupy the luxurious quarters which Miss Tucker surrendered to him."

A lot less influence was required to get the *New York World* on her side. When she appeared later that year at the Plaza Music Hall, the paper was plainly knocked over—and so was William Morris who held her over for a second week.

"Not in a great many years has a performer risen to the top of the ladder as quickly as Miss Tucker," said the paper.

"Miss Tucker is as great an artist in her line as Harry Lauder is in his. Don't look for a voice like Patti's or a petite comedienne in short skirts, but go there to hear coon songs as you have never heard them before, and the first thing you know is you will find yourself applauding until your hands are blistered."

Such praise couldn't be eked out by a press agent—let alone by Sophie herself buttering up a journalist, which she was getting very adept at doing. The blistered hands were a phenomenon being talked about in every Broadway café and every rehearsal room where vaudevillians gathered. The William Morris agency was bombarded by letters from other parts of the country asking when Sophie could go to their neck of the woods. When she did, they put out posters proclaiming the presence of this new "manipulator of coon melodies"—even though she tried to keep in whiteface most of the time. Now she had visiting cards printed—"Miss Sophie Tucker"—and placed them in her scrapbook along with those of a growing number of theatrical acquaintances.

When at Christmas 1909 New York vaudevillians sang

in Manhattan cafés for the "Star Santa Claus Fund" aimed at raising money for poor children, Sophie was proudly singing along with them. She posed for pictures wearing a big fur collar. Other photographs used for publicity purposes showed her wearing sexy off-the-shoulder dresses. Mama Abuza might not have approved, but Sophie Tucker was on the way to proving her point—and sure that one day the folks at Hartford would eat their words. To her it was spelling out the message: She had stayed off the streets and there was little sign she would ever have to resort to them.

As the New Year of 1910 dawned Sophie was back on the road and with her salary increased to over $100 a week was given a still more exciting billing, and this time it was to last. In Chicago they called her "The Mary Garden of Ragtime". It was a title she liked. Mary Garden was the big hit of the Metropolitan Opera and the way Sophie saw it, she was being recognised for what she was—an entertainer with class. She also sang her first really sexy song "There's Company in the Parlour, Girls"—full of double entendres, just the sort that she would make as much a trademark as her billing.

Again, the papers were interested in her activities. When she told them how she had scored an instant success at a command performance before Queen Wilhelmina of the Netherlands, the newshounds practically wore their fingers to a pencil point getting down every enticing detail.

The Queen was "shocked out of all composure" by Sophie's coon songs, they reported. It happened when Miss Tucker had the "unique distinction" of singing coon songs on her recent theatrical tour of European capitals. On the journey from Rotterdam to The Hague, sitting in a quiet parlour car of a train, she met an English concert company on its way to entertain the Dutch court.

"Why don't you join us?" the head of the company suggested. Sophie modestly put her hand to her chin, thought about it, and said she would be honoured to do so. Apparently, Queen Wilhelmina was delighted that she did. She allowed Sophie to kiss her royal hand, motioned to the grand piano in the ballroom—and asked for the entertainment to begin.

41

After the English troupe had performed selections from the classics, Sophie Tucker in all her finery lifted her statuesque form from the gilded chair on which she had been ceremoniously perched, and . . . in the words of the *Chicago American*, "assumed the mahogany piano stool and struck a chord."

"There was a perceptible straightening of backs'" said the paper. "'It was obvious as the American girl's fingers struck the keys that this was to be no classical music. . . . Miss Tucker's voice rang out with one of the popular coon songs."

When she finished, there was a moment's hesitation, but then the Queen herself placed her white gloved hands together and led the court's polite applause. Her Majesty presented the delighted Miss Tucker with an autographed picture.

Strange as it may seem, there is no sign of that picture among all Sophie Tucker's mementos. Strange? Well, perhaps not. In 60 odd years in show business there is no record of Sophie ever learning to play the piano. Just as strange is the fact that no one remembered seeing her leave the country. At the time that she said she was entertaining royalty, Sophie, in fact, was carting her own cases into a small hotel here, a theatrical boarding house there. She was doing well in vaudeville—very well indeed for a comparative newcomer to Big Time—but no one had yet commanded a royal performance from her and the only time she had been out of the United States was on that dreadful journey from Poland about 20 years before.

She was learning about newspapers. But either it didn't matter how big were her lies—because the newspapers themselves didn't care—or she just felt she could produce a quantity of wool whenever it was needed to fit over a gullible writer's eyes.

Sometimes it looked as though Sophie were growing too big for her own silk bloomers. Mollie seemed to think so. Soon after she had taken over the job of being Sophie's dresser, a coloured man called at the stage door. "I want to see Miss Tucker," he told her.

Mollie took her the message—"I'm too busy right now,"

42

said Sophie. "Tell the man to leave his name." He might have walked away at that moment but Mollie was not having it. "If this man is kind enough to want to meet you, you should be kind enough to meet him," she said. The man was glad of the encouragement.

"I'm a song writer and I think I have a number just right for you," he said. "Well," Sophie told him, "Leave it and I'll read it through."

"No," said Mollie, "let the gentleman read it to you now."

The advice was appreciated by the man—who by now had introduced himself. His name, he said, was Shelton Brooks.

Mollie took Sophie and Brooks towards the piano in the theatre wings—and began to sing the words as he played. . . . "Some of these days . . . you're gonna miss me honey. . . ."

Sophie smiled and said she would be pleased to take the song—and to sing it at her next performance. The following week, handbills were printed announcing "Sophie Tucker, the Mary Garden of Ragtime, will show you her own idea of putting over the big hit, 'Some of These Days'."

She was still at the threshold of her career, but never was Sophie to have a bigger number by which she could woo an audience.

Once more the papers were enthralled by her success. In 1911, they announced that Sophie was going to London for the coronation of King George V. But, she told them, she wasn't going to spend a fortune on her gown.

"Isn't it silly for a woman to pay hundreds of dollars for a dress? Yet we must, because the women in the audience force us to do so. For every new frill adds to the cost and there are some conscienceless inventors of frills. I really believe the reason American women pay so much for their clothes is because American men are so foolishly game. . . . He can't afford it, but he says to wifey, 'Get it'. She does. Then the woman next door doesn't want to be outdone and neither does her husband want her to be. He is both proud and game." So with those thoughts in mind, Sophie announced she was going to make her own dress that was going to force Queen Mary herself to sit up and stare. Her Majesty need not have worried. Sophie no more went to London than she had been to Amsterdam.

William Morris certainly didn't complain about his protegée's imagination. The stories were good for business. When he could announce that throughout the long hot summer of 1911, his theatres would become the "coolest spots on Broadway" because of the massive electric fans he had had built into the ceiling, he knew he wouldn't be able to keep the customers away.

The *New York Telegraph* appreciated the cool comfort inside Proctor's Fifth Avenue Theatre—recent scene of about the only flop in the careers of a child brother and sister act called Adele and Fred Astaire—almost as much as they liked the performance of Sophie Tucker, who "with her booming voice and jubilant personality took the audience with a rash. Her closing number is the most eccentric and ridiculous song heard around New York in some time. . . . In this number, Miss Tucker goes crazy about dancing with a bear on account of its shaggy skin. 'Put Your Paws Around Me' instructs the singer of syncopated melodies 'if you want to be my bear!'"

It seemed that the only person who could not "bear" Miss Tucker was her new cousin Mrs. Emeline Ellsmere— who was still smarting under the effects of Sophie's brass table wedding present.

Sophie called on the Ellsmeres one day when Emeline was out and was shown into the parlour by the family washer woman. She was disturbed to see that the table was hidden in a corner—and that one of its legs was rusty.

Insult was added to injury when the washer woman announced that the table was her property and that she was taking it away. "I bought this table and paid two dollars for it," she told her as she carried it out.

Sophie was so disturbed that she complained to The Bronx Women's League—an organisation of which both she and Emeline were members.

Raising herself to the full height of her assaulted dignity—and to show just how injured she had been, she signed her name, *Sophia* Tucker—she filed a complaint to the organisation. In her own handwriting, she wrote: "I

44

Sophia Tucker, prefer charges against Mrs. Emeline Ellsmere and your deponent declares that Mrs. Ellsmere acted in an unclubby manner, which your deponent wants a chance to prove it. I want her tried before the club and then censured by a unanimous vote of all the club members, which I am sure is going to be done. Then I want that she be expelled from the club and a piece printed in all the newspapers about it. Your truly, Sophia Tucker."

Syntax apart, the fact that Sophia Tucker wanted a piece written in all the newspapers about it rings truest of all.

In the end, the club did the most clubby thing of all and told both women to bury their hatchets elsewhere. But Emeline Ellsmere was added to the list of people Sophie Tucker didn't want to know about any more.

As for herself, nothing interested her more than her career—but even then, anxiety about other women would creep in. "When I open," she said about this time at Portland, Oregon, "I see some of the husbands out beyond kinder wriggle in their seats and steal a glance or two at their wives to see what they are going to do. By the time my first verse is ended, I can always tell whether or not I've made a hit. If I have, that husband has forgotten all about his wife and his wife is laughing as loudly as he."

Sophie was, however, finding it difficult to be accepted as "one of the girls". In 1910, at Atlantic City's Criterion Theatre, she saw her name in lights for the first time. She was headlining the bill.

C. B. Zittal, one of the most important influences on early 20th century entertainment patterns, was probably also the first man to use the word "charts" in terms of show business success. Writing in the *New York Journal* under the name Zit, he published a weekly "Vaudeville Chart" and week by week saw the name Sophie Tucker rise higher and higher. Then finally, that week in Atlantic City, she got to the top of the chart. Her prayer had been answered. She was now a headliner.

She was also, however, earning herself a reputation for toughness. William Morris knew the acts with whom he could argue the toss, fight for ten dollars here, five there. But Sophie was not one of them. She was strong enough to go into his office and demand the money to which she thought she was entitled. She and the man she always called "Boss" were to become close and devoted friends, but business would always be business. Now when Sophie brought out her handkerchief the tears were invariably used for the effect they could achieve.

She was earning $500 a week—big money by anyone's standards—and just as quickly losing it. Surrounded like other headliners by a coterie of hangers-on, she revelled in being accepted as their equal. There was a lot of time to kill between shows—some of it was used for shopping expeditions for new dresses, and for the furs which she was convinced represented not just success but also an advertisement for her act. She also took to playing cards—hard, tough games like poker. She liked to think she played well, but invariably was in at the losing end. Week after week her earnings went to the other players in the poker school.

The cards gave her an armour-plated exterior in which she was at first to glory and later to regret. Success was the almighty god, but so was having a good time and the good times were few and far between. Where other women of her age were settling down with husbands and children, she was plainly alone. When unattached girls had modest flings with young men, Sophie wasn't even approached for dates. How could she be? Who would be good enough for her? Convinced they would get rebuffed, the men didn't ask. Sophie worked and they played with other girls.

Even so, she desperately wanted to be liked. She had also inherited one characteristic from her mother that would never change—a love of charity. Other stars helped good causes, Sophie was obsessed by them. No sooner had she become a headliner than she was one of the acts listed as "An array of talent to play for the Newsboys Fund at the Herald Square Theatre".

Included in the "array" were "George M. Cohan—the Yankee Doodle Boy, *Erv*ing Berlin [which gives you some idea of how long ago this was] playing 'My Wife's Gone To The Country', Annabelle Whitford and 12 Brinkley Girls, Evelyn Carlton and Wm. C. Shrode, the Breakneck Dance Eight and Sophie Tucker."

46

It didn't matter that she was at the end of that list. The important thing is that she was there at all.

So what sort of a singer was this new headliner, Sophie Tucker? People were beginning to ask—and she had to find some answers. "You don't have to sing to be a coon shouter," she told the *Los Angeles Record* when she played in that still small West Coast town in 1910 while on a tour of the Pantages Circuit. "The orchestra takes care of the music and rags the melody till you just sort o' sway an' glide an' slide 'cause you can't help it." But Sophie could help it all right. Every sway an' glide an' slide was carefully orchestrated by Sophie Tucker herself to make the fullest impact with her audience. Her secret of success was that she was in control of everything she did.

To prove that was so, she signed up with the Edison Phonograph Company to make her first record sides—"The Lovin' Rag" and "That Lovin' Two-Step Man". She thought she was so good that she tried to see Thomas Alva Edison himself to get a long-term contract out of him, but got no further than a secretary who promised that the brilliant inventor would be writing to her. He never did.

The Edison publicity machine, however, did its job every bit as well as the cylinder recording and playback machines did theirs. The *Edison Phonograph Monthly* declared in June 1910: "Just to prove that her repertoire is not limited to coon shouts and rag melodies, Miss Tucker offers as her second contribution to the catalogue a comic song which she renders in the talking style of George M. Cohan." That was a very important development. It was a style that was to prove vital in later years.

The song was "My Husband's In The Country"—which requires little imagination to identify as a parody of Berlin's "My Wife's Gone To The Country". Women's lib came early in American show business. Certainly, Sophie Tucker was its greatest protagonist. The words for the tune, incidentally, were by Sophie's friend Zit—the man who had put her top of the charts.

The Pantages Circuit was introducing Sophie to a new kind of America—a West Coast that still had the feel and smells of pioneer country about it. In San Francisco it was

47

fun to see men flung out of saloons—and to play in a theatre where a man in a box laughed so much that his false teeth fell on to the stage in front of her. It wasn't the elegant East, but neither was Sophie the queen of café society—yet.

At Spokane, Washington—a generation later it was to become famous as the home town of Bing Crosby—she caused a sensation singing Irving Berlin's "The Yiddisher Rag". The local paper noted that the song "is out of the range of those who have never been where Yiddish is spoken or sung, but it is a hit just the same."

Yiddish, which Sophie never really learned to speak or write well, was also her main link with her past. She would write to her father in the language—sending him a few dollars here and there to replace the ones that she knew her mother was lifting from his trouser pockets.

In December 1911, she explained another reason for her generosity. It wasn't only her mother who was getting a cut from his "fortune". He was so used to digging down into his trousers for charity and for spongers and con men, that he never had anything left for himself.

"Poor Papa," she said at that time. "He doesn't have a chance to dig down much now. I send it home to Mama and she gives Papa what she thinks he ought to have.

"But, of course, that isn't like him having it all to himself to handle as he used to. So, I was just writing him to say nothing to Mama about it. So long as I've got a lung left, he ain't going to go without a merry Christmas."

In one sentence, as she sat holding court, talking to reporters without bothering to listen to what came out of her own mouth, she had finally said too much. Could that really be true? Sophie Tucker worrying about her father's Christmas?

She thought quickly. "I ain't asking him to change his religion," she countered. "I'm just asking him to be happy at the time when everybody in the country is—or wants to be happy."

Suddenly, her reputation for saying a bit too much was getting around. Out of nowhere, a reporter asked her why she had decided not to go to London for King George's Coronation, after all.

"I was billed to open in Manchester on June 25," she told a paper in Spokane. "But I backed out and came here. I wanted to see my own country first and then I'll go abroad." No mention now of entertaining Queen Wilhelmina.

The public liked Sophie and forgave her her indiscretions. But occasionally she did worry about the effects of her public image. She was beginning to worry most of all about the stories about her hardness and her ruthless approach to business. She told friends that she spent all her spare time doing embroidery—marking every piece of silk underwear she owned with a "gorgeous 'T' or 'S' in blue or pink."

Mollie had to be a part of this charade. For a time, she didn't like it to get around that she had a maid. "My dresses don't have hooks, so what do I need a maid for?" she asked. Mollie, any way, was so light-skinned that she could pass for Sophie's sister. For a time that was how she wanted it. Nothing, she decided, must interfere with the idea that she was just a simple, very feminine girl.

The Jewish festivals were times when Sophie began to look nostalgically towards home. Her biggest dream was to go to Hartford, headlining a show. But until then, her links with home were her letters in Yiddish and the very rare visits her mother made to New York, bringing Bert—"Son" as she called him most of the time—with her. The meetings between mother and son were not as warm as Sophie would have wished and the fact upset her. She had to learn from her mother and sister Annie which nursery school he now attended. But when it came to the Jewish festivals, her heart tried its best to go out to the family.

Into the scrapbook went the greetings cards—including one that said simply "All the best wishes for your happiness from your loving mother."

The scrapbooks were Sophie's most constant companions—and friends. Everywhere that she went, the scrapbooks went too. Into them she pasted every mention that she could find of herself—reviews of her shows, the ones that listed S. Tucker among a dozen also-rans, those that proclaimed her name in large capital letters, "the Mary Garden of Ragtime—always on the job". No one in 1911 thought that was

49

a not particularly nice thing to say about a lady. It definitely did not represent Sophie's sexual activities.

She liked noting her importance in the theatre industry —and revelled in the fact that when she opened in Chicago in a new revue called "Mary, Mary", 2,000 applied for places in the chorus.

"Mary, Mary" wasn't a momentous début for Sophie into the world of legitimate theatre. In fact, it ran for a mere three weeks. But before long, she had a new opportunity—in a show called "Louisiana Lou", about two families living down South, one Jewish, the other Irish; a sort of direct ancestor of "Abie's Irish Rose". The mind at this stage should not start jumping to conclusions. Sophie, of course, was perfectly equipped to be the leading member of the Jewish family. But . . . not quite. She played the maid—in the Irish family. From that point on, the audiences were thrown into a total haze of incredulity, with stock ethnic Jewish and Irish jokes about little people and long noses. Audiences loved it—and it didn't matter whether they were sitting in theatres in New York or Chicago or in towns that had never seen either an Irishman or a Jew.

It was the signal for Sophie to start talking about her own roots. "I'm a Jew," she told the *Chicago Examiner*. "There's nothing renegade about me." There was also nothing very clever about her either. Certainly, little to show that she had any knowledge of the history of her people.

"God," she declared, "is good to the Jewish. Sarah Bernhardt is a Jew—and so am I. And—hem—I too am a regular actress now. Here—don't laugh." And she recalled some of the ironies of her style. "I was blackface most of the afternoon and whiteface by night. Nobody would believe that a Jew would do blackface. Not even when I rolled up my sleeve and showed a white arm. There must be some-thing un-Jewish about my features when the cork is on."

But she used the cork very rarely now. On tour with "Louisiana Lou", she found that another Jewish artist was finding it less of a liability. A youngster called Al Jolson —real name, Asa Yoelson, son of a synagogue cantor—was touring the country making a name for himself as the best blackface minstrel of them all. In San Francisco and in

50

Chicago, they would chat together about their ambitions and their backgrounds.

There was a great freemasonry among the Jewish entertainers and observers of the show biz world who (notable exceptions being the non-Jewish Eddie Foy, George M. Cohan and John McCormack) practically dominated the scene.

One telegram to Sophie, ignoring her professed religious sensibilities, read: DON'T MIND THE OVER-WEIGHT OR A MUDDY TRACK BUT BRING HOME THE BACON BEST WISHES. ZIT.

Another used a traditional Jewish goodluck phrase: ZOL ZEIN MIT GLICK AND MAZEL MAY IT BE THE HIT OF YOUR LIFE MYRON GILDAY.

Sophie was concerned principally about making good herself. There was no doubt that "Louisiana Lou" was a sensation, and that Sophie was the main prop to that sensation. At the La Salle Theatre in Chicago, veteran actor Alex Carr, who played the head of the Jewish family, resented the applause that greeted Sophie's inelegant little dances. When flowers were brought on to the stage for her, he turned and walked off into the wings in a huff—instead of handing the bouquets to her, as theatrical tradition demanded.

"That's quite all right," Sophie said to the audience. "Mr. Carr would have picked up my flowers, but he's all worn out from my bows."

The flowers came in words, too—and in phrases especially tailored for the new scientific age that made people wonder what was going to happen next.

The *San Francisco Bulletin* said of her in July 1912: "Slim and sylph-like is Sophie Tucker. Slimmer and more sylph-like than when she was here last in September 1910. Not two years and in that time she has climbed. Climbed is not the word to use. She flew. She just stepped aboard the aeroplane called persevere and flew up and up until she reached such dizzy heights that people wondered and the theatrical astronerms announced the discovery of a new star. But it was only Sophie."

One Chicago paper dubbed her the "Marie Dressler

of Chicago"—a title that was to have certain repercussions about 20 years later.

Variety, with a little literary licence, reported: "American beauty Sophie Tucker cleaned up the show."

She didn't always clean up the show with her beauty, however—and perhaps the word "clean" isn't altogether appropriate, either. At one theatre, Sophie and Mollie were having trouble with a pair of harem pantaloons she was required to wear in a "Louisiana Lou" sketch. Sophie ran on to the stage minutes late—and the audience was near hysteria.

Now, for an artist trying to make the customers laugh, the experience of seeing them rolling around in their seats is more welcome than a cheque. On the other hand, when a singer goes on stage without a funny line in any of her material and sees the audience positively dissolve, something is wrong. Something was wrong that night—the pantaloons weren't buttoned up and Sophie was exhibiting parts of her anatomy that a young lady in 1912 never showed to anyone. But she was, if nothing else, a showgirl—and the show had to go on. So in one movement she desperately tried to sing her song, do up the offending pair of pants and try not to let the public see what they were never intended to see.

Afterwards, it was alleged to be part of a typical Sophie publicity stunt. The sweat on Sophie's blushing cheeks that evening convinced most people, however, that this was one hot spot she would rather have avoided.

Other tricks with garments were more deliberate. It was still the age of modesty. Sophie, to her own obvious delight, found herself mentioned in the newspapers for daring to walk through the streets wearing a tight sheath skirt that was split up the side—revealing her knees.

The skirt only got talked of and written about. Another item of clothing—and what she did with it—landed her before the District Attorney at Portland, Oregon.

The leader of the Portland Department for the Safety of Women was distinctly offended when she saw Sophie perform a number called "The Angle Worm Wiggle". As she sang this very slightly risqué number, Sophie's fingers —each encased in the cheap costume jewellery that she had

52

had specially made up for her—would caress her body. To the ladies of Portland in their long skirts and tight-fitting black straw hats it was evil.

Sophie tried to dismiss it all by telling her lawyer to "forget this dame and her society for the pickling of morals." But it was not as easy as that. The organisation called in Portland's Mayor for support—and he offered it. The case should go for trial, he decided. All that remained now was to convince the D.A.

That, however, was much easier said than done. The D.A. obviously was a lot less offended by Sophie's sensuous routine than were the morals squad or the Mayor and he decided he had no reason to prosecute.

To Sophie—and, just as important this, to the William Morris organisation and the Pantages Circuit—all that the Department for the Safety of Women had achieved was to provide a great deal of welcome publicity. The takings proved once again that Sophie Tucker was a headliner worth noting.

Now, she decided, the right thing to do was to feign modesty. "I ain't struck on starring anyhow," she told the *Chicago Examiner*. "I'm satisfied with this show at the La Salle. When I come on here, I hear 'em say, 'There's Sophie Tucker.' When I laugh, they laugh. That's pretty good for me. When you think how I started, the racket makes it sound as though nobody ever opened a lung before."

She was convinced that she was on the verge of something big—but even so, she admitted, she was now no chicken. On the eve of her 22nd birthday she confessed: "This is my last day, my very last, in the poultry department."

Meanwhile, the news from home was getting better. Word of Sophie's success had spread to the Abuzas' neighbours and the message bandied around in communal gossip was that . . . well . . . perhaps she wasn't such a bad girl after all.

She had started sending more money home too—more than her father needed for his gambling losses and enough to keep all the local spongers happy.

"I'm squared with my folks and that's a girl's good

luck," she said at the time. "My mother doesn't have to work. My kid sister has twice the range I have and she can have the vocal lessons I never had. And my brother—I'm so proud of him."

Finally, she was going to prove to Hartford what she could do—in the flesh. While the New York papers carried advertisements for Rothschilds of 10 West 23rd Street featuring Sophie wearing their fashions, bills went up all over Hartford announcing the next attraction at Poli's Theatre—"Hartford's own . . . Sophie Tucker."

That Lovin' Rag

She really could have been presented at Court—but nothing would have been as important to her as that opening at Poli's, Hartford, in October 1913.

Her parents were in the best seats in the stalls. Her mother's friends grudgingly accepted tickets, too—and snarled comments every time the rest of the audience dissolved into near-hysterical applause. It was difficult for them to accept, but Mrs. Abuza's fat, ugly daughter wasn't a whore after all. The programme notes supplied by the theatre said it all. Sophie was a star:

"It is with unbounded pleasure that the management presents Miss Tucker as this week's headliner, following her triumphs in musical comedy—for she is unquestionably the most popular and most successful Hartford girl who ever went on the American stage."

The theatre proudly informed its public that Sophie was "The Idol of Hartford—the Mary Garden of Ragtime". The name was beginning to stick.

To back their hunch about Sophie's drawing potential, the management decided to book her a suite at the town's plushest hotel. Mr. and Mrs. Abuza were not nearly as impressed as Sophie, the girl whose only experience of Hartford hostelries was via the scrubbing brush and the dish cloth. She took one look at her parents' sunken express-

55

ions and declared: "I'm going home. That's where I belong."

The trouble was that she had forgotten where home was. In the intervening years, the Abuzas had moved house from Maple Avenue to Barker Street. There, the ladies of Mrs. Abuza's circle came to peer at the celebrity, afraid to admit that this was proving to be the most successful Jewish family in town.

While her father waded through the dozen glasses of strong Russian-style lemon tea he allowed himself each day, Mrs. Greenberg and Mrs. Koppleman decided it was their duty to inform the young upstart that she shouldn't get too big for her boots. The fashion editor of the local paper might have been impressed with the white satin dress and the black lace skullcap she wore for her performance at Poli's, but to these women it was simply a "shmatter"—the Yiddish expression which can either mean an old rag or a piece of material of doubtful pedigree. Usually, it was no more and no less than a sign of rather intense jealousy.

Not that the neighbours were the only ones to pull Sophie down a peg or two. When she and brother Philip got into a heated argument, Mrs. Abuza decided it was her daughter who had gone too far. Star of Poli's she might be but that night she was treated to the experience of having her mother slap her face in front of the rest of the family.

Sophie would have liked to think that the proudest member of the Abuza clan was "Son". But Bert, now a student at Peekskill Military Academy, was more concerned with his grandparents, who with his aunt Annie's help had been so much closer to him. Bert apparently had been learning a few of the more gracious things in life at school—and wasn't too keen on his grandfather showing his prowess with the spittoon that was by his side at each meal.

Once Bert had told the old man that he didn't like his display of table manners, the spittoon was banished—something every other member of the family had been trying to do for years.

It was an eventful week for Sophie in a number of ways. It was the week when she decided to have nothing more to do with a professional gambler with whom she had oc-casionally shared a bed. A rousing boost of cheers from a

56

ticket-buying public fired enough adrenalin into her system to compensate for lost sexual fulfilment.

There was also another factor. On the same bill at Hartford was a piano player called Frank Westphal. He had a simple comedy routine that the audience liked. He came on stage wearing a raincoat, a souwester and a pair of rubber over-shoes. He sat at the piano, played a chord and took off the hat. He played another section of tune and off came the coat. With a third trill of the keys, he took off the over-shoes and then started to play.

He came on stage in the midst of Sophie's act, too—and said: "Excuse me, Miss Tucker—I forgot to play a song in my act. I know you won't mind if I do it now."

Now, most entertainers—and before long, Sophie was going to be one of them—would have made a beeline for their dressing rooms and torn up their contracts had the management allowed such things to happen while they were performing. But at that moment, something told Sophie to keep cool and allow the brash piano player to go ahead.

It went down so well that she decided to invite Frank to join her act. Before long, she was inviting him to join her in more intimate surroundings, too. A letter from one of Louis Tuck's close relatives altered life for her with a thud. Louis had died. It was a sudden blow that made her stop and think. When she had done her thinking and implemented her thoughts, she wrote a letter home to Mama: "I've married Frank Westphal," she told her—and then waited for the bombshell. This time, Mama couldn't suggest that her Sophela had to find a rabbi and have the marriage blessed in heaven—Frank wasn't Jewish. But Mrs. Abuza was nothing if not a realist. She knew it was too late to change Sophie's mind, so she told her that all she cared about was her daughter's happiness.

It all seemed to augur well when the civil marriage ceremony was held in Chicago. A dinner was organised for the couple at the swanky Café Royal and Paderewski, who happened to be dining there, too, played the Wedding March in their honour.

Sophie Tucker was at the top of a fluffy white cloud. The pinnacle of show biz success seemed to be hers at precisely the same moment as the fulfilment of her own personal happiness. She and Frank played the Palace—the place about which Judy Garland was to sing: "If you haven't played the Palace, you haven't lived." It was the Mecca to which all vaudevillians turned in their prayers. If Sophie asked God to make her a headliner, she would add for good measure—"and at the Palace, too."

She sang "Who Paid The Rent For Mrs. Rip Van Winkle?" and "There's A Girl In The Heart Of Maryland", but these were a mere fraction of her output at this time. When she went on tour again—this time a second and much more auspicious tour of the Loew picture house circuit—she was described as the girl who knows 300 songs. "And she will render these for the benefit of the visitors to Marcus Loew's houses," said a newspaper report at the time. In case this wasn't interesting enough, the paper pointed out that she could get through 150 songs each week. Not everyone took this for gospel. One paper enthusing at the notion of having her playing in their neighbourhood said that Sophie, "the Mary Garden of Ragtime knows more songs than the music publishers have printed."

The problem for Sophie's marriage was that no one seemed to mention Frank in reviews—or when they left the theatre, either. He was a funny incidental to her act and the William Morris agency, who handled them both, were making sure that Sophie got more money than he did. Frank developed an inferiority complex—a situation not helped by Sophie's determination to play the star at all times.

The *Los Angeles Tribune* reported in December 1916: "Sophie Tucker tucked her audience under arm at the Orpheum yesterday afternoon and just naturally ran away with the show. She responded to numerous encores and just left the audience howling for more. She sang old songs and she sang new ones. She did a little hula and talked to her friends in front and to those who manipulated the lights."

She thought that she could manipulate her family just as easily. As long as Sophie was the star bringing in up to $600 a week, who need grumble? Certainly not Frank—she was giving him a much better life than he would have without her. Absolutely, not her parents—they had never been so well off in their lives. Nor had Annie or her brothers. And then there was Son—pride of everyone and devoted to his military school.

Every autumn Jews throughout the world mark the beginning of a period of prayer, a time that commences with the New Year and culminates in the sacred Day of Atonement. It is a tradition at this time to send small greeting cards to friends and loved ones. To Sophie this was a time to get busy with her scrapbook. At the corner of one page of that book and surrounded by greetings from theatre folk, Sophie pasted a card that read: "Happy New Year to my darling mother—Albert." There was nothing about the positioning of this card to indicate that she thought anything particularly special about "Albert's" card. She just took it for granted that to him she would always be his "darling mother". What she didn't realise either then or later was that perhaps he wanted more than a reserved place in a Woolworth scrapbook.

Follow A Star

Sophie was everyone's idea of a headliner. Her prayers were not only being answered—the replies came in gold lettering. Early in 1917, she was recommending other performers to see the value of taking space in what she called the "newspaper in the sky", in other words buying electric signs with their names flashing on and off all over Broadway.

Billboard, the music world's paper, reported that by doing this she "woke up many vaudeville artists to a realisation of the value of publicity properly placed."

It was a lesson she did, indeed, learn—and before long with some disastrous consequences to her marriage. For the moment, she and Frank continued their act as before, getting a great deal of applause and enthusiastic laughter which seemed to suit them both. Frank was getting more attention than he would otherwise have justified and Sophie was drawing still bigger billing and still more publicity.

A series of engagements for the pair in New York nightclubs brought about the big change in Sophie's career and before long the big change in her marriage. In the Tokyo club on Broadway, Sophie sang while Frank played—and was suddenly joined by five youngsters in a jazz band behind them. Somehow, these boys—none of them was over 20— gave her a completely new sound and she liked what she heard.

Back in their hotel suite, all Sophie could talk about was

a new act. She had already worked out what she would call it: Sophie Tucker and her Five Kings of Syncopation.

"And where do I come in?" asked Frank. "You'll work on your own before I go on," she replied—without thinking that Frank might not like that sort of set up. The next morning, she phoned the "Boss", William Morris. "If you like it, Sophie," he said, "I like it. How long will it take you to set it up?"

She told him she needed two weeks. "You have it," he replied. All Frank could do was to agree to help Sophie round up the jazzmen—which he did.

The Morris agency got $650 a week for the new ensemble, with Sophie fielding $50 each to the "kings" and paying their travelling expenses. She figured it represented a sound investment. And, indeed, that was how it seemed.

Sophie Tucker and her Five Kings of Syncopation were a sensation wherever they played. They made her voice sound better and she liked that immensely.

She said she was going to call herself the "Jazz Queen" instead of the now passé "Mary Garden of Ragtime", but it took a long time for the papers to forget her old title. "Miss Tucker has a new act with the Five Kings of Syncopation," wrote one critic at this time, "a quintet of young men who add the spice of real pep to her accompaniment. She is known as the Mary Garden of Ragtime."

But the *Cleveland Leader* thought at Easter 1917 that Sophie didn't need any propping up by a group. "I can't report that Sophie is any politer since she was here before," said the paper's critic. "I cannot remark that the connection between Sophie and the week of Easter is wholly apparent to the layman. She sings songs that many of the others wouldn't dare to sing. And it must be admitted that Mlle. Sophie will never sing at the Metropolitan Opera in New York. Some-times her voice seems to be a phonographic reproduction of a foghorn.

"But for all that, Sophie Tucker seems to be able to take any old song, walk out on the stage and sing it straight between the eyes of the audience."

And that was the way she saw it, too. If Frank wasn't happy—well, it wasn't her fault, not completely anyway. He was beginning to drink a lot and as far as she was concerned it was a problem he was creating for himself. All she wanted to do was sing until she developed laryngitis. The louder she could sing the songs, the better she liked them.

In 1917, two events occurred that made her look again at the way Sophie Tucker, entertainer, performed. For one, President Woodrow Wilson had decided to abandon his previously stated pacifist stance and go to war against Germany. For another, there was a crisis back home at Hartford.

Ever since she had gone back to Barker Street with her success at Poli's ringing in her ears, her bond with Annie had grown remarkably strong. They wrote to each other three or four times a week—at first with news of Bert's progress at his military academy, then with just general chit-chat. But for more than a week she heard nothing. Her worries were compounded when, in her Chicago theatre dressing room, Mollie handed her a Western Union telegram that said simply: COME HOME AT ONCE PA VERY LOW ANNIE.

It was an overnight journey to Hartford. Sophie cancelled her evening performance and took the train home. By the time she got to the little house in Barker Street, her Papa, Charles Abuza, né Kalish, was dead.

It was a bigger blow than even she might have expected. After all, they saw each other only rarely. But the old man had represented one of the two strongest links with her roots. And, she said at the time, taking care of her parents was "the one great pleasure in life".

Abuza had missed his old neighbourhood. The restaurant and the delicatessen shop had closed and he no longer had much opportunity to play games of pinochle with his cronies. But as far as Sophie was concerned, he was beginning to "enjoy life for the first time". Now, all the money in the world Sophie could earn couldn't bring him back.

She confessed that she felt embittered. For once, she didn't care how she performed or whether or not she was creating the right image for herself. As she said at the time: "I was rougher in my work than ever. I simply didn't care. My one great joy in life had gone."

What she could not do, however, was sing comedy songs like "Who Paid The Rent For Mrs. Rip Van Winkle" any more. As the weeks went by, she developed a softer style and an altogether more sentimental approach.

Finally, she announced that she would do no more "coon-shouting" at all. "I never liked it," she said in Pittsburgh in 1917. "But the people liked it. It was pretty rough stuff but then everybody imitated it and that killed it."

In those days when individually-tailored songs were veritable trade marks for entertainers, the usual practice was to refuse to allow any other performer to use them. If they did, writs would fly round the courts. But Sophie was a lot more generous in this regard than most others. When she had finished with a tune, she would pass it on to someone lower down.

"I do all I can to popularise a song by giving it my personality, temperament and individuality as my talents will permit," she said. "And when I've used it for as long as I can I cheerfully surrender it and let others use it. They have to live, too, you know—and Sophie Tucker is big and strong and a hard worker.

"I know that my practice of giving away songs does not meet with the approval of all variety artists, but I lose no sleep over it. It helps less fortunate performers."

The war was having an equally generous effect on her nature and was not doing her publicity campaign any harm either. There was a desperate shortage of tobacco in the trenches of France. Sophie heard about it and started organising a tobacco fund for soldiers. During its first week, she personally collected $106 from the audience at the Orpheum Theatre in New Orleans. "Our boys should have the solace of their pipes in the camps," she said. "Everyone should do his part and I want to do mine."

When she wasn't entertaining for money, Sophie was singing for tobacco and cigarettes—and helping to sell war bonds at the same time.

At a rally at the Colonial Theatre in New York, she sang her newest hit, "The Dark Town Strutters Ball", and had the people yelling for more.

She set a Broadway benefit record for the fund—which now had the backing of the *New York Sun*—when an entertainment she sponsored at the Hotel Claridge, with the help of Eddie Cantor and Vivian Segal—not to mention Frank Westphal—realised $1,500.

The war had captured Broadway's imagination as if it were a new hit show. Because it had had that effect, Broadway was called on to help provide the "cast" for that "Show". George M. Cohan, who was never happier than when he had a large flag draped around him, presided at a rally addressed by General Pershing at which he called for show people to volunteer to go to the front. Sophie was one of the first to say she would answer the call—and promptly joined Cohan's newly-formed "America's Over There Theatre League".

From her stage box, she leaned towards the General and told him: "Sophie Tucker and her jazz band will go wherever called." Others like Otis Skinner, Billie Burke, John Drew and Walter Damrosch made the same sort of offer. As it happened, Sophie Tucker and her jazzband stayed in the States. But the work they did at home was vitally important, both to herself and her country.

The public, however, were electrified by the prospect of Sophie going to the front. "When Sophie Tucker gets to France," said the *Chicago Show World,* "the Bosches will think the Yanks are coming for fair!"

Both Frank and her brother Phil had joined the Navy, but Frank managed to get time off to perform at the Palace, New York, the same week as Sophie was headlining there. It was a difficult week with Westphal more drunk than sober—even on stage.

Early in 1918, he had a week's leave so that he could join Sophie's bill at Denver, Colorado. This time he was not only drunk, but exceedingly jealous of the impact Sophie had made at the Orpheum Theatre.

He himself had had an indifferent reception from the Orpheum's audience, but when Sophie and her Five Kings of Syncopation went on, the customers went wild. Just as the six of them were smiling and taking a bow, Frank stumbled on to the stage, determined to take a share of the action.

Then, assisted by a stage hand, he pushed his battered old piano on to the stage, took off his overcoat and cap and told the jazzmen to play with him. They looked at each other and decided the most sensible thing would be to agree. But Sophie had other ideas. "Stop," she called to the group in a very audible stage whisper. Frank knew what she was doing —and let the audience in on their embarrassing domestic tiff.

"What's the matter then?" he asked. "Is Mama mad with boozy old papa?" The best thing was for Sophie to give the OK, and by the time the curtain went down, the audience were under the distinct impression that it had all been arranged.

Her relationship with the men at the front was far happier than that with Frank. She was now being dubbed "The Smoke Angel of our Boys in France". And in one week, she sold $500,000 worth of bonds—$50,000 of them bought by herself—which gives some idea of how much she was worth at that time.

The publicity advantages of the campaign had not escaped Sophie, although at times these were less obvious than at others. Of the scores of postcards that reached her, one from a British "Tommy" read: "Dear *Sir*, Just a few lines to let you know that we received your tobacco and were glad to get it. Four of us boys divided up one package. We thank you American people very much."

Other thanks were more poetic—like this one signed by a "Buck private, Philadelphia":

"There's a bunch of prima donnas and
    a lot of dancers, too
There's a load of lovely women but none
    to compare with you.
You're The Queen of entertainers and
    like a Queen you reign alone
Your jazz band, your attendants and the
    stage it is your throne.
Gee, I wish that Bill the Kaiser could
    see you do your act
He'd forget about killing babies,
    he'd want to dance, in fact.
If he heard your Chocolate Soldier
    With the red light on your face
He'd yell for peace in a hurry
    when he'd think of his disgrace."

The poem, together with all the other messages from grateful smokers, was promptly pasted into her scrapbook. So was this Valentine card: "If you love me—as I love you.

No knife can cut our love in two."

Unfortunately for Mr. and Mrs. Westphal, the knife was cutting fairly deeply. For the moment, however, Sophie was relying on her war effort to keep her happy. As the dying months of the war painfully crawled away, she began using even her normal stage performances as opportunities to plug the allied cause. Only if there were interruptions from the audience would she lose her cool in public.

One day, she was so annoyed by the sounds made by four girls sitting in the audience constantly clicking knitting needles that she decided something had to be done. Whatever it was that the girls were knitting, it was in pink wool.

She stopped the band, leaned down towards the girls and told them: "Stop making that noise. But if you'd knit something in khaki, I wouldn't object." When Frank heard the sound of knitting coming from a box, he tried in vain to get Sophie to allow him to complain. So he simply got hold of two drum sticks and a long piece of rope and came on stage with them while Sophie was singing. He looked up at the box and said: "You haven't got anything on me."

The war also provided Sophie with a new link with her own people. For the first time, she was starting to raise money for specifically Jewish charities—firstly, for the Jewish War Relief Campaign, for which she entertained with Irving Berlin and Fanny Brice, and then for Jews behind bars, not in prison camps but in the nation's civil jails.

She organised Passover Seder services—on the first two nights of the festival when the story of the exodus from Egypt is recited in traditional ceremony in all Jewish homes—at New York State's Clinton Prison.

As a result of this, the following year convict No. 2583 of the Hebrew Committee wrote her:

"Having in mind your various expressions of kindliness towards those of us who have caused our faces to be turned against the wall, we address you, safe in the assurance that our appeal will at least be looked upon with favour by one who understands.

66

"The Hebrew inmates of the prison will be permitted to observe the coming Seder night, but since our abnormal existence lessens the possibility of the celebration being held as it should be in view of a lack of funds, etc., it behoves us to turn to our friends for assistance. There are at present, 100 Hebrews here."

Sophie did what she always did after receiving letters of that kind—she wrote a cheque.

She gave money to every cause that approached her. In honour of her charitable endeavours, the 71st Regiment gave a special dinner for her. The Idaho Cowboy Cavalry were so appreciative of her efforts on their behalf that they asked her to appear in the St. Patrick's Day parade with them.

The troops were a perfect foil for this vibrant young performer. Soon after the signing of the Armistice in 1918, Sophie stood on the deck of a tugboat, singing as loud as her ample lungs would allow, the chorus of "Some Of These Days". The boat moved alongside a troop transport bringing men back from France. Sophie pulled the corsage off her dress and threw it to one of the young officers standing on the deck of the bigger vessel.

"Here," she said, "give this to your best girl. And if you haven't a girl, come round and see me."

She was having a devastating impact on the people who bought sheet music. Sophie sang "Everybody Shimmies Now" and everybody, it seemed, wanted—if not actually to shimmy themselves, then to sing about everyone else doing it. But the war songs were the most popular. "I'm Crazy About My Daddy In A Uniform," she warbled—and uniforms had never before seemed quite so smart.

She was still, however, not so crazy about her own man—in uniform or out. Finally, she hit on what she considered to be the honest way out for both their problems. Frank would leave the theatre altogether and she would open a business for him. The New York papers carried the news about its opening. The only trouble was that, once again, Sophie saw more opportunities for herself in this enterprise than simply something for the little man to do. She called the operation "The Sophie Tucker Garage".

67

Advertisements for the garage at Baldwin, Long Island, declared that its proprietors were Frank Westphal and George McKay. And they promised: "We will store up your car at a much more reasonable price than you are paying or have paid. We will guarantee you better care than you are getting. Tyres—Tubes—Accessories."

Like most of Sophie's schemes for the men in her life, it was doomed to fail. As for her own career, it was about to take a distinctly new course.

Broadway Melody

The war ended with Sophie, the "Smoke Angel", personally being responsible for raising something like $3,987,000 for the tobacco fund. As the takings for the fund increased, so the Sophie Tucker Garage's income declined and with it Sophie Tucker's marriage, too.

The solace of new show biz success was as always strong enough to make up for what she was losing at home. But, now, the William Morris Organisation came to her with a proposition that she found difficult to accept—to go back to singing at restaurants—or at least one restaurant in particular, called Reisenwebers.

This was a building on three floors at the corner of 58th Street and Eighth Avenue. Performing for the customers on one floor was the dancer Joan Sawyer and her partner Rudolph Valentino. On the second was the Doraldina Room—Doraldina being the Hawaian dancer girl friend of Mr. Zittel, of *Zit's News* fame. The third floor, the company owning the club were ready to call before long the Sophie Tucker Room—with Sophie not only playing to the accompaniment of the Five Kings of Syncopation but with the Original Dixieland Jazz Band playing for dancing from the bandstand at the rear.

The rooms were long and narrow, perhaps 150 ft. long and 30 ft. wide. It wasn't a particularly smart place, but was

69

very popular with show people—the one audience most theatre folks tried to court more than any other. Finally she agreed.

Until her first night at Reisenweber's she wasn't exactly thrilled at the prospect. Although a Mr. Reisenweber had set it up as a restaurant, he had long since died and a private company had taken over the place. The three shows they put on nightly—with the last at two o'clock in the morning—presented a tough prospect for the artists.

But it did offer one important compensation: it meant she would be able to avoid those other pressures of vaudeville life which were conveniently ignored by the general public, but which in any other industry would long before have caused a massive strike. Theatre managers were often difficult to please—frequently insisting that even the biggest stars like Sophie change their material to suit the manager's own tastes. As for their theatres, they were often dirty, draughty and with insanitary dressing-room accommodation.

One of the worst problems of all was the difficulty of an artist getting herself heard in those days before microphones. In 1919, the New York theatre did go on strike. And she supported it enthusiastically—only George M. Cohan and Al Jolson gave it the brush off. "Maybe you don't smell anything rotten," she said then. "But I tell you those acoustics are rotten. The audience can't hear me and the critics can't see me. Me for the cabarets where a party has room to let out a pair of pipes."

A printed invitation in mock script went out to newsmen and show people:

Miss Sophie Tucker
requests the pleasure of your presence
Monday evening
December 23, 1918
on the occasion of the
premiere engagement of SOPHIE TUCKER and her
Five Kings of Syncopation
in the
Four-Hundred Club Room
REISENWEBER'S COLUMBUS CIRCLE
AND 58th STREET

She liked the experience and the nightclubbers who thronged Reisenweber's night after night liked her, too. In 1919, the *New York Dramatic Mirror* reported: "Sophie Tucker does not plan to play any vaudeville dates for some time to come, or at least until her money-making proposition at Reisenweber's begins to pall on her.

"Miss Tucker had established herself as an ever-welcome vaudeville act, a recognised big time single that always added strength to any bill. Then the Reisenweber offer came along. Miss Tucker had faith and the result was she has become a firm favourite at the Uptown restaurant. She plans a big night, June 30, when she will preside at the opening of the Paradise Room atop Reisenweber's Columbus Circle place."

The man who had helped make that triumph at Reisenweber's was William Morris, recovering from a now regular outbreak of TB at Saranac. Sophie organised a committee to present the "Boss" with a fire screen, as a gesture of their devotion to him.

Morris replied to Sophie: "WHEN I RECEIVED SCREEN I WITNESSED ONE OF THE GREAT MOMENTS OF MY LIFE WORDS FAIL ME." The soft heart of show business revealing itself again.

Sophie was working every (evening) hour God gave her. On Sundays, she would double at the Winter Garden, taking part in the concerts headed by Al Jolson—who liked the idea of having them because they gave him an opportunity to show his fellow showmen just how good he was. Later on, she would appear on the Broadway stage every night in a show called "Hello, Alexander" and then go on to Reisenweber's afterwards.

She had a chance to meet new talent—like the beautiful young blonde called May Gray who could shimmy like no other dancer in the '20s anywhere in the world, when people liked to see amazing things done with short skirts. Sophie spotted her at Reisenweber's, took her to Broadway and changed her name to Gilda Gray. Before long, she was known as "The Shimmy Queen".

The great thing about Reisenweber's to Sophie was the opportunity to play with people like Jolson, Eddie Cantor and Ted Lewis—who night after night would get up from their tables and join her in the centre of the floor. No greater tribute could anyone in the business enjoy. But all this new success and patronage did not mean that her vaudeville career was over.

After her first season at Reisenweber's she was back on the road once more.

She took part, too, in an extravaganza produced by Arthur Klein—a decade earlier, he had discovered Al Jolson—called Tic-Tack-Toe, described as "a musical outburst of mirth and melody".

And she went on tour once more. At Atlantic City, she tangled with the Prohibition Laws. Prohibition agents called at her home over the Café de Paris on the famous Boardwalk, searched her apartment and found a case of wine and five gallons of gin. She protested her innocence, but the stuff was confiscated and she was given a stern warning not to repeat the offence.

Touring meant, above all, Chicago. It was the city where she would try out every new routine before subjecting it to New York's approval: if Chicago didn't like it, New York never saw it. It was in Chicago that she admitted for the first time, that on Yom Kippur, the fast Day of Atonement, she was faced with a conflict between her work and her heritage. She went on stage as usual on the night before the fast and on the evening after it—but for 25 hours didn't allow a drop of water or a crumb of food to pass her lips. It wouldn't have had the approval of her rabbi, but was rather more than a token demonstration of the importance that day had for her. It also had a personal attachment. It was the day that memorial prayers were recited for dead parents, and with her father gone, a visit to the synagogue before the show provided a link with him.

It was while she was in Chicago in September 1920 that a buzz went round the town and landed firmly at the stage door of the Metropole Theatre. Was it true, she was asked by eager reporters, that she and Frank were about to divorce?

She wouldn't reveal anything and retired to the Sherman Hotel. There, the pressmen caught up with her. She

72

said she had a sore throat. But she added: "I'm not looking for anything like that said about me."

Frank himself was nowhere to be found. As the *Chicago American* noted, "He doesn't stop at the Sherman with Miss Tucker."

In fact, he was living on the North Side of the city and was about to open at the Chateau Club. "I haven't heard of any divorce papers being filed," he told reporters angrily. "If any news of that kind is forthcoming, I'd rather have Miss Tucker give it out."

Things were obviously very tense. Meanwhile, a telegram arrived at Sophie's Sherman suite. It was unsigned, but read: "WILL YOU MARRY ME WHEN YOU ARE A FREE WOMAN AGAIN?" There was no answer for the boy who brought it, but Sophie knew who had sent it. Like the others, it was pasted in her scrapbook—as though it were a note of congratulations on a new show opening.

In recent months, she had been having secret meetings with a sometime clothing manufacturer who was now a professional gambler. His name was Al Lackey. They had never been caught in any compromising situation, but vaudeville rumours were always rife and the one about Lackey and Sophie was that they had been known to sleep together.

Finally, in October 1920, the news was out. Sophie agreed, if reluctantly, that she was suing Frank Westphal for divorce. "Is it anyone's business if I do?" she asked angrily as she sat in her Sherman suite. But then she added a telling sentence: "Anyone who marries within the profession is foolish. Why, three years ago in this town I was married to Westphal and I had expected that after perhaps the hardest career of work, making others happy and getting little myself, I had at last arrived at the time in life when the real door of happiness was open to me—but the door slammed shut again and my hope of a happy married life is again on the rocks."

So was there more to life than singing and being surrounded by the adoration of cheering audiences? Apparently, there was. As she said: "Everyone seems to think that because a singer makes them happy, all is mirth. They seem to forget that she is acting. It was a contrast to what my private life was." And then she confessed that while she laughed on stage, at home she more often broke down.

The fact that Frank was seeing a lot of their shapely young cook didn't help matters in their relationship. When finally the cook left and Frank moved out, Sophie realised that another marriage had crashed to oblivion.

The divorce was granted and Al Lackey—a little man who, like Tony Pastor, barely came up to Sophie's bosom—moved permanently into Sophie's various hotel suites. Hotel staff reported on the quaint sight of the mountainous Miss Tucker sitting up in bed with a little lump curled up beside her. They seemed very attached—although some people noted that Lackey was taking an inordinate interest in the takings of the shows and was carefully watching the state of play at the card games which more and more were playing a part in the off-stage life of Sophie Tucker.

But Lackey had a strange effect on her. Most of the time she was still the best man in her crowd, taking the important decisions and implementing them without a bat of a false eyelash. But, despite the difference in their sizes, she could still go and sit on Al's lap and look girlishly coy. No man had been able to achieve that with her for a long time.

Nothing, however, did interfere with the various facets of Sophie's career. She announced: "I'm going to build, right here in Chicago, the Sophie Tucker Theatre, the Sophie Tucker Hotel and the Sophie Tucker restaurant. My name is the best kind of draw." It was the beginning of a string of investment ideas—some of which came off, some did not.

She didn't let the charities slide either. In October 1920, she received a letter from the U.S. Department of Labour at Ellis Island: "I wish you were here some Sunday to scatter some of your cheer among the hundreds of thousands of immigrants knocking at the gateway of the nation for admission," it said. She said she would be delighted to do just that another time—and did.

At Hartford, the leading Jewish charities combined to hold a bazaar and Sophie accepted the invitation to take part—to the accompaniment of Perlmutter's Orchestra.

The fame of Sophie's charitable endeavours spread very

74

easily to the Hartford Jewish community. But it was no more than any of them expected. She was merely following in the footsteps of her mother.

Every day, Mrs. Abuza would get the same streetcar to the Home for the Jewish Aged and other establishments and distribute largesse—in winter, wearing one of the wardrobe of fur coats that Sophie had given her. But that apart, she looked just like any other elderly Jewish lady of her age and times.

It was a Jewish area and even the tram conductor was Jewish. Day after day, he took her two-cent fare and they would speak a few friendly words in Yiddish together on the journey. But the old lady never said much about her business and no one asked—until one day the conductor could hold himself back no more.

"Tell me, Mrs. Abuza," he asked her, "You get this streetcar every day and every day you come back on the same one, too. Where do you go all these times?"

"Can you keep a secret?" she asked him.

"Of course," he said with a touch of indignation that the Yiddish accent magnified.

"Well, I'll tell you—I am taking piano lessons."

No one needed to give Sophie lessons in wowing an audience. Late in 1920 the *Davenport Democrat* was describing Sophie's new act as—"A riot—as usual." In March 1921, *Variety* covered Sophie's "farewell week" in Chicago and commented:

"Again this column proclaims that Sophie Tucker is the master show woman of the times, the most compelling personality of her class, a conscientious and sincere servant of the box office patrons."

Sophie went back to Reisenweber's—to become the highest-paid cabaret artist in America. And night after night, she was surrounded by show biz magnates who waved banknotes in her face—sure that the sight of all that green currency would make a more immediate impression than the detail of what might or might not be included in a contract.

The *Daily News* reported: "Miss Tucker's return to her famous battlefield of entertainment at Reisenweber's was sensational and unique in triumph." They noted, however, that Sophie had her eyes once more on the legitimate stage. As they said, "The buxom Sophie is bent on more august procedures than the uproarious blues song or jazz and the minor ditty. . . ."

But jazz and those minor ditties were making the audiences cry with laughter. She was perfecting her own way of talking through a song, but because the Five Kings were syncopating it in the background, the audience still went away humming. What was more, she was thinking about writing songs herself. In April 1921 she marketed one called "Learning". How much she produced of that herself and how much was ghosted for her in return for a share of the royalties, has never been established—but it was a convention in the business and Al Jolson for one made a fortune from staking his claim to some of the best songs he ever sang. The real writers of the piece didn't mind, since with Jolson's name on the credits, it was destined for a much greater success than it would ever have achieved without him. It was doubtless the same with Sophie. But in April 1921, she inserted a half page advertisement in *Variety* telling the world she was a songwriter.

It was headed "An open letter from Sophie Tucker" and read:

"To my many friends in this profession. I wish I could write all of you individually, but I'm glad to say there are so many of you that it is necessary to use this page in order to reach you all.

"Perhaps you have read that I have fallen victim to 'songwritis' and, as luck would have it, my first effort as a songwriter looks as if it is going to be a real hit. The title is LEARNING."

The capital letters didn't make it any more a hit than it would have been had she saved her money, but it was an important advertisement of Sophie's newest sphere of activity. As they used to say in Hollywood: "Doesn't matter what you write about me, as long as you spell my name correctly." They hadn't spelt Sophie's name wrongly for years.

In September 1921, Sophie was back at the Palace on Broadway. Abe Lastfogel, quickly rising in the William Morris office—he is now President of the company—sent her a telegram: MOST WONDERFUL PERFORMANCE I EVER SAW YOU GIVE. LONG LIFE SOPHIE.

Soon afterwards, she made her broadcasting début—singing "I'm Nobody's Fool" and "Dapper Dan" on what was quaintly called the "radiophone".

On tour, she was maturing into being even more of a hit than she had been before. The *Washington Star*—a paper which, with Al Jolson as a favourite son, knew something about Broadway headliners—noted that "her pleasing personality carried a 16-inch gun of reserve power", and added "she is the possessor of well-stocked brains as well as a pleasing presence".

"Her programme embraced several new songs of which 'My Mammy' was the best. Its rendition puts Al Jolson in the also-ran class." Such things had never been said about Jolson before.

Back at Broadway's Palace, she was more of a sensation than even before. She shared billing with Lou Dockstader, the famous minstrel, and Houdini who escaped twice-nightly from a water cell, but the adoration from the audience she shared with no one.

In 1922, she changed her act—radically. For a few nights, she brought Bert on to the stage with her and sang a specially composed number to him—"My Boy." A few moments later, a little white-haired old lady came on the stage—and she sang to her a·number called "Don't Cry, Mother". That was precisely what she wanted the old woman to do and what the audience wanted her to do, as they dug into their own handkerchiefs and Sophie sobbed not so quietly into hers. The woman was an out-of-work actress and Mrs. Abuza, wearing her new mink, sitting in the best box in the house, enjoyed it all immensely.

But more lasting changes were on the way. The Five Kings of Syncopation weren't getting on well together and Sophie began to think they should part. She had two young men in mind who she thought could revolutionise her performances. One was called Jack Yellen, the other Ted Shapiro.

77

Me and Myself

The trappings of stardom hung from Sophie like silver bells on a Christmas tree. They glittered and shone not simply to look pretty but to create the (now well-founded) impression of success beyond the reach of most other show folk.

They were evident in the best hotel suites in which she stayed and on the cars in which she rode. They were fairly obvious, too, in her clothes and in those of her mother—who excused the frivolity of her appearance by telling friends: "It's not right for Sophie Tucker's mother to be seen wearing the same dress two days running."

It also became evident in the people around her—although here, the investment was far more calculated. The first of these investments came with Sophie's decision to take on her own songwriter. She found a well-read young man called Jack Yellen who had just written "Down by The O-H-I-O" and was about to produce such standards as "Happy Days Are Here Again" and "I Wonder What Became of Sally".

Sophie offered Yellen a proposition that was too good to refuse: "Write me special songs and I'll give you a weekly salary." The catch was that the songs would never be published and would be Sophie's own property—that meant that no one else could ever sing them or, indeed, even know them unless they heard her sing them. It, of course, didn't prevent him writing other songs on a freelance basis.

This turned out to be a good deal. He could produce a comedy number simply by sitting down with a yellow pad in front of him and bringing a smile to his lips.

"Hard-hearted Hannah" and "You Can't Sew A Button On A Heart" were two of the numbers that gave Sophie a special edge when she performed them.

When he joined Sophie at the beginning of the '20s it was the start of a love affair—platonically speaking. He had all the devotion for her of a son—and in many ways he was treated better than was her own son. As for Sophie, she said in her book "Some of These Days" that he was the best friend she had—next to William Morris.

The coming of Ted Shapiro was less auspicious. He arrived in the wake of the dismissal of the Five Kings of Syncopation. They quarrelled over the money Sophie paid them and when she told them to behave, they united to present her with an ultimatum: either they got more money or they wouldn't open with her the following Monday at the Palace, New York.

It was a tough threat, but Sophie's pride was bigger than even her estimate of the future. It was also helped along by the Morris agency who thought it time she worked as a single. She told the boys they could—and should—go. For a time, Sophie found her old pianist Al Siegel to take their place, but he didn't last. So she did what most people in show business would do in that predicament—she sent the word round Tin Pan Alley that she was looking for a piano player. And the call was answered—by Ruby Cowan, a publisher.

Cowan told her about Shapiro, who though no more than 22 had already had a wealth of experience in vaudeville and cabaret. The son of a Jewish tailor, he had left home at the age of 14 and become a "candy butcher" selling confectionery on commuter trains in and out of New York. He had graduated to vaudeville where he worked on the same bills as Fred and Adele Astaire and later as accompanist to Wellington Cross and Nora Bayes.

Now, Cowan said he might make a good deal with Sophie. "She's at the Claridge Hotel," he told him. "Go and see her."

During the day, a number of other musical contacts rang with a similar message: "Sophie Tucker needs a good piano player. I told her they should see you."

So many people had recommended Shapiro, in fact, that Sophie became quite sceptical. She thought it was a frame up—which is precisely what it looked. When the thin young man in horn-rimmed spectacles called in at the Claridge that night, Sophie was anything but warm in her greetings. She suspected she knew a come-on when she saw one and Mr. Ted Shapiro looked like one.

It was three o'clock in the morning when they met at the Claridge, Al Lackey was in the room with her. She had just finished three shows at Reisenweber's and, although a night person, she was feeling very tired.

There was a piano in the room and on it she placed the "lead sheets" for 26 songs—songs that she would sing in her own key and with her own interpretation of the lyrics. As she made clear at that meeting: "I don't sing songs just as they are written. I start here," she said, pointing to the top line of a song, "and I go down and do one chorus. Then I go back, do half a chorus again. Then I skip down to the third part."

She wasn't giving any demonstrations at that moment and she didn't ask Ted to audition. Fortunately, the youngster was convinced he had a photographic memory and he bundled the music gratefully in his hand and set off for his apartment in Brooklyn. When he got home he sat down at his own piano and started tinkling the tunes as the great Miss Tucker had shown him to do.

It was the early hours of Saturday morning and she wanted him to be in the first show with her at Reisenweber's that evening. It was a daunting prospect. But as Shapiro says now: "I was going to show the people who recommended me that I was as good as they told her I was. I wasn't going to let my friends down."

He worked the whole day through and memorised each of the 26 numbers. At 9 o'clock that night he was at Reisenweber's in his best tuxedo.

The bandstand was at the rear of the dance hall. There were no microphones and he knew that he was going to have to make himself heard in such a way that Sophie would dominate the proceedings. Just before the first show, he went up to her: "Miss Tucker, which numbers do you want me to play?"

Then came the first moment of shock. "I don't know, kid," she told him, "I'll tell you on the floor." The trouble was that his photographic memory wouldn't allow him to jumble the songs up without being able to establish some kind of order.

Her first number she sang facing the audience with her back to Ted. He couldn't hear any of her instructions and was totally lost. The audience could tell he was in trouble. There were uneasy stirrings at the tables in front.

The next few numbers were just as bad. At the end of the performance, Sophie walked off to polite applause and didn't even look at the piano player. He heard her say to Cowan, who had decided to watch the show, "So this is the great guy you recommended to me! I think he's terrible."

Cowan took the sad tidings to Ted's dressing room: "She doesn't think you can handle it," he told him. "You'll play out the week and that's all." He did the second and third shows that night, both slightly better than the one before but not much.

The young man's pride and his reputation might have been in tatters—had not Sophie just had no alternative but to put him to another test the following night, Sunday. This was by tradition guest night. The place would be full of stars—Al Jolson, Eddie Cantor, Fanny Brice were likely to be in the audience and Sophie would pick up their bills. In return, they would be expected to perform.

Jolson was there that night. He sang "April Showers" and Ted, working on a small piano now that had been wheeled out into the centre of the floor, asked him which key he wanted it in. "Oh, I don't know," said the great "Jolie", "I'll start to sing and you pick it up from there." And he did—while Sophie watched in disbelief from the wings. When he scored similar successes with Eddie Cantor singing "If You Knew Susie," she was amazed. "Is this the same fellow who played for me last night?" she asked Mollie. "He's great."

After that Ted felt he was on safer ground, although

81

Sophie said nothing to him. Eventually, he plucked up enough courage to approach her direct. "Miss Tucker," he said, "I have the feeling I was not pleasing you before, but is it better now? Are you keeping me on?"

Brusquely, she said: "I'll tell you later." She never did—not for 45 years. They never had a contract between them and he never called her anything but "Miss Tucker."

Ted went everywhere that Sophie did. He played for her on the stage, in nightclubs and on her charity visits. On one occasion, they played at a TB clinic for war veterans. She was enjoying herself as much as the inmates, quite oblivious to anything she couldn't actually see. The magnetism of her audience was enough for her to feel that at that moment she was being loved.

She certainly didn't notice a thin, ageing man in a dressing gown sidle up to Ted. "Do you think I could play just one number for Soph?" he asked, using the abbreviated name first coined by journalist Jack Lait and now more and more used by her intimates. He whispered his name—but asked Ted to say nothing about him. Having had the promise, he disappeared until the show was about to end. Then he sidled into Ted's seat as the younger man slipped away. He began to play the opening bars of "Some of These Days". Suddenly and instinctively Sophie turned round —and seeing the piano player she burst into tears, totally unable to finish the number. The stand-in pianist was Frank Westphal, attempting a cure for the tuberculosis he had picked up during his naval service. They didn't see each other again after that.

Together with Ted, Sophie continued her musical prison visiting. One of her favourite "cons" was Fanny Brice's husband Nickie Arnstein, in jail for a half-million-dollar robbery which he was supposed to have masterminded. "Masterminded?" Miss Brice is supposed to have commented, "he couldn't mastermind an electric light bulb into the socket!"

Other lesser-known inmates found Sophie to have a sympathetic shoulder on which to cry. From Ossining Prison in New York, James B. Gourlay, Prisoner No. 69942, wrote her: "The night you made your appearance at the prison, someone promised you a beaded girdle and that fact was drawn to my attention.

"During my spare time I have been making beaded work and I have completed a bag that I'm going to forward to one of the best fellows it has been my good fortune to know (yourself). Don't hold your head too high. The bag in question is a very flashy piece of work and you can rest assured you will never meet yourself coming down the street."

And she continued her work for what others considered to be more deserving charities. A whole-page advertisement appeared in the Hartford newspapers. The message ran:

"This page is dedicated to Miss Sophie Tucker for her untiring support given to the Menorah Home—an institution similar to the one where her dear mother is dispensing light and hope and happiness for the aged and infirm."

It was also demonstrating Sophie's attachment to Jewish charities in particular. Her friends continued to send her messages of encouragement in Yiddish and back home at Hartford she was not just the Abuza girl, but the "Yiddisher meidel who did good." They had forgotten some of the less pleasant things they had once said about her.

When Sophie went to visit her old *alma mater*, the Brown School, she led the children in a singing lesson. Her mother went along, swelling with pride—until she heard her sing "Onward Christian Soldiers".

"How can you sing so enthusiastically about Christians going to war?" asked Mrs. Abuza. Sophie gave her an answer that made the old lady smile, but might not have gone down so well with the school. "I should worry if they fight and kill each other," she told her.

Soon, an entirely new audience was going to fight over tickets for a Sophie Tucker show. She told Ted Shapiro that she had taken William Morris's advice. She was going to pastures new and was taking him with her. London was going to learn something about America's taste in entertainers and Sophie Tucker was going to do the teaching.

Round in Fifty

London represented more than just a new potential audience, it was a whole new world. To a brash entertainer like Sophie it was also a very unpredictable one.

On the journey across the Atlantic on the *Homeric*, she was like an excited schoolgirl. Not since Mrs. Kalish had brought her to America as a babe in arms had she been to a foreign country. Her enthusiasm was transmitted to young Ted Shapiro—who now felt fairly secure in her employment, bringing home a regular salary of $150 a week.

On board ship, she was fêted as a star, and like all stars making the trip was expected to entertain the captain and the other passengers. She readied herself to sing with Ted at the piano. He was joined by another pianist called Jack Carroll. Sophie liked the way the two played together so much that she decided to keep the act that way in London.

London itself was as quaint as she imagined it. Perhaps a little too quaint. She recorded in her diary on her first day: "Arrived London, 7.30 p.m. Mr. and Mrs. William Morris and Junior and Harry Foster [he was the British impresario handling the tour on Morris's behalf] met us at Waterloo Station.

"Can you imagine a taxi loading 10 trunks and baggage and passengers and hauling all over to the hotel? Fare 1s 6d—25 cents—and two shillings—14 cents—tip for all?"

Her arithmetic was a little astray there. If 25 cents was worth one and sixpence, 14 cents was less than a shilling (or a bob as it would have been called by her taxi driver).

The diary entry went on: "Registered at Piccadilly Hotel. Beautiful, big spacious rooms and bath—£1. 6s. a day ($5.12). No steam heat, charged 2s. 6d. a day for a fire (47 cents)."

Now what more could be asked by an American who really wanted to see London as it was in the '20s?

As she said, with a typical piece of American chauvinism, "Everything smacked of the ancient days, plumbing of 1492 vintage."

But there were happier touches: "Very courteous servants, page boys and all the help. . . ."

"Dined with the Morris family, Joe Laurie of *Variety* and Harry Foster at the Piccadilly grill. Very nice, but oh, for an American band! English bands know only one kind of music, 'classic' and that lets them out."

On her second day she noted: "We lunched at the Cavour, lots of Americans there . . . lots of friends. Did enjoy my coffee. English people cannot make good coffee. Cream with coffee priceless!"

But if she were tough on the English coffee and harder still on the local crop of bands, she was practically speechless about British vaudeville, known as "music hall". As she recorded: "Went to the Coliseum matinée—worst vaudeville show I've ever seen. So slow, such stage waits. English artists, dirty-looking. Majority, red-nose comedians, no class. Very, very poor."

Now, having said all those less than kind things about Britain and its vaudeville, Sophie was about to find out what they thought of her own brand of entertainment. A full music-hall tour had been booked by Foster on behalf of the Morris agency, but her early experiences on the other side of the footlights made everyone wonder whether she could, in fact, translate American style entertainment to Britain. Perhaps, she wondered, British audiences like red-nosed comedians who didn't look particularly clean? Perhaps long stage waits were appreciated?

Foster decided to take no chances. He booked her into

one of the toughest music halls in London—the Stratford Empire. But he didn't tell its customers about it.

All that was posted on the easel at the side of the stage was one word: "Deputy". Nowhere could you find the name Sophie Tucker. When she walked out on to that stage, there was barely a ripple of sound from the audience—or at least, the ripple that there was came from the conversation of the people in the auditorium.

Certainly, a few did notice that Sophie's gown was glamorous and when she began to speak, her voice made a number of them chuckle. It was five years before the birth of talking pictures and few if any of the people out front had ever heard an American accent.

She sang her first number in utter silence. Her second song was more noisily received—although none of the noise was particularly appreciative. By the time she was ready with her third, she was positively frightened. Everything about the theatre worried her—the sloping stage, which was common in British theatres, was totally strange. Ted Shapiro for his part was only scared that the piano would roll into the audience and give them something to really laugh about.

The men out front, most of them wearing open shirts with mufflers around their throats, some in caps, nearly all smoking—which was totally unheard of in American theatres—seemed to present a threat to their safety. Who could be sure they would leave the theatre in one piece after this fiasco? But Sophie wouldn't give in, even though by now she was really desperate. How could she break into a hardened audience like this one at Stratford? She decided on talking to them in their own language—little of which she really knew. She told them her next song was going to be "It Takes A Good Girl To Be Bad" and then added:: "You're just going to walk right into my kitchen", which with someone as loud and obviously well fed as Sophie, was too enticing a proposition to be ignored. History records that moment as the time the hearts of London melted. The audience was applauding. By the time she had finished her fifth song, they were cheering.

The next night, there was a similar experience at the Finsbury Park Empire. But this time with a slight difference.

The theatre always had a large Jewish clientèle and before long the audience was shouting her words of encouragement in Yiddish. That night marked the beginning of Sophie's warm relationship with Britain, a relationship that was to last and blossom with the years.

Even after that reception, part of her time in London was spent watching the competition. At the Hippodrome, she saw Britain's biggest music-hall star, George Robey, receiving the devotion of audiences to whom he was "Prime Minister of Mirth"—combining cockney humour with the sort of risqué dialogue which would have had him drummed out of an American vaudeville theatre.

Robey was starring in a show called "Round In Fifty"—an updating of the Jules Verne classic, "Around the World in 80 Days", but which assumed the trip could now be done in a mere 50 days. Sophie enjoyed it—so much so that when she was invited to play a small part in the show herself, she jumped at it. She jumped, perhaps, a little too eagerly. "Sophie Tucker says she will show George Robey a thing or two," a newspaper reported. Robey thereafter reported that if anyone was going to do any showing it would be he, not this upstart from the States.

The show was a revue—with the linked theme of the world travellers seeing the local entertainment in each of the countries en route. Sophie played a night club entertainer in one of the American scenes.

On the first day of rehearsal, Robey was noticeable by his absence. Sophie hoped he would come along to wish her well, as stars usually did for guests of her calibre. But there was no Mr. Robey. By opening night, Robey was still making it plain he didn't want to meet her.

Now, according to her own autobiography, on that opening night she knocked on his dressing room door and apologised profusely for being so insulting in the newspaper article—in which, she claimed, she was totally misquoted. "I just can't go out on that stage with you sore at me," she says she told him, yet the big star still refused to talk. She walked slowly to the wings, her eyes brimming over with tears. Finally Robey appeared, apologised that his mind had been on other things and wished her well.

Like so many other Sophie stories, it wasn't quite like that. In truth, it was days before they spoke. And then, only after Sophie decided she could stand it no more.

She gave him no choice but to listen—and then virtually brought down the walls of his dressing room by shouting at the top of her lusty voice: "Look here, George Robey. I know you don't like me and think I've come over here to take away all your glory. But let's be fair. Come down and see my act."

Robey, his vast eyebrows twitching, decided he would be fair. "Yes, I will," he told her, then in her company walked to the wings. After her act, he patted her on the back as she came off, bathed in sweat. The cheers of the audience made the chandeliers tingle.

Sophie was in the centre of some other problems backstage, too. The stars wanted radio sets in their dressing rooms—"wireless receiving sets" as they were quaintly described. But the Post Office said No—because Sophie Tucker was an American.

Mr. W. A. Bennet, a Hippodrome official, was given the news by a sombre civil servant. As Mr. Bennet reported: "The GPO officials seemed ready enough to let either Mr. George Robey, Mr. Barry Lupino or myself have the necessary licence until they heard that Miss Tucker is an American. Then they flatly refused to grant a licence to anybody at the Hippodrome."

The sombre official quoted Section Two of a document entitled "The Authority for the Use of Receiving Apparatus". It read: "There shall be no divulgence to any person (other than properly authorised officials of His Majesty's Government or a competent legal tribunal) or any use whatever made of any message received by means of the apparatus."

As Sophie had for long had—again using the phrase of the time—"an installation" in her New York home, she just reacted in the same way as she did to the lack of central heating.

The newspapers were not quite certain about Sophie the performer. The *Daily Express* commented: "I found Round In Fifty going as strong as ever at the Hippodrome yesterday, but Sophie Tucker, who has just joined the cast, does not, I think, add appreciably to its picturesque side, and certainly not to its humour.

"I am possibly not educated up to an 'American Jazz Queen' (a throne, by the way, with innumerable claimants), but I am as tired of brass-throated syncopation as I am of Alabam, Georgia, sunny Carolina, Tennessee and Dixie, and on this occasion, we had the whole lot."

The part of her act that caused a note of discontent in the audience was when she referred to the Prince of Wales. American audiences were used to hearing their Presidents taken to the edge of ridicule, but the British theatre-going public of the early '20s was still treating the Royal Family as though they were part of the retinue at Bethlehem. Before long, the Lord Chamberlain, Britain's theatrical censor, would step in. For the moment Sophie was regaling her audiences with stories like:

"When he was in America, the Prince of Wales said to me, 'Sophie, be my sweetheart and you can have everything.' I said, 'Come back when you're King. Then you can talk to me'."

That didn't please the Lord Chamberlain at all. A message was passed to the manager telling him that the routine just would not do. So she changed her references from the Prince to Sir Thomas Lipton and his tea. Everyone seemed happy, particularly Sir Thomas.

Equally delighted with the presence of Sophie Tucker among them were a gang of kids in East London who offered her one of their precious hot cross buns on Good Friday 1922. Sophie liked them so much that she ordered trays more of the delicacy—and gave one to every child on the estate. The newspapers were calling her "the Chicago Blizzard".

It was a marvellous tour for Sophie—and for Annie who came along too, shielding her from the pressures of over-enthusiastic fans and the demands of benefit concert organisers who would get up bills purely on the strength of hearing she was in town. Some of the causes were less deserving than others and it was a difficult job sometimes knowing which one she should accept. To the Chicago Blizzard every clapping hand represented a heart beat. Without them she would have preferred to be dead.

Sophie sang five songs in "Around In Fifty". A few days after her opening, the name Sophie Tucker blazed away in lights outside the London Hippodrome, as it was now accustomed to doing in New York and Chicago.

She stayed in "Around In Fifty" for about three months. On her last night, Robey led the applause of everyone connected with the show—the stars, the chorus, the orchestra, the stagehands and the audience. On stage, he presented her with a solid gold jewel box engraved with the names of the entire company. It was the first time such a presentation had been made to a single member of the show's cast.

All the time that Sophie played at the Hippodrome, she doubled in cabaret at the Metropole Hotel in a late show called the Midnight Follies. Both in the hotel and outside it she continued to delight and shock society figures who were barely able to contain themselves at the sight of so much female leg offered by the new fashions. Sophie always liked carrying a big handbag. One evening she and English actress Heather Thatcher were discussing fashion and the subject turned to that handbag. "Why do you need such a big one?" asked the pert Englishwoman. "Oh," said Sophie. "I always have to carry an extra pair of drawers." Apparently Miss Thatcher was unamused.

Most of the other night owls, however, loved everything she could give them.

The critic of the *Sunday Graphic* reported: "The most congratulated woman in London yesterday was Sophie Tucker, who came to London unknown and has become a star in half an hour.

"When in the early hours of Saturday morning a stoutish woman with fuzzy blonde hair and a very pink complexion stepped from her table at the Midnight Follies on the dance floor, took off her ostrich feather hat and plonked it on the piano top, the guests wondered what was going to happen.

"The anxiety was heightened when a tall, thin, pale young man with large tortoise-shell rimmed spectacles

90

seated himself at the piano and strummed ultra-rag rhythm. But in less than two minutes the doubts were turned to electrical enthusiasm.

"The woman was Sophie Tucker, an American who has the temerity to poke fun at Rockefeller, the President, the Jewish writers who write of songs about Dixie and—herself. She even included a reference to the Prince of Wales which, in cold print, might seem offensive but which was, in fact, just genially precocious.

"She plays constantly on her shortcomings in looks, form and voice and in a woman with less talent and individuality, nothing but ridiculousness would result. As it is, her profound charm dominates the effort and you laugh with her." Her rhythm had to "come from the Southern States."

As the paper reported, "Miss Tucker will do much to brighten London."

Al Lackey sent her a telegram from Berlin: TICKLED TO DEATH OVER YOUR SUCCESS. LOVE AL.

But with Sophie as with her entire generation, the messages that thrilled were those from her contemporaries in the business who had seen for themselves just how well she was doing. One of the most treasured read: GLAD TO BE A WITNESS TO YOUR BIG LONDON SUCCESS CHARLES DILLINGHAM. Dillingham was one of the big three of Broadway—after Ziegfeld and the Shuberts. While the others have gone down in history as tyrants, Dillingham is remembered as a gentleman, no mean feat in the environment in which he operated.

Sophie's London success was shared by others in show business almost as avidly as she enjoyed it herself. One man even took a full page advertisement in *Variety* to tell the profession how good she was.

His name just happened to be Tucker (Tucker, the singing violinist) and he also just happened to come from Hartford—but there was nothing closer in their relationship. From an address in London's Holland Park, he assured the show biz bible's readership: "There seems to have been some doubt about the sensational success of Sophie Tucker during her stay in England. Allow me to state that Miss

Tucker was one of the biggest hits that has ever come to this country. Had she decided to remain, I feel certain her success in England would have continued indefinitely."

The telegrams kept pouring in—some of them again emphasising that definite link among the Jewish people in show business. One said simply: "Success—Morris Mish-buhah" (a corruption of the Hebrew word mishpachah, family).

Around the same time that the "success" telegrams poured through the letter box of her Piccadilly Hotel suite, another equally simple message was received. Before long it found its way into Sophie's scrapbook. It just said: "BEST OF LUCK AND SUCCESS ON MOTHER'S DAY—ALBERT."

Despite his few visits to the theatre, it wasn't difficult for even Bert to become bitten by the show biz bug. But his grandmother was determined that he wouldn't follow Sophie's example. "One member of the family on the stage is enough," she declared and the word of the matriarch of the family went out from Hartford and had to be honoured. Sophie, of course, was in no position to dictate anything to "Son", but she told him that she wanted him out of the entertainment industry, too—certainly for as long as Mrs. Abuza lived.

Apart from the cracks about the Prince of Wales, Sophie had them roaring when they heard of her success in taming wild men. "When they're too wild for everybody else"—at which she loudly snapped her fingers—"they're perfection for me."

The word was that in 1922 Sophie Tucker, the American star, was a sensation to watch.

After London, Sophie and Ted went on tour—Sophie staying at the best hotels, Ted "in digs", lodging in theatrical boarding houses and tiny bed-and-breakfast establishments. Today, he remembers one particular feature of that brand of accommodation: "Man it was cold!" He was handed a succession of hot water bottles, but only when a kind landlady said he could put up on a couch in the front parlour of the house was he happy—the room was sufficiently warmed by the gas fire which had been on all day.

Ted Shapiro was a smart young man enjoying every moment of working in the big time—even though he was sleeping in less exalted circles. But he could bask in the glory accorded to the former Mary Garden of Ragtime who was now being described as "a syncopated Marie Lloyd".

It was the syncopated Sophie Tucker who had the society figures begging for more. But the sentimental Sophie was having more than a few moments all her own, too. In theatre after theatre—or to use the terminology of Britain of the day, in "hall" after "hall"—she told audiences: "Now, I'll show you why I came to England. It's my mother." Mrs. Abuza was still happily dispensing charity back home at Hartford, but to the more gullible British audiences, she was a little white-haired old lady who sat at the side of the stage bawling her eyes out.

The *Daily Chronicle* was not very impressed. "This sob stuff may go very well in unsophisticated America," it said, "but really, England has just been through a war." That remark didn't endear the *Daily Chronicle* to Sophie any more than had—after reflection—the reporting of her assessment of Mr. George Robey.

Was the woman really crying? The *Chronicle* accepted that she really was on the night they saw Sophie's performance—"because she had just heard from her 'boy'." The paper had the presence of mind to ask: "Whether she meant her great-great grandson or her young man, I could not guess."

The sarcasm had its effect. The tears on stage brought laughter from the audience. Eventually, "Mother" was told she was wanted no longer.

Sophie was seen hugging the old lady as very definitely real tears rolled down the woman's cheeks. "I've never had so much loving in all my life," she told her stage "daughter".

Sophie was at work almost as soon as she returned to London, regaling the Press with the news that not only had she been a tremendous success at Reisenweber's but that she owned it, too. In addition to owning—as she did—the garage that Frank had managed for her she told them she also had her own gramophone record factory.

The only time the reporter of *The Star* newspaper could

93

get to see her was at three o'clock in the morning. As the paper said: "Folks has to hustle some when she gets the gotch on a new idea.

"When she gets really busy she will deal with a reporter with one hand, rehearse her two piano boys with the other, talk to the stage manager about the lights and build up some more songs in her spare moments."

Charities were not forgotten on this trip. St. Dunstan's, the organisation aiding blinded ex-servicemen, were the beneficiaries of one concert, the Church of England Home for Waifs and Strays of another. The Home for Aged Jews received a total of £1,300—a veritable fortune in those days—from a charity show she actually organised herself.

She and Ted went all over the country and even in the very English city of Nottingham there was one man who hit the nation's headlines by shouting out after her first entrance: "Mazzeltov to you!"

At London's Hotel Metropole, she sang in cabaret and one of her most appreciative fans was the Duke of York —later to become King George VI—who obviously shared his elder brother the Prince of Wales's love of American show business.

Sophie was terribly nervous about the royal visit—particularly since she had to descend a long winding staircase as part of her act. In the end, she did exactly what she feared she would do—and tumbled down the steps virtually into the Duke's lap. The papers had a field day then—one after the other headlined their stories: "Sophie Falls For the Duke of York."

She also fell for the Mountbattens, the most glamorous young people after the Royal princes. Lord Louis and his young bride, Edwina, were star-struck and America-mad. They were almost as thrilled at meeting Sophie as she was to know them.

Most of the aristocracy seemed to be taking to the American visitors just as warmly. At the stately home of the Earl of Sefton, Sophie and Ted were treated to the delicacy of the house—and did all they could to avoid spitting it out. No one had ever offered them cold, poached eggs before but they had to eat them.

Finally, in November 1922, they got ready to leave for home again. There was a full-scale theatrical farewell for them at the Metropole—where Sophie kissed 35 English show biz people who stayed behind after her final show. George Grossmith, one of the top musical comedy artists of the day, made a speech after the "Midnight Follies" at the hotel. No one really understood exactly what he meant. But he told Sophie:

"While there are no beauty roses in England, the roses will be beautiful when Miss Tucker gets them."

The sentiment at least was appreciated and Sophie got her roses, in a basket taller than she was.

The papers had described Sophie's trip as a "syncopated visit". Certainly, it was the beginning of an entirely new facet to her career.

I Know It

The return home of Sophie Tucker the Conqueror was as sweet for this over-sized shouter of jazz songs and sex homilies as it had been for Caesar when *he* got back from England.

She had done more than conquer an entirely new public. By succeeding beyond imagination she had brought prestige to her own people. As it was for Caesar, the journey home was one long parade of love and homage.

In Paris, she called at the salon of Paul Poiret and bought an outfit which she declared top secret until she was ready to unveil it. At another couturier she bought a magnificent long black gown with a black and silver fur wrap. At a stage designer's emporium, she spent $1,000 on patent leather drapes which she thought would help her act. No matter how big a fortune she seemed to be pulling, she was having to spend a vast percentage of that money on what other people in business would describe as "overheads".

In Germany, she had a chance to recoup that lost fortune. *Variety* trumpeted that, at a casino, Sophie won a million—and then casually added it was in the already crumbling German marks and not dollars. She found enough of those marks, however, to buy two German police dogs—animals whose sinister potential had not yet even been guessed.

When Sophie and entourage passed the Statue of Liberty, an idea of the enthusiasm awaiting her came with the hooting of the tugboats' sirens and the coming aboard of a gang of newspapermen. When Sophie heard that among them were a group of cameramen, she decided the time had come to reveal all. She appeared on deck wearing her Poiret creation—a royal blue trouser suit. That, as Sophie herself declared, did it. She had beaten Marlene Dietrich to being the first woman celebrity in trousers—even if La Dietrich did fill them better.

If proof were needed of how important Sophie was regarded outside the business, it came through Reginald Warrenrath, a baritone at the Metropolitan Opera. He wanted someone to debate with him the respective merits of jazz versus classical music—and, views of purists to the contrary, there was no better exponent of jazz to his mind than Sophie. By all accounts, she acquitted herself brilliantly at the debate.

A few days to rest and Sophie was back on tour again, with Ted Shapiro and Jack Carroll back on two pianos. In Chicago, she was once more being feted as the local girl made good—her second home was showing its true loyalty. It was there that Mollie, Sophie's confidante who had been waiting patiently for another trip round her home country with her "Patsy", was taken seriously ill and couldn't continue on the road.

Sophie was now part of the Pepper Box Revue, a show that was little more than her own act with a few supporting turns to give her a chance to catch a breath. When this was over, she was back in vaudeville again, going from one luxury hotel room to another until she reached the West Coast—where she cooked hamburgers for Fanny Brice and had a film test with the Warner Brothers. It is not on record as to whether Miss Brice, Queen of the Second-Hand Roses, was more satisfied with her hamburgers than were Warner Brothers with the film test.

For this first attempt at confining the formidable Sophie form on screen the Brothers Warner placed her in a gingham dress in the middle of a farmyard and told her to imagine she was a farmer's wife. For a girl whose experience with chickens was confined to the soup they made this was not exactly inspired casting—and the fact that Sophie heard no more about it from the studio seems to have proved the point beyond question.

Being in California enabled Sophie to see something of Bert—who was living in lodgings in the area because it was thought it would help cure his sinus problems. But the mother instinct in Sophie was never as strong as the one that told her to go out on a stage and belt her lungs out.

For two years, the vaudeville trek went on—frequently a strange sort of vaudeville it was, too. Not only was there Sophie the star, one or two of the other two-a-day greats, and the usual mixture of acrobats and red-nosed comics, but Helen Keller was on the bill as well. No one thought it demeaning for a deaf, dumb and blind young girl—who through her own brilliance and that of her teacher had learned how to communicate and speak with a strange high-pitched voice—to become a vaudeville turn, but that was what she was. Perhaps her teacher thought it better than the circus. Sophie remembered the girl as having a tremendous sense of humour. It is not difficult to understand how much she needed it.

As for Sophie, she was the star wherever she went —"Sophie Tucker assisted by Ted Shapiro and Jack Carroll." Before very long, Carroll was to leave the act and not be replaced, but it was very early on that Ted Shapiro established himself as the more senior of the two and the one who was almost a son to the woman he still persisted in calling "Miss Tucker". She was more of a mother to him than she ever was to Bert.

When they returned from Europe, Ted's salary was raised from $150 a week to $225. A year later, he approached Sophie's brother, Phil, who was now her manager, and said: "I think I'm due for a raise." He immediately said: "Right" and offered another $150, an offer that was gratefully accepted.

Ted earned that money. He was very young, very enthusiastic and loved every excruciatingly exhausting minute on the road. It would be his job to get to the theatre at 8 o'clock in the morning to be sure to get the number one rehearsal check—the one that would ensure that no one else sang her songs and also that her dressing room was just right.

He had also learned the art of matching Sophie's unerring gift of dealing with an audience with his own ad-libbing.

It was established very early on that he was more than just a pianist. And as soon as it was established, he began getting away with statements that the audience would never have accepted from Sophie herself. On stage, he could insult her all he liked—and all she had to do was smile. Had she been rude to him, it would have looked as though she were merely putting an underling in his place.

In Chicago one night, Sophie came out behind the footlights, wearing a white dress that positively shimmered with the reflection of the lights playing on the beads that covered it. And as the lights shimmered, Sophie collapsed into fits of laughter—so much so that the beads were shaking with her own rolls of fat. Ted said to the audience: "Did you ever see a big white mass of jello before?" The audience loved it. But it succeeded simply because it was a fresh ad-lib, one made to measure for the occasion.

They had a sketch where Sophie was supposed to be bemoaning her fate as the fat girl whom no one loved and who was always without a date. At the end, Ted would disappear to come back a moment later with a beautiful girl on tow. As he disappeared into the wings, he would say to Sophie: "Well, I'll see you two girls later!"

It was an amazing relationship between employer and employee. It was while touring that the pair hit a problem. They had to travel from Chicago to St. Louis, but they could only get one sleeping compartment for the two of them.

That was the time when they would play the Palace at Chicago for two weeks, then go away to another theatre for a month before returning to the Palace again. This time, they had to be in Chicago on the Monday morning, and there was no alternative but to share the sleeper. Ted wasn't exactly ecstatic when Sophie told him the news, but the idea of its being anything but totally decent didn't strike him—or her—either. She would be in the lower berth and he in the upper. As it turned out, they didn't have much in the way of sleep, either of them.

To Sophie, it was a gift from the gods. She could have planned it that way—and probably did. For, as far as she was concerned, there was no better way to rehearse her new act than by holding Ted "captive".

For every opening, Sophie Tucker had to have new material—material that had to be taken and then honed to her idea of perfection. By the time the train steamed into Chicago at seven o'clock in the morning, Ted knew what was expected of him at the Palace theatre that night. What was more, he was first into the theatre for the number one rehearsal check.

Only once did Ted and Sophie have a row of anything like serious proportions. She was the type of woman who took for granted that the people around her would give of their best—all of the time. But she never gave anyone the satisfaction of an out-and-out compliment. The nearest she ever got to doing that was by allowing a younger artist to appear on a bill with her.

Gilda Gray, the Shimmy Queen, was one who benefitted from a moment of Tucker generosity. Julia Gerraty, a big ungainly girl with a voice that could make the rafters rock, was another. Sophie decided to take Miss Gerraty under her own ample wings—and would give her the chance to sing while she herself was making a change. It was on the first night of this experiment that Sophie realised she had bitten off more than she could chew. Miss Gerraty was stupendous—singing so lustily that the audience just wouldn't let her off. All the time that she was singing, Ted was having to look after the "interloper's" musical arrangements, watch the lighting and hope that "Miss Tucker" wasn't getting too angry about the customers' response. But she was.

Sophie took over and had the kind of response from the people out front she had come to expect as a right. But she was still niggled by the appreciation shown to the newcomer. It didn't matter that Miss Garraty was there as a result of an invitation from Sophie herself.

At the end of that show, Ted's stiff white dress shirt was limp and soaking wet from the strain of the evening's

100

happenings. As Sophie sidled up to him, he knew she was going to make some unfavourable comment about the new singer and was expecting a word of thanks for his efforts, too.

The comments came thick and fast—but no thanks. Instead, she said: "You were lousy out there."

It seemed an incredible reaction. As Ted says now, he may have played the odd note not quite correctly, but no way did he feel he had been lousy. Sophie was standing by her statement—much to the young man's disgust. "If I said you were lousy," she told him, "you were lousy."

Ted was full of pride. Nothing would let him stand for that sort of treatment. "Well, in that case," he told her. "I think you had better get yourself a new boy." The next engagement was two weeks hence at Atlantic City and he informed her without much ceremony that he wouldn't be going with her there.

Word got around the business that there had been a row between Soph and her boy, and the night after the rumours started spreading the Chicago music publishers were at the Palace to see the fun.

What they did see was Ted giving Sophie the usual insulting patter—but refusing to look at her while he did so.

The usual procedure was that at the end of the week, Ted would go round to Sophie's dressing room and collect his cheque. At the end of the first week after the row, Sophie sent her maid with the money. Ted refused to look at his boss either on stage or off. But one evening in the second week, he happened to walk past the star's dressing room.

The deep gruff tones of the Tucker voice called out: "Teddy—come here."

In the tiny room, the big Sophie sat, tears in her eyes and with a very sad expression on her face. All she would say was "I feel so bad . . . I don't feel good." Nothing more. No words of apology. But a natural instinct as Ted heard that she wasn't feeling good, brought him to tell her: "I'm sorry." She handed Ted his cheque and together they boarded the train to Atlantic City. She never did say "sorry" to him—or to anyone else for that matter.

My Yiddisher Mama

Sophie Tucker could squeeze emotions out of a song as though it were a sponge. The gift with which Jack Yellen presented her in 1925 was a super-absorbent one, labelled "My Yiddisher Mama".

Yellen, as we have seen, adored Sophie. By writing her that number, he was not only earning his salary, he was stating clearly how much of a mother figure she already represented to him. The sentiment came easy to him in other ways, too. He was a religious man in the Orthodox Jewish sense of the term. He had a profound knowledge of Jewish history. From such roots, it was not difficult for him to think in terms of an old "Yiddisher" lady sitting in an ancient East Side tenement building. Neither was it difficult for him to write the song in Yiddish.

His own command of Yiddish was extremely fluent. Despite the legends, Sophie's was not quite so good even though it really had been her mother tongue. She would spend hours writing laborious letters in the language to her mother. She would be delighted to read—as she often could—lavish praise of her performances in the Yiddish press, but she would freely admit that an average-length article would take her an hour to get through.

The Yiddish lyrics of "Yiddisher Mama" were written down for her phonetically and that was how she learned them. She developed right from the start a form with that tune that would be with her throughout her career. She would first sing it in English, then Yiddish—and always the tears would roll down her cheeks like falling rain.

The song was a link not just with her own Yiddisher mama who, as the years went by, became more and more an idyll as well as an idol to her, but also with her past.

Brought up in a kosher restaurant, she developed an inordinate liking for forbidden foods like shellfish and banned culinary treats like lashings of butter on her steaks. To her knowledge, she never ate ham, bacon or pork, but the chicken salads she would enjoy out of town were not always all they seemed. The idea that to be kosher all meats had to come from animals killed in a certain way never struck her at all. But when she was out on the stage—one Yom Kippur eve, fasting as usual, she sang it taking over from Cantor Josef Rosenblatt who, of course, wouldn't appear at all—"My Yiddisher Mama" was an act of religious dedication. She might even have felt a better "mama" herself by singing the tune, although Bert never had reason to prove it. He was pining for affection, but it never came from the one direction from which he had a right to expect it.

Sophie took the new song everywhere she went—to audiences for whom it was as warm and reminiscent as a plate of steaming hot chicken soup, and to people who had not consciously seen a Jew in their lives.

And she sang it in jail, too. The Hebrew Brotherhood at Sing Sing wrote to tell her just how much they enjoyed "Yiddisher Mama". And at San Quentin prison a pale, dejected prisoner whom Sophie thought she recognised wept at the sound of the melody. His name was Herman Roth, one of the most prominent "sheister" lawyers of his day who told her he was behind bars after being double-crossed. Sophie went to see the prison warden and the governor of the state and was convinced she was responsible for his release in time to die in his own bed.

Round about the same time as the tears from "Yiddisher Mama" were drowning unsuspecting theatregoers, Sophie was getting a new title for herself on almost—but not quite—similar lines. She was being billed as "the Last Of

The Red Hot Mamas", although no one had found out who her predecessors had been.

She sang a song called "Red Hot Mama, Turn Your Damper Down", standing over a box from which a red light glowed, while an electric fan blew tissue streamers looking like flames around her. It was Ted Shapiro's job to make sure that the box was ready for Sophie's opening when he took the morning rehearsal check. On one occasion, it was not ready.

"Right," he told the theatre manager, "We're not opening." The theatre man couldn't believe what he had heard. A youngster like Shapiro deciding that the biggest star in vaudeville was not going to open? It was laughable—but he phoned Sophie to check. Ted was put on the line and she asked him: "What's the matter?" He told her and the phone was passed back to the manager. "If Ted says we're not opening," she told him, "he's got good reason. We're not opening." The red box and the electric fan were ready for that evening's performance.

Late in 1925, the box, the Red Hot Mama routine and the sheet music for "Yiddisher Mama" were all packed up ready for an ocean voyage. The Morris agency had got a return booking for her in London—this time at the prestigious Kit Cat Club.

The club was in the Haymarket at the corner of Jermyn Street and next door to a cinema. It was a magnificent place—with a wide, winding staircase down which everybody was guaranteed to be able to make an entrance; every guest on the main ground floor, wearing full evening dress, had to walk down that staircase.

If the men wore dinner jackets or lounge suits, they were consigned with their ladies to the balcony above. The night that the Prince of Wales came to hear Sophie sing yet another song about him—for the moment she had still not learned to do things the Lord Chamberlain's way—he, too, was shown to a table above the platform from which she performed.

The Prince said he was delighted to hear her sung comments about his recent tour of the United States, but before very long the censors ordered the offending line to be

104

removed. Sophie put up such a fight about it this time that her booking at the Kit Cat was almost terminated. It was thanks to Lord Beaverbrook's order for his papers to drop the story completely that the matter was finally allowed to die down.

A few years earlier she would doubtless have embroidered on her royal associations to show that she had been presented at court. As it was, she did no more than say she dreamt she had been.

"A man asked me—'Do you know how to curtsey?' So I put him right. I told him: 'Why, I've taken more bows than the King and Queen put together'." At which point she sauntered up to the majestic Queen Mary, tapped her on the shoulder with her fan and said: "Come and hear me sing while I'm at the Holborn Empire."

That was the point at which she said she woke up. Believe her? Why not? What her money had failed to achieve, she was as free as anyone else to dream. And if it wasn't true, who would know? As she herself said: "Fancy a ham actor like me dreaming a dream like that. I suppose only a ham actor would dare."

And perhaps only a ham actor would pretend to get as steamed up as Sophie did on hearing that in his will a wealthy bachelor had left his house to "women aged between 18 and 28"—with the instruction that "no fat women need apply".

Said Sophie: "I've sung 'Nobody loves a fat girl' but a lot of people do love me. This old skinflint obviously never loved anyone in his life."

The critics took Sophie to their collective heart every bit as much as they had on her previous visit. Said the *Daily Sketch:*

"A banging of tables announced the American queen and I saw—beginning low—an exquisite pair of feet and ankles and two legs delicate enough for a marquise. Then a plump, good-natured bust and a really funny face, crowned with a forest of yellow hair. Miss Tucker surveyed the diners like a seasoned campaigner and then proceeded to cast her spell. I confess to becoming one of her victims at once."

The writer added: "There was a quality of sincerity and

105

burlesque about her singing that made the feet restless and yet touched the strings of sentiment and even pathos with the deftest of technique.

"When she sang about her 'Sweetie', one could see that she knew the term was absurd, but nothing else could describe the young man of her choice."

She showed her usual charitable strain early on. When Ian Maxwell Stewart, son of a London producer, was charged with murder, Sophie immediately contributed to a fund to raise enough money to retain a K.C. for his defence. The young man got off.

Seeing who was going to the Kit Cat was almost as entertaining as seeing the show oneself. Other entertainers would go every night after their own performances and have the club's midnight supper—a snack and a bottle of wine. In one evening, there could be Gertrude Lawrence, Melville Gideon and Jack Buchanan all cheering Sophie ecstatically from their seats in the balcony.

Most acts were booked into the Kit Cat for five to six weeks. The club owners knew that with the experience of Reisenweber's behind her, this was Sophie's home ground. So they booked her for six months. And they were right. With an intimate night club audience, Sophie could get nearer to her public than she could ever be on stage. There was a two-way magnetism that sparked electricity between them—and if the atmosphere grew hot, as it frequently did in those pre-air-conditioning days, she always had her chiffon scarf to wipe away the sweat. The scarf was becoming as much a part of her costume as her stunning gowns and hairstyles.

"I've been away from London for so long that I have lost 28 pounds fretting to get back," she told her audience and they screamed for more. She gave it to them.

She talked as Ted played: "It makes no difference how old you are. It's just how young you feel.

"Good looks today don't get you very far.

"It's just like a waggon without a wheel."

It was the sort of lyric that no one sang in the bath, but matrons would secretly ask her for the words—and she would have them duplicated and sent off to all who wanted them, with Jack Yellen's blessing.

She told *The Star* soon after her arrival this time: "I hope to add to the gaiety of London." After one evening at the Kit Cat, it was clear she had done just that.

Yellen was now on ten per cent of everything Sophie earned. Naturally, if she were paid £400 a week to appear at the Kit Cat, Yellen got a £40 share. But if she got £50 for a private party that no one knew about, Yellen—much to his surprise—would find himself having earned £5 of that, too.

The parties were becoming an essential part of her time in London. And it was at one of these that Sophie was introduced to the Prince of Wales for the first time. He was at a party at Talbot Square. There were only eight in the group, but the host phoned the Kit Cat and asked if Sophie would mind giving a private command performance.

After that evening, Ted Shapiro played for the Prince's own private parties—as he learned to dance with his current girl friend, Poppy Morton.

Miss Morton lived at Bryanston Square. Nobody knew about her or about her romance with the Prince, except the very small coterie of titled people whom Edward felt he could trust implicitly. The only outsider, in fact, was Ted who followed him from one party to the next.

Finally, as the time to leave Britain drew close, Shapiro told the Prince he wouldn't be able to play for many more of those parties. He said he understood, and Alistair Mackintosh, the Prince's equerry, told him: "There'll be a cheque on the way to you." It never came.

Later, the Prince danced to the tune he called his favourite foxtrot—"If I Had You," a standard written by Shapiro while at the Kit Cat.

But two shows a night at the Kit Cat and one private party afterwards only made Sophie Tucker feel unemployed. While playing at the club, she thought she could earn a little pin money playing at the Alhambra Theatre, too. It was then that tragedy hit the famous Charlot's Revue at the Prince of Wales. Its star, Maisie Gay was constantly ill, and when her understudy came on, she found she didn't know the words of any of the songs. Could Sophie help out? She did—while continuing at the Alhambra, the Kit Cat and doing the odd private party in one evening.

The *Sunday Referee* newspaper noted: "A ray of sunshine (and some ray) fell across my path when Sophie Tucker came along from the Alhambra to strengthen the show. Sophie would prove a veritable tower of strength to any show. She is a very remarkable artist." And Hannen Swaffer declared: "What Mistinguette is to the little Paris midinette, so Sophie Tucker embodies the very spirit of American sentimental and syncopated emotion. In England, we have Marie Lloyd; in Paris, they have Mistinguette. Sophie Tucker is no less a triumph for America."

Charlot didn't know what to pay Sophie for her life-saving contribution to his show. "Send me a bunch of flowers," she said. And it was flowers that she got—doubtless laced with a cheque or two as well.

This one-woman productivity drive—with Ted Shapiro still enjoying it as much as any of the paying customers —went on even after the Alhambra engagement came to an end and when Maisie Gay was well enough to go back to work.

Sophie did a variety act twice nightly at the Victoria Palace, two shows at the Kit Cat and also took a straight part in a musical play at the Duke of York's Theatre called "The Monkey Talks". In this she appeared as a clown, singing the prologue and a number called "The Broken Hearted Clown", just like Pagliacci.

Her nightly timetable now read like this:

7.15 Victoria Palace
9   the Duke of York's
9.30 Back at the Victoria Palace
10.30 The Kit Cat
12.30 The Kit Cat again.

As Sophie said at the time, the Americans couldn't understand why she worked so hard. "If I did (slacken off), they would say, 'What's Sophie out after now? Can't she stick to her jazz? Hasn't she made enough money at the old stuff?'"

So why did she do it? The temptations were simply too big for her to refuse. She went through 50 songs in a day and ended that day exhausted. But, she said in 1925, "that's what they like me for." And above all, Sophie had to be liked.

She was, however, always willing to experiment. While still at the Alhambra, she did a number called "Tall, Dark and Handsome." Ted Shapiro had been to a party which lasted all night and much of the early day too and by the time he got to the theatre for the matinée he was almost comatose.

The number began with the famous Tucker talk of the verse. She would say "Isn't that right, Teddy?" and he would say "No. It's not" and go on to tell a completely different tale, much to the audience's delight.

That afternoon, she said: "Isn't that right, Teddy?" and all Teddy could do was to try to pinch himself awake. . . . "What . . . what . . . wha. . . ." was all he could produce from his mouth. He sounded tired and looked drunk. The house collapsed. It was great theatre and very natural. It was so good that they decided to keep it in the act. But it never worked again. The spontaneity had gone and they were professional enough to see that it had.

While in England she took advantage of the short distance across the English Channel and saw something of Europe. She went to Paris, Brussels and then to Berlin—a city crowded with transvestites and prostitutes and restaurants serving the best food she had tasted since leaving Hartford.

In Paris, she was shocked by the nudity of the Folies Bergères. "Not even Ziegfeld would have dared to go that far," she quipped. But the girls were beautiful and she could appreciate that—if not in the same way as the men customers who queued to get in. The Folies were showing how mistaken were the fashionable dress designers in trying to banish the bosom. The girls at this most famous French theatres not only had pretty faces, they also had the most beautiful breasts ever put on public view.

Sophie was earning between £800 and £900 a week in London—more than almost any other artist and still more than the average working man saw in eight or nine years. The Ministry of Labour decided it was time to investigate. They said they were "viewing the situation with some concern"—since income tax only became due after six months' work in the country.

But even the threat of the Board of Inland Revenue

couldn't stop Sophie Tucker's insatiable thirst for work and the rewards that it brought. Late in 1925, she signed a contract to play in a show built around her. It would be called the Sophie Tucker Revue.

Sophie was going to receive £225 a week plus 15 per cent of all the receipts over £1,000. Before long it would be called finally "So Long Sophie"—a twist on a title already registered by the producers called "So Long Lettie".

Theatres were booked at Birmingham, Glasgow, Liverpool, Manchester, Leeds—and Bradford.

That, though, was one plan that didn't come to fruition. Early in January 1926, Sophie received the message that inwardly she had been expecting for years—certainly the one she had feared most. Her mother was seriously ill. At the age of 78, Mrs. Jennie Abuza was not expected to pull through.

The trouble was that Sophie was 3,000 miles from home and the only way to get there was by the next available ocean liner—the Leviathan which was not due to sail for several days. It wasn't a moment to think about contracts. She told the Kit Cat she would be leaving, sent similar word to the organisers of her other engagements and told Julian Wylie she wouldn't be going to Bradford at the end of the month for the revue. Bradford was renowned as Britain's toughest theatrical town—you had to break your back falling downstairs to the roll of drums before you got any applause there. But despite the legends about Bradford, that wasn't the reason for her breaking the contract. She said she was sure Mr. Wylie understood. He didn't—and made it very clear he was going to sue her for £26,000 for breach of contract if she didn't honour the agreement.

For once, a Sophie Tucker show would not go on. Her Yiddisher Mama had to take first place. But there were those days to go before sailing and the best way for her to fill them was by working. Meanwhile the Kit Cat planned a last-night party for her.

Lord Londonderry, until recently Education Minister for Northern Ireland, was among the celebrity guests. And as Sophie sang "Me and Myself", the people in the club swarmed around her joining in the song. Lord Londonderry was with his friend Lady Carlisle. Other society figures included Lady Portarlington, Lord Westmorland, Lord Wimborne, Lord Londesborough, Sir William Wiseman, the Viscomtesse de Sibour and her father Gordon Selfridge— who was almost a member of the titled aristocracy himself.

And there were her contemporaries from show business there, too. Ethel Levey sang a song from the gallery. There was a duet from Peggy O'Neil and Lew Hearn, and Heather Thatcher did a child imitation.

All this, however, was but a prologue for the big, totally unrehearsed show of the evening. That began with the entry of a little man with curly black hair accompanied by a taller, elegantly dressed young woman. It was Irving Berlin and his bride, Ellin Mackay, making their first public appearance since their elopement. Berlin, born in Russia, of poverty-stricken parents, had "dared" to woo the daughter of a Catholic millionaire. By actually marrying Berlin, she had been disinherited. Only Sophie, Berlin said, could bring his bride and himself out of hiding.

He had a reputation for being the shyest man in show business, but that night Sophie put him in the spotlight and together they sang his newest hit "Remember"—while Ted Shapiro played for them.

As they sang, Ellin stood on a table to hear them and was immediately followed by almost everyone else in the room doing the same thing. Never had so many tables stood up to so much wear from so many well-heeled feet.

"Sophie and I began together," said the songwriter in the little voice that inspired comedian Joe Friscoe to say: "You gotta hug him to hear him". It was almost the hit of the evening, although that came when Sophie herself made a little speech. As Ted lightly dusted the keys behind her, she said in the rhythmic voice usually reserved for advice to other women: "I hope to see you all real soon again. I give you my word, it breaks my heart. Someone calls me home."

That morning there had been more news from Hartford. Her mother was worse. "She won't make the grade any more. I shall go straight to her bedside and stay till it's all over. Then . . . this sort of thing will start all over again."

111

"This sort of thing," she explained, was working her heart out.

The tears rolled down her face and down the faces of dozens of other people there that night. And they continued in her hotel suite. A procession of people called to say good-bye. Flowers and farewell gifts arrived. A little Jewish girl—whom Sophie had almost adopted while trying to get her a visa to America where the child's father had fled from Russia—came and cried with her. And there was even a farewell message from the Prince of Wales.

Sophie had sent the Prince a bundle of her records. Major General Trotter wrote her a note that said: "His Royal Highness desires me to say that he regrets to hear you are leaving England and is glad you have had such a pleasant visit to this country, also to express his good wishes for a safe voyage to the United States."

Even in 1926, there could be no guarantee that a transatlantic voyage would be safe. The omens certainly were not good. After a rousing send off from Waterloo station with Rudolph Valentino at her heels, Sophie told the crowds: "You have all been absurdly kind"—she boarded the Leviathan on what was probably the worst voyage of its life.

The waves were like mountains and the furniture inside the ship rolled around like the table and chairs of a dolls' house being carried in and out of a child's bedroom. The stomachs of the passengers rolled as much as the furniture and the doctors had never been more busy.

Sophie was asked to take part in the ship's concert, but she said she had no heart—or stomach—for it. She was more concerned about a message that might any minute come out of the ship's radio room.

Finally, Rudolph Valentino persuaded her to sing a few songs. She said she would—if he went to see if there were any messages for her. He was away a long time. When he came back Sophie was in the middle of her last song. The look on Valentino's face told her what she was scared of most. He handed Ted Shapiro the telegram and disappeared. When Sophie had summoned up enough courage to take the form from Ted, she could have told him the message without looking at it. It said simply: MA PASSED AWAY.

The Broadway Blues

"SOPHIE TUCKER TOO LATE". More than one news-paper on both sides of the Atlantic put it as simply and as bluntly as that. And no one was more aware of that fact than Sophie herself. When her father had died just a few years before, she could barely forgive herself for not being with him and then for missing the funeral. Now that it seemed she had done it again, it was more than she could bear to think about.

The rest of the stormy voyage to New York was totally unbearable to her. When the Leviathan docked, the presence of Moe and Annie at the dockside made her feel only slightly easier. She took it for granted that they had come to the pier direct from the funeral. Mrs. Abuza was strictly Orthodox and without any question burial would have already taken place. It would have been regarded as a mark of respect to the pious. But she was not too late. Mrs. Abuza knew Sophie would want to be at her funeral and had made the family promise to wait for her elder daughter's arrival.

As soon as Sophie arrived at the small house in Hartford she ran straight up to her mother's room to say a few last words and plant a final kiss on her brow.

The funeral was the saddest experience of her life. The poor and the old waited in the cold January wind for the coffin to be lifted slowly out of the house, followed by Sophie and Annie, Philip and Moe—all weeping profusely. The only one in the party to be composed was Ted Shapiro who offered more support to his "Miss Tucker" on the way to Hartford than her close relatives could possibly have done.

The coffin was borne into the funeral home, while at the side of the small chapel Ted sat with the family. The rabbi stood silently for a moment, looked down at the coffin in front of him and then at the mourners, each person weeping louder and wetter than the one sitting next to him.

"You my children," he told them, "you just don't know what you have lost." If the Abuza family allowed themselves to forget their tears for a minute, the full meaning of that statement might have registered. They didn't know what they had lost? They had just lost not simply their mother but the very lynch-pin of their existence as a unit.

Still the rabbi went on: "She was an angel . . . but you don't know what you have lost."

The coffin was then removed from the chapel and a long procession of visits began. First it called at the Jewish orphanage, then at two or three of the other charities which Mrs. Abuza had helped; finally, just before burial, it was taken to her pet cause, the Jewish Home for the Aged. There, as everywhere else, the coffin was brought in and set down on a platform. The rabbi began yet another eulogy, this time directed at the celebrity in the family:

"Mrs. Abuza was such a darling lady," he said. "But Sophie, you don't know what you've lost."

By the time the funeral procession arrived at the cemetery, Sophie knew precisely what was lost. Her emotions overcame her completely. As the coffin was lowered into the ground, Sophie tried to jump in the grave after it. Only quick thinking and a strong arm from Ted prevented what could have been a very nasty scene.

Mrs. Abuza left a will—not a legal document because Sophie, with all the superstition that Jewish daughters have about doing such things for their parents, wouldn't hear of getting her to a lawyer and her Moe wouldn't dream of aiding and abetting such an act either.

She simply left a note to her next door neighbour—which the neighbour's daughter had written down for

114

her—and said it should be produced after her death. She bequeathed her jewellery to Annie, her bedclothes to Annie and Phil (Moe would have got some of it, too, but he wasn't married, she explained) and her clothes and mink coat to Mrs. Ettie Greenberg, her best friend. But what about Sophie? Mrs. Abuza thought about that. "And to my daughter Sophie," she wrote, "who gave me everything, I leave nothing—because she don't need anything."

It was a long time before Sophie could think of working again. The only thing she needed was her mother. For weeks the only song that ran through her mind was "My Yiddisher Mama" and every time it did, she would dissolve into more and more tears.

Finally, William Morris—still the devoted "Boss" —persuaded her to go back to the stage and do a few benefit shows. She did them—but uncomfortably; knowing that anything she did on the stage, the girl serving at the speakeasy next door could do equally well. As she said in "Some of these Days", it was a mechanical Sophie Tucker, not the real thing.

The stage which had long since ceased to be Sophie's happiest medium was not the place for her return to normality. Eventually, it was William Morris who hit on the idea that would bring her back to a still pining public. He opened a night club on West 52nd Street, between Broadway and Seventh Avenue, and called it "Sophie Tucker's Playground".

Among those there on opening night were Mayor Jimmy Walker, Jack Buchanan, Bea Lillie, Gertrude Lawrence—all reliving Sophie's triumph at the Kit Cat—Texas Guinan, Joe Frisco, Harry Richman and the man who had been the first to tell Sophie Abuza to leave Hartford and try for the bright lights of New York, Willie Howard.

Variety reported: "After five years absence from Reisenweber's, Sophie Tucker's debut at her Playground Wednesday evening was the scene for the heaviest first night in Main Street cabaret history. The frenzied shouts and cheers came from the throats of the town's most front-paged. Over 500 celebs sat down in the same place at the same time, peacefully—a Broadway record."

115

It was a place where the show business greats would gather to talk—and sing and swap gags. When Sophie announced that Al Jolson had just had a successful tonsilectomy, comedian Jack Rose quipped: "I offered him a million dollars for the one with the mammy song in it."

It was the place for celebrities to be seen enjoying supposedly private parties. When millionaire Charles Schwartz won the British Grand National, he decided he would hold the celebration 3,000 miles away at the Playground.

Everything seemed rosy for Sophie again—except that in London Julian Wylie was still determined to wrest £26,000 from her for failing to keep her contract. Normally that would have meant her having to go to England to fight the case, but Mr. Justice Avery agreed to take her evidence "on commission"—that is, second-hand—with her swearing a document in New York and then being represented in the British courts for the action.

Sophie was well represented. One of the great aces of the Bar, Sir Patrick Hastings K.C., was her counsel.

But she lost her case, officially. Wylie was awarded damages of, not £26,000, but £100—hardly enough to make Sophie even once dab her eyes with the chiffon handkerchief.

There were other consolations and money from other sources. She posed for corset advertisements in the New York papers—without baring an inch of flesh or showing a centimetre of pink suspender. The name Sophie Tucker in association with a firm's products was enough.

She also looked to the future in her business, too. On May 28, 1927, the *New York Times* announced: "When the invention of television was made public recently, Miss Sophie Tucker with an eye to the money-making possibilities secured an option on the rights to broadcasting scenes from revues." It never happened, but it was not just an interesting idea, it showed her finger was on the pulse of the future. Who in 1927 knew that television would ever have more than peep-show possibilities? She may never have brought other people's revues to the screen, but she would one day find that television was as

116

exciting a medium as standing in front of a nightclub crowd.

But there had never been a crowd quite like the one at the Playground when Eddie Cantor and George Jessel, both members of the Tucker generation, came along for what they described as "an evening of fun". That fun consisted of introducing a young dancer, whose name they would only announce after the audience had shown whether or not they liked him. The people politely gave the impression that like him they did. After making an introductory announcement there was nothing for the visiting celebrities to do but reveal the youngster's identity—Bert Tucker.

Sophie didn't know whether just to be annoyed or to warmly congratulate him. She compromised. She said she would send him to dancing lessons. But even then, as the youngster tried to do something important under his own steam, Sophie found it simply impossible to be warm. In her book, she made the incredible statement that she thought the young anonymous dancer looked "a lot like my son".

Sophie had joined a revue called "Le Maire's Affairs", an attempt by a leading executive of the Shubert empire, Rufus Le Maire—and a very big name in Broadway circles in the late '20s—to go it alone in the big time. The show was most notable for Sophie's launching of the period hit, "When The Red, Red Robin Comes Bob, Bob Bobbin' Along", yet another tune that was soon to be taken over by Al Jolson as his personal property.

Bert made his show biz debut in this show—carrying a placard in a minstrel line up. The other members of the company used to tease him—not because he was Sophie's son so much as because he was green to the business. He got tired of being sent out for the keys to the curtain. Before long, he was joining another company on his own and doing a fair soft-shoe shuffle in the show as well as a parody of his mother performing her burlesque number "A Turkish Towel", complete with white bath towels.

In Chicago, Sophie went to see him—and made a curtain call speech to the audience: "For the 14 years that I have been coming to Chicago you've accepted me in everything I've had the pleasure of bringing for your approval. Not once have you let me down. Today, Sophie

117

Tucker, the mother, gave you her son and you accepted him, for which I am deeply grateful." The cynics might have said that she was most grateful if at all for the big round of applause she got herself.

In May 1927, she announced that Bert would star with her on Broadway in the spring edition of the Winter Garden's spectacular. For once it seemed that Sophie and Bert were really at last building up the right sort of relationship. Sophie took him backstage at the theatre, chatted with the other members of the company and talked enthusiastically about the future—the thrill of seeing their names up there in lights together.

The thrills and the fun lasted just four days. On the fifth day, Bert was taken to hospital after a complete breakdown. It would only be temporary, Sophie reported, Bert would be back. Those lights would spell out the names of Sophie and Bert Tucker before long. When he got better, he would go back to the family home at Barker Street in Hartford and then—watch out Broadway. Broadway never got that chance. It was the nearest Bert got to stardom and probably the nearest he got to his mother.

She would spend a lot of money on him, buy him clothes and luxuries, but there was none of the affection he desperately craved, even after that experience. It just was not natural to her. Casual visitors to a room where Sophie was sitting with Annie would notice the gruff, almost aggressive way in which she would talk to her younger sister, but no one ever doubted there was a strong loving bond between them. With Bert there was no wool to pull over anyone's eyes.

But she was more generous to her immediate family than to some people she met casually. She would find it convenient not to have any coins on her when it came to tipping a hotel bellboy. "See to it, Teddy," she would say to Shapiro who might give the boy a quarter. "What did you give him so much for?" she would then ask. "A nickel would do."

She, of course, was coining in enough money never to be anxious about another hotel bill in her life. But for the first time in years, she had reason to worry about how long it

118

would all last. Rufus Le Maire had been doing so well with his "Affairs" on the road that he decided the time had come to open in New York. The only problem was he didn't want Sophie. She, he concluded—and with the connivance of his backers—was box office poison in New York. That was not a sentiment echoed by the Shuberts or the management of the Palace, but Le Maire thought he knew the more sophisticated Broadway revue audiences. He wasn't exactly correct. The show closed without her six weeks after it had opened in New York.

Certainly, the Palace never had reason to complain. She did a week there, standing in for her old adversary Nora Bayes, and was a sensation. Miss Bayes was hardly delighted about that—a few nights before she had walked off a benefit bill in aid of the vaudeville artists' benevolent fund because she said Sophie was getting better billing and a more choice spot on the bill than she was. And she still couldn't forgive her for having the audacity to attempt to upstage her in the 1909 Follies, although Sophie, to her eternal credit, had no such compunction.

As a result of her difficult behaviour, Nora was banned from the Palace for life—although she did once persuade the theatre's manager to place her photograph on the easel in the theatre foyer for just one morning so that she could drive past it and imagine that she was still the theatre's principal star. Two days later, she was dead.

Despite the views of Mr. Le Maire, however, Sophie Tucker's career was far from dead.

The Winter Garden revue, "Gay Paree", duly opened with Sophie doing her usual, comfortable, single act. It did so well that the newspapers were suggesting that all the cast could safely rent themselves apartments for the year. The show lasted throughout the summer and then went on tour.

In Detroit, she worried about the need for publicity. With an act devoted to giving sexual advice to other women, she knew what would make newspapermen sit up and take notice. "Less clothing for the girls," she declared to be her new crusade. It was, she assured her shocked readers, the only way young women could benefit from the advantages of the American summer sunshine. "I won't be satisfied," she

119

said, "till I have women free to appear on the street as they do in 'Gay Paree'." With that Sophie doubtless tightened up her own corset and went to the Shubert Opera House for her next performance.

In Chicago, the *Examiner's* critic wrote: "I want to run when Sophie sobs. For then, she is more deadly to me than Al Jolson singing 'Mammy'. But even Sophie, in an intelligent manner of speaking, slobbed and I stayed where I had been put. It seemed to me that this was the best revue the Messrs Shubert had produced since Mr. Jolson left the Winter Garden. It was certainly the nakedest." (Which gives you some idea of what Miss Tucker had in mind). The review of the revue went on: "The employment of the nearly nude is done with more feeling for art than for nature."

The critics were not Sophie's only friends in Chicago. When she made her tours of the nation's prisons, the Chicago underworld figures there were her loyalest fans. They were constantly looking after the interests of the entertainer whom they regarded as one of the best of "the boys".

She was playing poker in her Chicago hotel room one night—with the "other boys"—when Ted called her to the phone. It was personal and sounded important. "Soph?" asked the voice at the other end. She muttered something like "and who do you think you are interrupting an important game of poker?" but all the dismembered voice would say was: "Don't wear your ice tonight." He wouldn't tell her why, he simply repeated: "Never mind, just don't wear your ice."

For Sophie to be told to go without her jewellery was like being instructed to walk down Chicago's State Street completely naked. It would probably worry the people who saw her as much as it worried herself. But it was also an instruction which she could afford to ignore at her peril. She was very friendly with Chicago's famous Mayor Thompson. What would he advise?

"Stay there," he ordered. "Don't take your own car to the Tivoli Theatre tonight. I'll send a squad car."

Winter had turned into spring, but spring in Chicago

can be bitterly cold. It was with the Windy City's most blustering gales blowing all around them that Sophie and Ted went that night to the Tivoli—in an open touring car, courtesy of the Chicago Police Department.

Nothing more was heard about it for a week. Then there was another phone call. Again Ted picked it up and again, in the same gutteral gangster's voice, there was the same instruction: "I wanna talk to Soph."

"Who is it?"

"Never mind. Let me talk to Soph."

"Is there a message?"

"No. Let me talk to Soph."

Ted told her there was a tough guy who wanted to talk to her. "Tell him to come up," she ordered. He came. Ted opened the door and a typical Hollywood-type hoodlum was standing there, a noticeable bulge under his coat. He walked in, past the five men sitting round the hotel suite table, poker cards stacked in front of them.

"You don't know me, do you?" he asked Sophie, who was totally unperturbed about his visit. "No," she said.

"Well," he told her. "I'm the feller who called you and told you not to wear your ice."

At that point, Ted stepped into the picture. He thought it was a soft touch. "Is there anything I can do for you, or anything you want Miss Tucker to do?"

He replied that he wanted nothing at all.

"No, I was just sitting in the bar," he explained, "we love Soph here and I heard two men talking in a booth that they were going to heist her for her ice. Now as I said we love Soph here and we're not going to have that."

As Ted looked suitably gratified, he added: "Besides, they were out-of-town boys." And that was a much bigger crime than simply heisting Soph's "ice."

The man wouldn't even take a drink. He walked out and everyone breathed a heavy sigh of relief. Not least of all, Sophie's friend the Mayor.

On another occasion, playing at a Chicago nightclub, a man pulled a gun at a girl sitting at a stage-side table. He called to Sophie: "Get that broad out of here and nothing will happen. Just get her out." It seemed that the gunman was

121

shocked to see his old flame out with another man—on his first night out of jail. But he knew that Sophie was a "square guy"—he had been one of the prison inmates to benefit from a box of matzos sent by her for their Passover celebrations.

After "Gay Paree", Sophie joined Earl Carroll's Vanities—which was yet another attempt at copying the magic of the Ziegfeld Follies. She wasn't happy about being sandwiched between so many beautiful girls—she knew that no matter how big a star was she could only be intermission fodder for the important part of the show, girls with plenty to reveal.

After the "Vanities", Sophie decided to go back to one of the most dedicated audiences she knew, in London—although there would be a family celebration first. Annie was to be married and Sophie organised the kosher wedding supper that went on all night—following a service conducted by the most celebrated cantor of the age, Yossele Rosenblatt.

Sophie, who stood next to her sister under the wedding "chuppah", the canopy that symbolises the blessing of heaven on the newly-weds, could only think how much her Yiddisher Mama would have wanted to be there. She might also have reflected on how she would have liked to be in the bride's place herself. With Al Lackey dancing attendance on her that day, there was every chance it might happen sooner rather than later.

Rightly, *Variety* covered the nuptials as if they were an opening on Broadway. The paper reported: "Soph stole the show. She looked like two million dollars—in cash."

Sophie entertained the guests with her favourite song of the moment, "Mama Goes Where Papa Goes", and Al got the message. Usually, she did it pointing a gun. That night she didn't do so—and judging by the look in Mr. Lackey's eyes she didn't need it, either.

He travelled to London with her, shared the same hotel suite—where this little, thin, almost frail-looking man would persist in calling over to his girl: "Hey, Soph—come over here." And she would. Lackey, the man with the Napoleon complex, was trying to prove to Sophie that he really did love a fat girl. She certainly thought that he did, and that was all that counted.

Recently, he had become a clothing salesman, but officially his visit to London was as her manager—a role her brother Phil had been fulfilling in fits and starts. Would Sophie and Lackey really marry?

Sophie was against it at the time. After all, she had had two attempts at matrimony and both had been disastrous. There was really little point in their going to the trouble of organising a ceremony. She had him without responsibilities and neither objected to sleeping together without the blessings of a rabbi. In later years, she was to say that her love life had cost her $1 million. In 1928, she was still trying to decide whether or not to continue working up to that total.

When newspapermen wanted to know about the little Mr. Lackey she fenced them off with statements like: "There are other things that come first, my brother, for instance. I must get him married off before I think about myself." Moe was working as a lawyer in Brooklyn but was taking his time about finding a wife—a crime in Jewish circles of the age.

"I've seen my sister happily married," said Sophie. "But there still remains my brother. He is a bachelor of 35 and he must have a wife. It is one of my jobs."

Deep down, there were fears that Sophie could be just repeating her previous mistakes. It was difficult to keep up a marriage when a partner was in the same business—and Al now liked to think that he was. It was particularly a strain trying to make jokes all the time, and that was how he liked it.

As much as anything a London visit was a chance for Sophie to see her name in print in a whole bunch of newspapers again, newspapers that would find their way into the bulging scrapbooks which were now kept and catalogued for her by the Morris agency, but only after she had personally cut out everything and stuck every item in with her own hands. A paper had only to mention her name casually in the midst of a very long article or list her among 200 other personalities, and the whole article would be assiduously cut and then fixed in her album. Most stories were syndicated by the wire agencies and they would be printed word for word in every newspaper in the United States. Since Sophie subscribed to a press cuttings agency that cut up every single newspaper in the United States, she would receive every one of these identical articles—and every single one of those articles would be stuck in her book.

Before leaving for London, she sent off messages to leading British journalists—like the *Daily Express's* Hannen Swaffer, who was becoming a personal friend, every bit as important to her as Sime Silverman of *Variety*. She knew that most of them would print the news of her imminent arrival in their papers and they, of course, did just that.

Her principal job in London was to go back to the Kit Cat, which by now had overthrown its rule that every guest should be a member of the club, and was just a smart restaurant. She "doubled" there with performances at the Alhambra, the Coliseum, the Palladium, the Holborn Empire and the music halls of the East End. She completed her six months in England by doing a Greek drama and a nightclub engagement at the Grosvenor House Hotel in Park Lane.

Before she started work, she went on a tour of the theatres to see what the "opposition" was like. At the Winter Garden Theatre, she held the curtain up for 15 minutes while the audience stood and cheered—and admired her newly bobbed hair.

When she finally started work, she decided she would earn £750 a week—and she did. But she worked for it, and so did Ted who was with her all the time she was on stage, wherever it was.

When she went to bed in the early hours of the morning, she had sung no fewer than 48 songs since starting work the previous evening.

Each of those songs was specially tailored for her audiences. Unlike other entertainers—Nora Bayes was one in particular—she was never afraid to adjust her material if she thought it might go down better with changes. This time, there were no jokes about the Prince of Wales. But she did sing a ditty about Winston Churchill—then the wild rebel of the Tory Party—and another about Oxford losing the Boat Race.

For reasons best known to themselves, Sophie and

Britain's two prestigious universities were on very good terms. She went to Oxford and sang there to the Union. There were also special Eton and Harrow nights at the Kit Cat, which Sophie loved. "You've no idea how excited these boys got when I went on," she said delightedly after the first of these.

Perhaps that put her in a ready frame of mind to do what everyone said was the impossible. She took part in a Sunday evening performance of the play "Socrates"—playing the philosopher's mother.

It didn't quite go according to plan. The white robes she wore were so voluminous that she tripped and fell immediately she got on stage just as she had in vaudeville years before and again before the Duke of York. Then she couldn't remember any of her lines. The audience fell about almost as much as she did. She later blamed the sandals she had to wear—after years on high heels, they just weren't any more suited to her than was her toga.

The producers—who were quite serious in their intentions to introduce Miss Tucker to the better things in drama—really ought to have known what they were letting themselves in for the moment that Sophie agreed to do the play.

"In the play I'm called Xantippe," she told excited reporters, who suspected this could be just another one of those publicity stunts. "I'm called Xantippe, but that's the same as Mrs. Socrates, all right. So now you know why the old guy took poison."

Sophie saw the funny side of the Greek role.

"I think it's the biggest joke that has ever been made," she said. "Every time I think of it I want to laugh. I believe in trying anything once, and I am going to put my heart and soul into Xantippe."

The play was really going to be called "Xantippe and Socrates". "But," she explained—in case anyone had any other ideas—"there's not going to be much Socrates about it. I'll see to that. I just don't let the old boob get a word in edgeways. I've never before had such a mouthful to say, and I enjoy brow-beating the old bearded boob so much that at rehearsal they kept on telling me not to say things that are not in the book."

125

By this time, she was tremendously excited by the opportunities this drama was going to provide for her to emote. As she noted: "Say, Xantippe must have been a regular cat. I suppose that's what comes of making women wear these long baggy curtains instead of skirts. In the play, Socrates comes home at dinner time, but refuses to eat the goat flesh and garlic sauce I've cooked for him, so there's a nice how do you do with me as the principal talking machine. When I've finished, it's no wonder the poor guy is glad to die."

The Sunday Play Society, however, were equally glad they had Sophie Tucker to breathe life into their otherwise staid production at the Adelphi Theatre.

The normally cold *Morning Post* woke up to the revolution threatened by Sophie Tucker and commented that it had been "a little wearying in spite of the respective charms of Miss Viola Tree and Miss Iris Hoey.

"But when Miss Sophie Tucker strode on as Xantippe to give Mr. Edmund Breon as Socrates a bit of her mind for coming in half an hour late for his roast goat and garlic sauce, somehow the whole theatre woke up to delight. It was the touch of genius over writing that was in itself quite clever, and the thing ended with cheers."

The play was produced by André Charlot, whose revue she had saved on her previous visit. Now she told him she would like to do so again—and possibly have Bert with her. It was an idea that came to nothing.

But she did go on tour with her variety show—working for no salary, but taking a hefty percentage of the profits out of which she would pay everyone else on the bill.

Sophie became ill during the tour—nothing serious, but she needed a doctor. He came, gave her some pills and then refused to take a fee. She felt she had to do something in return for his kindness. Finally, a deal was made. She agreed to do a charity concert for his hospital, which she did.

Her favourite audiences were in London's East End. As she repeated time after time: "These are my own people." She spoke to them in Yiddish and the audiences answered her back in the same way. They opened up their hearts to her so warmly that she broke a rule that she had up till then

126

felt she would keep for the rest of her life: she sang "Yiddisher Mama" to them in Yiddish. After her own mother's death, she had decided it would be too great an ordeal to sing that version. But once done, she could do it again—although perhaps with less genuine emotion. The first night when she sang it in the East End, however, her chiffon handkerchief was wringing wet.

Everywhere she went—singing "Yiddisher Mama", "Some Of These Days" or "Me and Myself"—the people who paid the tickets wouldn't let her alone. At Grosvenor House one night, the guests clapped solidly for 15 minutes before they would allow her to go off. At the Kit Cat, Lady Edwina Mountbatten, the Marquis de Case Maury, Lady Brecknock and the young American millionaire "Laddie" Sanford were hemmed in by the crowds at the top of the normally spacious staircase and just couldn't move.

The chefs from the kitchen, the hairdresser from the restaurant's own salon and the cocktail shaker from the bar came out to hear her.

"That shows what a reputation can do," said the *Daily Mail*. "Listening to Miss Tucker, it was inevitable that one should try to analyse her immense appeal. It is certainly not one of mere looks. Her most popular songs are based entirely on references to her plump appearance. Nor is her voice, though full, of high quality.

"The reasons why she can command her enormous income—and in a relative manner, by the way, her contract must be of pleasurable interest to the Chancellor of the Exchequer—are her enunciation, her slurring of words that the audience know or guess and her bell-like peal at the point where she is getting her effect.

"But perhaps most important of all is her marvellous memory for faces. Both before and after her songs, she would stop and exchange greetings with people she had met only once before, making them feel like her oldest acquaintances."

The *Daily Mirror* completely agreed: "What an extraordinary woman she is—the possessor of an overpowering personal magnetism and the singer of the most attractively silly songs. She is as perfectly turned out as a blancmange.

She is devastatingly efficient. Her hair is waved just like the pictures in the advertisements.

"If someone wrote songs worthy of her 'putting over' powers, she would make the Albert Hall dance a jig."

Again, she sang for the Prince of Wales—at the Derby Ball—and again she did a string of private parties. Sir William Joynson-Hicks, the Home Secretary, best known as "Jix", liked her so much that he invited her to entertain at a party at his stately home at Newick Park, Sussex. It proved, said the *Star*, "that he is much more of a gay dog than is popularly supposed."

At a charity performance for ex-servicemen—the Haig Fund—The Duke and Duchess of York came to renew their acquaintance with her. They came again to the Kit Cat. When Sophie wrote the words of her next song on a blackboard for the people out front to join in, the members of the royal party seemed reluctant to do so. The Duchess, now the Queen Mother and loved for her unstuffiness, pumped one man in the party on the back and said: "Sophie said you should stand up. Do what Sophie says." The room dissolved.

Other professionals came to her for tips. Maurice Chevalier, about to make his first trip to America, wanted to see how a big star from the States operated.

Finally, at the end of 1928, Sophie revealed there were "family reasons" for her wanting to go back to the States. She wouldn't go into them any further—and no one ever knew for sure what those family reasons were. It could have been a problem with Bert. It could have been Al. No one was saying.

But when she made her final appearance at the Holborn Empire on the last night of the tour, it was as though the family was some 1,000-strong and none of them had any problems at all.

For 55 minutes, she sang to the people at the Empire —some of whom went there in the evening dress they wore at the Kit Cat. They sang "Auld Lang Syne" together and Sophie was crying her eyes out. By the time that the final curtain came down Sophie was in tears again.

Later, she couldn't walk out of her dressing room until

a path had been cleared through all the flowers sent to her by devoted fans. They all went off that night to local hospitals.

Around one of the bouquets was tied a small puppy. Sophie took to it immediately and got ready to take it back home with her.

To her hotel suite, a messenger brought a clock, inscribed: "For breaking all records". It came from the management of the Holborn Empire.

There was nothing left to do now but pack her trunks and collect up the bric-à-brac she had acquired on the trip. She also took home her coffee percolator and the remainder of the stock of Maxwell House coffee she had brought to England—because she couldn't stand the British variety.

It was the only thing she couldn't take in England—apart from perhaps the lack of central heating in most of the places in which she stayed.

On September 5, 1928, Sophie returned home on the Leviathan—with George Arliss among the other first-class passengers.

Four months later, a newspaper shouted: "How A Fat Girl Can Love". Finally Sophie had married Al Lackey.

Who Wants 'Em Tall, Dark and Handsome?

Sophie Tucker (neé Kalish Abuza) and Al Lackey (né Albert Lackerman) were married in New York on December 14, 1929. Sophie later said that she should have known better, but all the outward signs that day were that they were glad they had taken the plunge.

To Sophie Al represented the refutation of her own adage that "nobody loves a fat girl" and that did her now frequently sinking ego a lot of good. To Lackey, who adored bullying people because he didn't think anyone would otherwise ever do anything for him, Sophie was comforting. She was certainly that when he cuddled up to her.

But no one ever suggested that they were in love. In 1929 they were already too old for that to matter very much.

For a time, however, they certainly had a lot of laughs. Al gave up any pretence now of being in the clothing business—he sold dresses or men's suits, according to which paper you read—and concentrated on being Sophie's business manager. What that really meant was that he had access to new contacts who would then lend him new sums of money with which he could gamble.

Soon after their marriage, he returned home from the Saratoga Springs race track and poured $20,000 into Sophie's expansive lap—his day's takings from the race meeting. Two or three days later he had lost every cent of it again.

Al would borrow from anyone who would take a chance with him. Most of these generous souls got their money back—from Sophie. In the early days of their marriage, she didn't seem to mind her husband's mental blockage when it came to working out how much of a mug's game gambling could be, but before long it took serious toll on their joint existence.

For the moment, however, everything seemed to be coming up roses for them. He would watch Sophie's performances and when she sang "Tall, Dark and Handsome", the look in her eyes was undoubtedly directed at this very short, paunchy, fair-haired man she had just married.

News of the marriage took three weeks to get out. For the first time in her life Sophie was concerned about her privacy. She was also concerned about her appearance. There would be no honeymoon, she announced, until after she had had her face lifted.

In fact, the facelift was not done simply to satisfy Mr. Lackey when he ordered her to bed. More, it was with Messrs Albert, Harry and Jack Warner in mind. The surviving Warner Brothers—brother Sam died the morning after their greatest triumph, the première of Al Jolson's "Jazz Singer", the world's first "talkie"—invited Sophie to Hollywood.

Never deterred by advice on the folly of trying to copy anyone else, the Brothers Warner announced that they were going to turn Sophie Tucker into a new Marie Dressler. They were going to star her in their film "Honky Tonk".

It was set in a New York nightclub and Sophie, of course, was the night club queen. So far so Sophie. But the story called for her to yearn for her fireside—and for men who usually had too much to drink. In the end, her daughter denounces Sophie's sinful friends in front of her nightclub clientèle. It was all aimed at extracting every tear an audience could give, and then, when the eyes were still sore, bringing everything back to a more even keel to knock 'em dead in the aisles.

The Warner Brothers studios were a strange outfit. The brothers themselves still hadn't got used to the idea that they had made it big with talkies and that the near-bankruptcy that had forced them to think about the gimmick of

Vitaphone sound films had now receded into the past. Every day, their mother would bring their lunch down to the studios for them in a picnic basket.

For Sophie, working for them was yet another opportunity to prove how much money she could make. She was not merely holding down a three-figure weekly salary from the studio but was doubling at the Los Angeles Orpheum Theatre in the evening, too. There were also the inevitable private parties.

One person not needed while she was on the Warner lot was Ted Shapiro, but he continued to get his usual weekly salary, and so did Jack Yellen. But Shapiro struck it lucky with Warner Brothers, too.

Very early on in the shooting schedule, the director, Lloyd Bacon, whom Shapiro knew, asked him: "Ted, have they signed you yet?" When he said, no they had not, Bacon said that he ought to be on the payroll because he was needed as a technical adviser.

The following day, Ted received a telephone call from the casting director at the studios, Eddie Manix. He told him: "I've just talked to Lloyd and he needs you. Will you come down to the studios to talk?"

They met the next day with Ted worrying himself silly about how much he should ask. Bacon had suggested he ask for $1,000 a week. But that seemed too much—especially if the studio ever found out he was being paid by Sophie at that time. What if he were just shown the door? He would end up still having to do it for nothing because Sophie ordered him to work.

At the time, he was getting $350 a week from Sophie. He decided to tell the studio he had double that figure. "I'm getting $700 a week from Miss Tucker for our normal work. . . ." he began, at which point Manix interrupted: "You wouldn't want more than that, would you?" It was the moment of truth. He could have asked more, but now it was too late. A deal was struck and he was going to get $700 for giving advice.

Weeks went by, but no one ever asked Shapiro for any advice, or to do any work either. All they did expect him to do was to go along to the lot on Fridays and collect his salary cheque. He did so every Friday until Sophie and Al packed up their belongings and moved East again six months later. He did so for three months after shooting stopped. He never told the studio he was leaving—so the pay cheques could still today be mounting up in the name of Mr. Ted Shapiro.

The response for "Honky Tonk" was a lot better than the picture deserved. None of the lyrics for the songs Sophie sang in the film were right for her and she definitely missed the rapport she always had with a live nightclub audience that was never more than a couple of feet away from her. But the papers found it exciting. Particularly in England where *The Times* commented:

"Miss Tucker . . . gives us a series of songs rich in sentiment and humour and interpreted in a way which can only be described as dynamic." The critic went on to add: "Here is Miss Tucker employing all her arts of dramatic song recital with disturbing generosity and telling giddy young men and erring daughters what she thinks of them.

"In its rather brazen way, her personality is an entertainment in itself and her lines contain many flashes of wit and homely sentiment. Interspersed are as much dancing and melodrama as a hearty appetite for these things could desire. The whole production is extravagantly mounted and of its own kind, notwithstanding crudities of feeling may be called a success."

The *Daily Express* was slightly less kind: "People who like added sentiment and slushy banalities of one kind and another will find ample entertainment in Miss Tucker's ripe performance, but there is little for the intelligent picture-goer."

A certain Arab sheik was much more impressed. In fact, he was quite overwhelmed. Sheik Abel Rey proposed marriage on the strength of seeing the picture.

"I saw yourself in cinema play 'Honky Tonk'", he wrote from Port-ou-Bain, beginning his letter "Honoured Madam". And he went on: "I wish to tell you I think you are the most beautiful lady I have ever seen. Your generous proportions appeal to me more than I can say. I am a very rich man and have an old splendid house in Algiers with 18 rooms and much silver and gold.

"If you will do me the honour to come to Algiers, I shall make you the favourite of my harem, give you your own chamber with bath and many lovely gowns and shawls. I also have a pet monkey which I shall be honoured to present to you."

Sophie was suitably overwhelmed, but said "No thank you." And she explained, "I'm afraid my husband, Al Lackey, might not like it."

For the moment Al and Sophie were staying faithful to each other. Wherever she went, he went, too. "It's too bad if husband and wife have to keep running away from each other," she said in October 1930. "That puts marriage on the rocks. What about the marriages where husbands and wives only meet for breakfast? That isn't marriage. That isn't love. That isn't happiness. That's glamour. And glamour is bunk—for the average girl."

So what was Sophie's secret? In 1930, she was back to her old tricks, making statements which she either knew to be untrue or which she had told so many times that she was unable to distinguish fact from fiction.

"I eat pretty much what I want and feel healthy and strong always," she said in June 1930. "I eat meat and lots of tasty vegetables and I never diet. I've never had so much as a facial or a mud pack in my life." She made no mention of the facelift she said she was having for "Honky Tonk".

Then came another fib. Never dieted? When she left for yet another trip to Britain, she announced she was going on a strenuous diet—to put on weight. Her bulk, she declared with newsmen's ears and eyes straining for whatever titbit they could gather, had gone down from 219 lb. the last time she was in London to a mere 164. And London liked her fat—because she was funnier that way.

A Professor Straussberg, a European specialist—an acceptable name to the publicists—had guaranteed that by following his diet regimen she could put on 25 lb. in 10 days. "It calls for four meals a day and a lot of rice," she explained.

And that was the spirit in which she, Al, her sister Annie and her husband, and Ted boarded the Ile de France for the

134

Above
She was always well prepared
– in this instance, "In Case
the Red Hot Mama Got Too
Hot" 1925

Left
That First London Visit 1922
Sophie is second from the
right – with Ted Shapiro on
her left

Sophie in 1934 She always liked to
call the tune

With Jackie Coogan in 1937

journey to Britain, where she was going to star with Jack Hulbert in the show "Follow A Star".

Before leaving for London, Sophie had suffered one of those sad periods in her life she called "heartaches". Mollie, the maid who became one of the principal influences in Sophie's professional career, was dying of cancer. Sophie moved into the hospital with her during her last days and as she said in "Some Of These Days", when the little coloured woman died, "She took a piece out of my life when she went."

The trip to England was uneventful most of the way, with Sophie doing what she liked to do best, sunning herself on deck, eating lots of food—not necessarily with rice—and entertaining in the evenings.

Before her performances began Ted would go to the piano and start playing. One evening, as he played, all hell seemed to be let loose as a giant wave thrust the huge liner on to its side and furniture, passengers and crew all fell about in a mad frenzy. Women screamed, men started praying and in the first class lounge where Ted had begun tinkling the keys, limbs cracked and snapped as did the crystal glasses being carried into the room by the stewards.

The piano and its stool, which were permanently fixed to the floor, were the only things that weren't sliding hideously around the luxurious room. Over the noise of the screams and shouts, Ted kept playing.

The ship righted itself very quickly, but the screams and the prayers and the twisted nerves of the passengers continued. Walter Damrosch, the eminent American conductor, sidled up to Ted: "For heaven's sake keep playing." He did and before very long, all was calm again.

Damrosch was the first to go over to Ted and congratulate him, followed by film star Norma Talmadge and Hattie Silverman, wife of the Editor of *Variety*—which turned out to be not so good for Sophie, who was among those spreadeagled by the lurch of the ship.

Once she had dusted herself down, Sophie made her way to the radio room of the ship and dictated a message to the wire agencies in New York. It was a good time to do so, because she didn't think anyone was around to hear or watch. She described how the singing of Sophie Tucker—who in reality had not opened her mouth other than to scream a couple of times—had calmed down the near panic-stricken passengers in the first-class lounge. She forgot to mention the help of a certain Mr. Shapiro.

Unfortunately for Miss Tucker, Hattie Silverman heard about Sophie's message and dictated one herself—to her husband Sime. The following week and much to Sophie's embarrassment and surprise, *Variety* came out with a story about *Ted Shapiro's* calm show-must-go-on performance that night.

What Ted had actually played no one could remember. Chances are he wasn't playing anything very important or very well, but what he did was considered very brave indeed by the owners of the ship, the French Line. They gave him free passage on their ships for life.

Arriving in London, the word was out that "Soph's back". More and more people were dropping the "ie" from her name, although she would always keep it for her billing. Dressed in pink and black, she was met at Waterloo station by an entourage from the Foster agency and by the various people she had worked with on her previous trips. On the cheeks of each and every one of them, she planted a kiss and muttered something that sounded like: "Oh, my darling oh. . . ."

They were just a section of the crowd that always gathered at the railway station to greet Sophie. When she arrived this time, among those cheering her was Prince George, later to be the Duke of Kent—accompanied by two bodyguards.

"See," she told her friends back in the comfort of her hotel suite, "see I've lost my tummy." She actually sat still for five minutes at a time—which prompted one of the Foster executives to ask, only half mockingly, "Soph, old girl—what's the matter with you?"

Soph was the much sought after guest at the big society gatherings. Her near namesake, Sophie, Lady Wavertree, invited her to her garden party at Sussex Lodge. But when the entertainer arrived, she politely declined the invitation which her Ladyship had intended to go with it. "The two

Sophies are going to play tennis," she announced while the guests clapped politely. "Oh no, they are not," replied Sophie Tucker. "You'll have to find someone else." Which she instantly did.

But she wouldn't have wanted anyone else to take her place in "Follow A Star".

Hannen Swaffer, the "Pope of Fleet Street", invariably her most devoted admirer in London, with his flowing untidy hair and the cigarette ash that always decorated the front of his blue serge jacket, put his feelings into type. In the Daily Express on September 18, 1930 he stated categorically:

"Sophie Tucker, making her London debut as a musical comedy star, scored last night an enormous personal triumph.

"The first act of 'Follow A Star' full of novel ideas is one of the most interesting I have seen in a musical show for a long time. Although the second is not so good, it is a clever show.

"But it was Sophie Tucker's night. She is the wife of the world's worst conjurer who discovers in a New York cabaret that he is an English baronet. . . .She proved when she stepped out of the play towards the end and sang seven or eight numbers with Ted Shapiro at the piano, that she was the cleverest artist of her kind in the English speaking world.

"She sang about how fat she was, told women how to make love—'lonely wives, you should worry; that's what God made sailors for'—and she sang about her size, and how red hot she could be and how cruel she was. Nobody believed it, but it brought down the house.

"Beautifully gowned in white, with her golden hair shining and with her face beaming with sauciness, Sophie held the house for number after number, daring, challenging and yet so attractive. 'Follow A Star' with Sophie is splendid entertainment. Sophie is the star to follow."

Incredible as it may seem, everything she was doing on the stage now seemed so fresh that it was almost automatically greeted as a new Soph doing a new thing.

Sophie herself declared herself pleased with the way things were running. The show, she said, will run for years. If it did, she would keep it fresh by changing her numbers. But she wouldn't change her dress style—nor would she do what so many gay young things were doing and walk around with bare legs. "If I were slim and young and full of sex appeal, then bare legs perhaps—but not for me . . . not that mine aren't very nice legs. . . ." Mr. Swaffer obviously believed they were.

Why was she so successful? One reason was that she always carried the rest of the company with her. Other stars ignored the lowly acts on bills with them. Not Soph. Before every important opening—and "Follow A Star" at the Winter Garden was one of those, all right—she gave out presents to everyone with whom she worked. Every girl in the chorus had a piece of jewellery; every stagehand a sweater.

All Maurice Chevalier got when he went along to the Winter Garden was a long, passionate kiss. "I think you are the most wonderful artist of your kind that I have ever seen," he told her once he had come up for air.

She was such an important commodity in England that she was appointed Chairman and Governing Director of a newly registered company—Sophie Tucker Enterprises Ltd.—which would produce its own plays and films.

"Give me a month or two to get used to the job," she declared, "and I will try to show you just what a fat girl can do when she becomes a governing director and chairman." As things turned out, she did very little—and so did the company. There was talk of her linking up for a film with Jewish East End boxer Kid Berg, but it never amounted to anything.

As always, her biggest fans were the Jewish people who came to see her, first at the Winter Garden, then at the Kit Cat where she did yet another season and at the Palladium where she appeared in a number of charity benefits.

She was in London for Yom Kippur 1930, obeying her conscience and declaring as usual—but this time only after deep-hearted consultation with Hannen Swaffer—that she would do justice both to her job and to her God by working on the sacred day but without a drop of water or a crumb of bread passing her lips.

Some British Jews were not so impressed as her American fans had been. Doris Franks wrote from Kilburn in North West London to declare:

"People of the Jewish faith must be very thrilled to learn that Sophie Tucker is going to fast and also work on Yom Kippur. While it may be good for her figure to 'refrain from eating, drinking or smoking', it is contrary to the letter of the law to do any manner of work.

"The mere cancellation of the matinée on the day of the fast will hardly count for much, as doubtless Sophie Tucker intends to go through with her part on the previous evening. This is equally important to Jewry as the fast begins at sunset.

"Do please tell her how delighted we are to hear that she is 'remaining a Jewess and also doing her job'. Professing Jews and Jewesses will be getting on with the job of fasting and would be obliged if the usual bunkum that appears at this time of the year in the papers would be cut out."

Just to show how international Sophie considered her work, she replied to that by announcing she was going to start singing in Gaelic.

She was, however, deeply in love with Britain—and particularly with the British theatres. She didn't have to work so hard there as she did at home, where she was expected to do five shows an evening—completely ignoring the fact that she tried to do as many shows herself as her income tax situation would allow. She said: "You can't be an artist five times a day in a theatre where the back seats are so far away that the audience don't hear the first song till you are halfway through the last."

If there were five performances a day of "Follow A Star", she would have been able to fill the theatre just as many times.

She really wasn't that much of a hit for the show that Jack Hulbert had been planning. She came alive only when all pretence at a plot was thrown to the wind, but that had been enough.

Finally, in November 1930, Sophie announced she was leaving. As for Jack Hulbert, he said that without her the show couldn't continue as it was. So he announced it would

139

lay off for two weeks to recover from the experience of having Sophie dominating everything in it.

Yet she wasn't leaving England, not just yet. There were plans for a provincial tour but for a time she contented herself with writing a daily column in the *Daily Express* that always managed to read like one of Jack Yellen's lyrics. For example, there was this one:

"Some of these modern girls think it's swell to lead a crowded life, but there are some things you just can't crowd out of it—and love's one of them.

"Oh, yes; I know, everyone likes to jeer at love; what they are really jeering at is sentimentality. You've got to know the difference.

"Never care what they say to you—give your heart the lead of your head and even if you get it broken, believe me, you'll have had a bigger slice of life helping and standing by the man you love than living on late nights and bright lights and too many sweethearts—until you lose your good looks and find you've never had anything worth remembering."

In another of these gems of journalistic style, she wrote: "There's three things girls always talk about when they get together—men, clothes and money. They talk about money and clothes, the most, but think about men the more.

"And what a lot of women get wrong ideas from this one little bad habit! Take it from me, any girl who talks about men as a collective noun has got a disappointment coming. Take Sophie's advice and be a one-man woman. And if you can't, keep quiet!

"Plenty of girls measure their success in life by the number of men they get. Show me a girl with a dozen boy friends and another with one man to love, and I'll tell you who's having the good time.

"The funny part of it is that the girls who collect men like postage stamps, always get the wrong sort. They fall for some high-polished grease ball with a smooth line of talk and all their experience doesn't prevent 'em being left cold.

"They think it's swell to eat fancy food and doll up in their glad rags every night and have a new sweetheart every time the weather changes. Say, d'you think they wouldn't give their shirt, after a few years of it, to change places with

140

some home-town girl who's had one man and stuck to him, and knows the meaning of together?"

"Together", of course, was one word that Sophie never did know the meaning of. But no one bothered to ask from the bottom of whose heart the ghost-writer was speaking.

But she may have been on the right wave-length with this: "Whenever a woman starts pulling the companionate marriage stuff, you can bet your last dollar her marriage is a failure. Sometimes, she doesn't realise it. Tells you she's broadminded and what a good pal her husband is when they have time to be together. She also tells you a bunch of boyfriends keeps a gal young and her husband up to scratch. Now that's all very well if you don't care two cents for your husband and are counting on separation." As she said, if that ain't the truth, then "Sophie doesn't know husbands."

The *Express* called these daily slices of wisdom "Philo-SOPHIES". The most revealing was probably this one: "Whenever I see a woman cry, it sets me thinking. There's something wrong in crying, beyond the cause of your tears. Don't tell me that every woman has something to make her blue. I know that better than most people. Do you think that because I sing every night and get called a good fellow I never have a heartache?

"Heartaches? Maybe I have more than most. But, I'm too old and wise to show it. There are some silly folk in this world who hold that tears have a cash value—but don't you believe it. Tears never got a girl anything but a red nose.

"Tell me you can't pay your rent . . . tell me you're fired from your job, tell me your man's left you and you'll never have a new sweetheart. But will Soph prescribe that good cry and feel better for it?

"Not on your life.

"Here's a wisecrack that's part of my philosophy: the tougher the break, the broader the grin.

"If your sweetheart deserts you, it isn't salt tears that are ever going to bring him back. It isn't sticking around and sobbing and letting him see you're crazy for him. Believe me, holding a man is very simple—after you've lost one or two.

"So take it all with a smile as part of the training, and

141

put on your smart clothes and your best smile and go out and enjoy yourself. If your kisses can't hold the man you love, then your tears won't bring him back."

The journalism bug bit deep—and the same day she was giving one of her philoSOPHIES in the *Express*, she was writing an article in the *Daily Sketch* called "The Worst Of Being A Woman"—which she said amounted to having to sit in the comfort of the back seat of a car, while outside in the cold and rain a man was changing a flat tyre.

In fact, all the evidence was that she was writing as frequently as she had been performing. Not only was she doubling in two national daily papers, but she was writing a weekly agony column in the *Sunday Graphic*—called "Sophie Tucker's Post Bag".

One of her answers to questions in the *Graphic* went like this: "Many girls often take up the stage as a means of livelihood. Maybe—well, just say they have a hunch it would be rather nice to act.

"Girls, if you are lucky you will end up in the back row of the chorus. If you're unlucky, you'll end up in the ditch. You've got to be prepared to sweat blood. If you're not, I advise you to take up some comparatively easy job like aviation."

Sophie herself did try aviation, donned a beautiful white flying suit, got up to the door of the single-engined plane and then thought better of it.

But her advice about the stage was sound. At one time, there had always been a chance in the chorus line for a girl who felt she had greasepaint in her blood. But the coming of sound to the cinema had altered that. Already, only two years after the showing of "The Jazz Singer", American vaudeville theatres were closing as if they were houses made of playing cards. In a way, they were—the ace had been pulled away from under them. In Britain, where things always took longer to develop, the same trends were already discernible. Small towns were closing their music halls and opening up cinemas in their place.

It was as much Sophie's achievement to keep on working as it was to constantly get star billing and over-the-odds salaries. At the Kit Cat she had taken over from

Beatrice Lillie who had earned £400 a week. Sophie's take was £500 a week.

Above all on this trip, Sophie had perfected the art of singing the right songs to the right people. Audiences in large theatres couldn't react to "point" numbers that she had to put across intimately as though they were part of a private conversation. So for them, there were always "Some Of These Days" and "Yiddisher Mama" as well as the latest hits. Yellen's speciality pieces were left for the cabarets.

Whether she realised just how much she also owed to Ted Shapiro at this time, is debatable. What she didn't seem to appreciate was that the strong, loud voice with which she had bewitched the customers at Abuza's restaurant and had the people at the German Village flocking to hear, was going. Not yet 50, she was losing her finest asset. That she didn't also lose her stardom is due almost exclusively to Shapiro. Without telling her he was doing so, he started dropping the key in which he played for her. He would make new arrangements for Sophie without saying a word. She had not yet reached the stage where she just talked her songs, but that day was fast approaching.

Of course, Shapiro by now was the lynchpin to her act and Sophie was big enough to appreciate it. He undoubtedly had the biggest billing ever given to an accompanist. She never appeared anywhere without the posters and marquees declaring: "Sophie Tucker, accompanied by Ted Shapiro". At one theatre, the manager even twisted it round the other way to read "Ted Shapiro accompanied by Sophie Tucker". Sophie saw it, Ted told the manager to take it down but "boss" wouldn't hear of it. The sign stayed that way for a week and Sophie apparently enjoyed it as much as Ted. It was one of those gestures that at times set her apart from other stars—the pity was that for much of the time she was concerned only about herself.

Ted Shapiro was as vital to Sophie Tucker as a guide dog to a blind man. She would stand by the piano, twisting her chiffon scarf around her fingers, but it was Ted in his horn-rimmed glasses who could see how the audience was reacting.

She would turn back to him and say: "Are they

laughing?" and Shapiro, speaking out of the corner of his mouth like a ventriloquist, would answer: "Keep smiling, keep smiling." She could get very nervous at moments like that, despite her fame and success.

Sometimes a number wouldn't go right and Ted would sense this before she did. So without saying anything to her, he would change the music and she would change her routine to take up the song, too. She was the boss of the outfit off the stage, but on it, he was the one in charge. She never questioned his judgment.

In Britain that judgment was faultless. Word of it had crossed the Atlantic. In New York, the *Evening Graphic* reported: "Sophie Tucker took London like Grant took Richmond".

She not only wrote for newspapers, she appeared in advertisements in London, too—recommending the delights of Ecko radio sets, or rather wirelesses.

From London she decided to see something of Europe. She had a booking to sing for the first time at Paris's most famous music hall of the period, the Empire. It would be nice to recall now that she transferred the tremendous overwhelming success and response of Broadway and London to Paris. But it wasn't like that at all.

An indication of what went wrong comes with the headline in the London *Sunday Express* of February 22, 1931: SOPHIE TUCKER HISSED.

She was terribly nervous before going on. "Will they get my stuff?" she kept asking—and while nerves on most other occasions melted into instant communication with the audience, this time they twisted her intestines into knots that would not unwind.

Everything about her performance was a mistake. She began by attempting to sing "Some Of These Days" in French—the words had been translated for her by Edwina Mountbatten, but that was unfortunate. The lyrics were totally unintelligible to the Paris audience.

She found it impossible to get across to the audience. She knew no French at all and the audience couldn't understand her talk songs.

They grew restless and when Sophie started using a

megaphone, they erupted still further. It was a combination of things going wrong. But there could have been nothing in her whole career to compare with the reaction to "My Yiddisher Mama". The hisses turned to boos and these changed to downright anti-Semitic shouts from one side of the house, countered only slightly by a demonstration from a small but vocal Jewish element in the audience.

Finally, she ran off the stage while the audience was still shouting.

Other evenings were only slightly better. Sophie wore gowns made for her by Jennie Dolly, one of the world-famous Dolly Sisters act. Maurice Chevalier came to see her and there were flowers smothering the stage—all, it was later discovered, coming from the Dolly Sisters.

Someone shouted from the stage: "Why don't you bring on a tree?" The house dissolved and Sophie left in tears once more. In the wings, she covered her face with her hands and would neither see nor talk to anyone.

Wherever she went, language was an insurmountable barrier for her. She only began to breathe when Ted discovered a restaurant called Zelli's. Mr. Zelli was Jewish and that helped. Most important, he spoke Yiddish. While in Paris, Sophie went there for consolation.

Finally, she took refuge in the Dolly Sisters' Riviera chateau.

From the South of France, she went to Vienna where she didn't attempt to sing. But she did discover that every record shop in the city was featuring "My Yiddisher Mama" and by all accounts it was selling like hot begels. This made her feel slightly better.

From Vienna, Sophie went to Berlin—where she was invited to sing "Yiddisher Mama" on the radio. Ironically there were none of the outward signs of anti-Semitism she had experienced in Paris.

All in all, it was not the triumph Sophie had expected. When she returned to Britain, there was the crowning touch—she was arrested and charged with evading customs duty on three silk dresses after stepping off the Golden Arrow boat train at Victoria Station.

She said that all her clothes had been bought in London

before leaving three weeks earlier. But the customs men could not agree. The silk dresses looked French—and brand new.

She finally told customs officer Maurice O'Flynn "You're right. I'm sorry for the trouble I've caused. You've been very nice about it."

The dresses were found to be worth a total of £30. At Westminster police court, she was fined £40—and her counsel, Mr. B. M. Cloutman, K.C., said she had "exercised a woman's privilege and changed her mind several times".

The *Daily Express* commented: "Miss Sophie Tucker, who was fined £40 for smuggling silk frocks into this country, has the slight excuse that the female conscience does not regard such an act as unpardonable. But Miss Tucker might have remembered that she is a foreigner who has exacted heavy tribute from us for her syncopated charms and not grudged the small sum which conformity with the law would have demanded." She did not mention this part of the tour in her autobiography.

The Lady Ratlings enrolled Sophie as one of their new members and she joined in the patter with the rest of the ladies of the "profession". The Magicians Club made her their first female member. There was talk of her buying the Kit Cat for her new company but it never happened.

From London she began another exhausting tour of the provinces. In Glasgow, she was given the sort of welcome she craved in Paris. In Edinburgh, she had the audience rolling with her latest jokes interpolated between the songs. At the Belfast Hippodrome she assured the audience: "I Don't Want To Be Thin". At the Manchester Hippodrome she was her usual sensational self.

The *Manchester Guardian* reported: "Sophie Tucker was called back to sing again last night half a dozen times after she made her farewell. Some wanted one thing and some another.

"She stood at the front of the platform, the object of the surge of voices, laughing and then throwing back the voices with her hands.

" 'Not "Yiddisher Mama",' she said. 'You want to be cheerful tonight.' She sang something else, and then the people who wanted 'Yiddisher Mama' became audible again through the clapping. . . .

"This is the sort of thing Sophie Tucker can do with people in the cross-rhythm jazz of which she is master. The jazz is neither highly melodious nor easy to copy, nor in itself directly expressive; but it releases for her the profundities most often of humour.

"They gleam in her eyes, they are delivered from her mouth; the slight movement of the body even suggests that now she has a hand on a situation and will strangle the truth out of it.

"Sophie Tucker gives a testimonial to life every time she opens her mouth. She gives a wide and generous view of it all."

She had reason to remember that Manchester visit. Early on in the run, she was handed a cable just before she was due to go on for the evening's second show. It said: WAS MARRIED TODAY TO A FINE JEWISH GIRL LOVE SON.

Stay Away
From My Door

Sophie's relationship with Bert was the one big failure in her life—much more of a failure than her trip to Paris or her attempts at being a good wife. To make things worse for her now there were already rumblings that she and Al were not doing so well.

As far as her husbands were concerned they were disposable merchandise. When she had needed comfort in bed, there had never been a shortage of men ready to oblige, although she always feared that there would be. When she married them she always suspected they had proposed simply for what they could get out of the match, and in Al's case that was certainly so. Once the marriages were over, she tried, not always successfully, to forget them.

Bert, on the other hand, was a constant presence. She knew no more how to be a good mother than she could change a tyre on her car, but every now and again she would try to pick up the threads—only to have them constantly tangle up before her eyes yet again.

During Bert's childhood and adolescence she was up there on a pedestal, an unreachable goddess but a goddess just the same. As a young adult, he felt that he had failed her. But all the time there was a craving for a love as deep for him as the way she demanded the adoration of audiences.

148

Just occasionally, Sophie would feel the pangs that her neglect had brought to her conscience. If these coincided with yet another signal of devotion from Bert, it could be a touching experience.

Early on in her British tour, she received a telegram from Bert that touched her to the roots of her now dyed blonde hair:

FOR THE DEAREST AND MOST LOVELY MOTHER IN THE WORLD I AM PRAYING CONSTANTLY THAT YOU WILL ACHIEVE THE GREATEST SUCCESS OF YOUR ENTIRE CAREER. I LOVE YOU DEARLY AND MAY GOD BLESS YOU ALWAYS LOVINGLY YOUR SON.

When Sophie received that cable, she was deeply moved. "That's why the show was a success," she said afterwards.

Receiving the new telegram from "Son" brought back the old doubts, the old miseries. She knew she hadn't been a good mother and she didn't deserve any better. But she was distraught just the same. Not only was she not at Bert's wedding, but he hadn't considered it essential for her to be there either.

So what was their relationship going to be? Back in America, it became very obvious. "Son" talked of going into show business, but Sophie knew that he was not much good at it and she didn't want him to spoil her act. She bought him a shoe shop, but it failed.

His mother didn't like Lil, his "fine Jewish girl", very much, but that was no reflection on Lil. She would not have approved of any choice he had made. Lil tried desperately to win her affection, would run errands for her or do her other little favours, but Sophie never regarded them as anything more than chores by yet another "hanger-on". Sophie would always ask herself—and sometimes the question was aimed directly at the person involved—"What do they want from me?"

All Lil and Bert wanted was some love, but it was never really there. She made them an allowance, but it was never enough for more than a small West Side apartment in New York, facing a blank wall. Had she been just a very little

149

more generous, they could have lived in luxury. It was a story that was to continue until Sophie's death and would never cease to gnaw at this couple who committed the number one sin in Sophie's book—they didn't succeed.

All the love and care she had denied Bert she showered on other people.

Early in 1932, she telephoned William Morris with an important message: "Say Boss, I hear that Eva Tanguay is very ill. Let's get up a show for her."

Eva Tanguay, the "I Don't Care Girl", had very nearly nipped the Tucker career in the bud before it had got started and did all she could to ensure Sophie wouldn't make a name for herself in the Ziegfeld Follies. Now she was going blind and was very ill, but Sophie saw no reason why her past relationship with Miss Tanguay should interfere with her helping with a benefit.

Eva had, in fact phoned Sophie several years before and asked if they could get together. Much to Miss Tanguay's surprise and embarrassment, Sophie agreed without asking any questions. Eva walked into the Tucker apartment, made straight for the bedroom and on to the bed dropped a large knotted handkerchief rolled up into a ball. As the handkerchief spilt open, from it tumbled an assortment of bracelets, rings and necklaces. Eva said she wanted to make up for the past. Sophie decided not to let her former rival's conscience rule her head and refused to take any of it.

Now, Miss Tanguay had contacted Sophie again. She wrote a letter, telling her just how ill and broke she was. "But nobody will believe me," she said. "No one will understand my plight. I am sick and destitute and if I can't get help, I know how to end it all."

Sophie saw her plight for herself when she was touring in California. For the next months she and her maid wrote 3,000 letters to friends, to people in the entertainment business and others known to have both big hearts and large bank accounts, asking for help for the former star.

Every one of the letters was written by hand. Sophie didn't think a typewritten appeal would be nearly effective enough.

Her ploy worked. A total of $3,700 was raised. Later,

150

"With Ted Shapiro at the Piano" as all the billing said (circa 1952)

"Some of These Days" — the original sheetmusic. Her biggest hit

Sophie paid for two operations on Eva's eyes. She even persuaded her friends at Chicago's Sherman Hotel to provide Miss Tanguay with a suite for life for only $1.50 a day.

She also drew up a budget for her to live on: one dress, $10; breakfast, 25 cents; dinner 50 cents; supper 40 cents; 10 cents for bellboy who brings up the newspapers.

Eva wrote Sophie another letter in thanks: "Precious friend—I thank you for this year or two of life. I once felt sorry for those who died in the prime of their careers. But now I think how lucky they are. They say that people cling to life, but in some strange way life clings to me. I can't get rid of it. I have come to think that the hardest thing in the world is to die. Some of us just can't. We must live. But there must be a way that I can escape this cruel reality that served me so many years, yet fooled and trapped me."

The pencilled letter on lined exercise book-type paper went on: "I know you have you troubles but you at least have your work. How I envy anyone who can work. I envy the bellboys, the waiters, the chambermaids. I envy the news-boys. I envy the street-cleaners as I look down upon them from my windows. They can work and you can work." And that from a woman who once tried—and nearly succeeded —to see that Sophie never worked again. But as she said at the time: "We're like marionettes. No one believes we're real or that any of us ever need money."

Sophie was generous in many ways—particularly with praise for other artists. She wrote this to the leading Yiddish actor Maurice Schwartz:
"Dear Maurice,

After seeing your performance last night at the Yiddish Theatre, with your most marvellous company playing Yoshe Kalb, I'm happy to send my little note to you in commenting that I'm proud I am a Jew and proud of you."

For all this, Sophie's jealousy could take strange forms. One of the many newspaper profiles of her in the early 1930s describes a time in her youth when she was "so poor that the famous *star* who later became her maid went out and bought her a dress for $35 to wear at the audition. . . ."

The interesting thing is that one can only guess (but

151

with some degree of certainty) that the writer of the piece was describing a famous "star". For although the long article is preserved perfectly in one of Sophie's scrapbooks with all the other things written about her, the word "star" has been neatly scissored out. The vacant space fits the four-letter word perfectly. For all her professed love of Mollie, was she jealous or incensed that some generous writer could call her a star? Mollie may have been a two-bit hoofer, but the exaggeration hardly hurt Sophie's own reputation.

There were also always other aspiring artists who were disappointed by their confrontation with Sophie, even though she liked to think she encouraged new talent. Eddie Gor, a bellhop at Sophie's hotel, was one of them.

He used to walk up and down the hall in front of Sophie's room carrying a pitcher of iced water, and singing at the top of his lungs. He was sure Sophie would run out and shout: "What a marvellous, wonderful voice!" Instead, Sophie poked her head out of the door and admonished him: "Kid I called for ice water, not vocal gymnastics."

Still, it was her own performances that brought the loudest tributes. In February 1932, Ed Sullivan recorded in the New York *Evening Graphic*: "Sophie Tucker returned to the Palace this week and when I say returned, I mean that she came back and tore the roof off the place."

In fact, although Sullivan was not to know it at the time, a few days later Sophie was to help stop that roof being blown off.

It was four days after the Palace opening. Sophie was on stage singing "Some Of These Days" and Ted Shapiro was doing his ventriloquist act. In the middle of the song, while smiling to the audience, he told Sophie quietly: "When you've finished the number, walk off. Don't take any curtain calls. Just walk!"

She knew he would not have said that without good reason. She did as he told her and together they retreated into the wings while the asbestos safety curtain was lowered behind them. "Why did you tell me to walk off?" she asked him. But there was no time to answer. Putting his jacket round Sophie's shoulders, they made a dash for the stage door. "You didn't know it," he told her as they ran. "But the manager kept calling me from the wings: "'There's a fire. Get her off.'"

The theatre was not destroyed—only the flies and the orchestra pit were damaged—but as Sophie says in her autobiography, the Palace was never to be the same again. She also tells how she avoided panic in the audience—who knew nothing about the fire while she was on stage—by telling them: "Take it easy folks. Don't run. Give everybody a chance to get out."

It was a heaven-sent opportunity for Sophie's imagination and that insatiable thirst of hers for publicity to find an outlet. The newspaper stories at the time sang even stronger praises of Sophie (and her press agent).

Reuter reported: "Miss Tucker at once took the situation in hand. By impromptu curtain talk, she was able to calm the audience."

And a New York paper told the story of the manager telling her: "You can't go on, Miss Tucker. We'll have to ring the curtain down." "Nonsense," she is supposed to have replied. "Just put the fire out. That's all you've got to do."

A report published in the London *Daily Express* was probably nearer the truth.

"Sophie was hastily dragged off the stage shouting: 'Don't lose your heads. . . .'" And it told of Sophie's reactions: "Horror laid hold of me. . . . The stage lights went out and voices called hoarsely to me in darkness illuminated by the great bonfire overhead. I stumbled blindly to safety and fearing a catastrophe might ensue."

You paid your money and you took your choice as to which story you believed.

Sophie certainly was deeply affected by that fire. In a way, it was a watershed, if a fire can be so described, in her own career as much as it was in the history of the Palace, which was now almost the last surviving outpost of vaudeville in Manhattan.

For the first time, things seemed to be going wrong for Sophie Tucker and each episode seemed tougher than the one that went before.

The first indication of trouble came with an offer from the Capitol Theatre—another temporary survivor of the

153

vaudeville age—of an engagement at $3,500 a week. Hardly peanuts—especially for 1932. The problem was that only a short while before, Sophie had made $4,500 there, topping the bill. This time, not only was she being offered $1,000 a week less, but she wasn't even at the top—that was a place reserved for Lilyan Tashman, described as the "best-dressed woman in pictures". It was another indication of the extent to which the movies were taking over.

She didn't want to take the job but the Morris agency, Ted and Jack Yellen, all persuaded her to do so. In the end, she was glad she did. The cast—including a violin player-comic called Jack Benny—presented her with a suede handbag, inscribed: "For Sophie. Still the tops in show business and a regular gal."

Unfortunately, coming half way down a vaudeville bill was not tops in show business, although the "kibbitzers" in the theatre industry were showing her how big their hearts were. The biggest thing in entertainment was now the movies and, after "Honky Tonk", the studios were not exactly lining up outside her front door begging for more.

Equally important to an entertainer was radio, now rapidly moving into every home in the nation. If you had a regular radio spot, you were made. If you couldn't get one, the word got around that you were a has-been. Sophie tried desperately to get a radio contract, met all the right people from CBS and NBC but none of them would bite. "Sorry Soph," they all seemed to say. "Radio's not for you."

For someone like Sophie Tucker, whose craving for adoration was even more vital than that for beaded gowns and chic hairstyles, it seemed like a death sentence.

Other signs were on the horizon to show that 1932 was not going to be a good year. The death of Florenz Ziegfeld—and Sophie's name seemed to crop up in all the obituaries—was followed soon after by that of William Morris, "the boss". Without him, Sophie felt she was minus a right arm. But the Morris Agency was still with her, and still
catered for her every whim. If she wanted to play at a certain theatre, they would arrange it. If she wanted a white car to greet her at the station, they would lay it on. Now the man in charge of the agency was Abe Lastfogel, once Morris's male

secretary—he didn't like women as secretaries because he was always afraid they would go off and get married, leaving him flat—who promised to watch her interests and always did so.

He got her cabaret spots—first at the restaurants that were nightly being filled by visitors to the Chicago World's Fair, and then in New York and in Florida. For a time Al Lackey would go with her. But he was becoming an embarrassment—yet another problem for Sophie at a time when she felt she was having a full ration of these.

On one occasion, he called out to a waiter at one of the restaurants where Sophie was playing: "She's going somewhere else next week. I can't stand your food." On another occasion, he slapped her face in public when she refused to give him some more money with which he could gamble.

Rumours of a split between them first began circulating in 1933. Then in April 1934, there were stories that she had been secretly divorced in the Chicago court of Judge Desort. Sophie's press agent was worried about the effect that could have on her image. "Totally untrue," he said. "Miss Tucker is happily living with her husband."

But then it was revealed that she had been divorced as long before as September 1933. Sophie's money and her husband's cruelty—caused because she refused to share the money with him—were cited as reasons for the break.

This was one story that Sophie was anxious to keep out of the papers. She refused to discuss the divorce with anyone, but Al could be found—and he talked, rather sadly but with a false smile, about his lost marriage.

"We've been separated because of my alleged association with horse racing. But what got my goat was that I've had nothing to do with the nags." How long had he and Sophie been living apart? "Oh, about long enough for a filly to have a good two-year-old."

In court, Sophie said there had been three specific acts of cruelty. She testified: "It was at our apartment at the Central Park Hotel on September 25, 1932. He asked me for money and because I would not give it to him, he slapped me. Then again in our rooms in the hotel. He asked me for more money. I refused and he slapped me. Then he left me."

Rumours were circulated by her press agent that they were going to get together again. "It's all too distressing," she told reporters. "I won't talk about it."

"It does not seem possible for us to get along any more although he is a fine fellow," she said, tears making the mascara she always wore work tramlines down her cheeks. "Call it temperament if you like."

There was probably more love in Sophie for Lackey than for either of her two previous husbands. She stuck by him for the longest period of all. She even turned down a proposal of marriage from a British aristocrat, a banker whom she had met at the home of Lady Wavertree.

Strangely, with the hard things said in the heat of the court action behind them, they continued to be friends—which meant that Sophie continued to pay Al's gambling debts.

But now, after five years of marriage and at least two of living together before they were married, Sophia Lackerman—as she appeared in the legal papers—was officially on her own. She had asked no alimony. But what of her future, gambling debts apart?

She had even less reason than before to cry on Bert's shoulder—and certainly less right to do so. He was now trying desperately to build a life of his own—living with Lil in uncle Moe's apartment in Brooklyn where he hoped he could learn something about the pharmacy business, but he had little more luck there than he had had on the stage. Even if Bert had wanted to take his mother into his confidence and show her love, Sophie was incapable of reciprocating with any warmth of her own.

She could, however, bestow the Sophie Tucker accolade on others and find them grateful for it. How the "Eight Handsomest Men In The World" reacted to being selected by Sophie in November 1934 is not on record. But the list does present an interesting indication of her taste: 1) Mussolini—"his face is a mirror of strength, self-confidence and intellect", she decided; 2) King George V; 3) H. G. Wells; 4) George Bernard Shaw; 5) Einstein; 6) Lindbergh; 7) Roosevelt; 8) The Prince of Wales.

As usual, she showed her heart by doing good works for good causes. Charity never began at home for her and the

156

nearest that it reached was when she sang for the Hartford Jewish Home for the Aged.

She told the *Hartford Courant* that her real pride came when she saw how well another Hartford girl, Katharine Hepburn, was doing in Hollywood. She felt very deeply for Hartford—if the *Courant* were listening. That was why she kept dropping the place name in various spots in her act—and had even done it in "Honky Tonk". Her real ambition, she said, was to retire and live near her brother Phil in her old home town. The tears ran down the cheeks of the *Courant* reporter but the William Morris agency knew better. They thought they had found a much better cure for the Tucker blues.

Command Performance

If America wouldn't appreciate Sophie Tucker, London would. So now, with the nagging doubts about her future dominating much of her thoughts, she was going back to a country that had been showing nothing but affection for her ever since the night she caught the cockneys by surprise at the Stratford Empire.

The Morris agency had done more than find her a prestige new booking at the Café de Paris and another at the Holborn Empire; they had landed her on just about the biggest and most prestigious bill in British theatrical history—the Royal Command Performance. She was going to sing before the King and Queen of England at the London Palladium.

That would be something to tell the folks back home. For someone like Sophie who was so concerned with image and the value of publicity, it was a gift from heaven. Unfortunately for her, it looked as if she was to be denied even that pleasure.

The Palladium said they had no knowledge at all of the offer to Sophie. Before hearing that denial, Sophie swept into a press conference and announced: "I am very excited because I have been told that I am to appear before the King and Queen in next Tuesday's Royal Command Performance."

Immediately hearing that, Mr. George Black, the

158

Palladium's enterprising managing director, countered: "Miss Tucker has not been asked to appear at the Command Performance."

As *The Star* newspaper commented on getting the two announcements side by side: "It's all a muddle." It certainly all seemed like another Sophie Tucker publicity stunt, if this time one that was backfiring inconveniently, to say the least.

"It is a surprise to me," said Sophie sheepishly, not sure whether perhaps she had been sold a pup to entice her over the Atlantic. "Until I see my manager in the morning I can only say that the invitation to appear at the Command Performance was conveyed to me by him and I have no reason to suppose that I have been misinformed."

It turned out that the Palladium were playing Sophie's game—without consulting her and, therefore, giving her even more nightmares. The rest cure that Lastfogel had promised was raising her blood pressure alarmingly.

The papers, however, had come to the conclusion fairly early on that the Palladium were up to a trick or two. The trade press were revealing, too, that Sir Cedric Hardwicke and the Mills Brothers would be on the bill with her.

"The fact is," said *The Star*, "a suggestion was made that Miss Tucker should appear, but that everybody concerned was implored to breathe not a word about it. It was intended that she should appear with several other celebrities as a surprise item."

Indeed, on May 8, 1934, the "surprise item" appeared on the stage at the Palladium while George V sat with Queen Mary in the Royal box, clapping politely. The Queen took out her lorgnette and holding it six inches from her eyes, regally surveyed the woman still known in London as the "Chicago Blizzard".

Sophie and Ted had been given strict instructions as to the etiquette to be observed: "You walk out on to the stage, bow to the box on the upper left. Then, when you have come to the end of the act you bow to the box, bow to the audience and walk off. You don't come back for any more bows."

Sophie, a bundle of nerves, was more concerned than anything else that she wouldn't yet again trip over her long white lace gown.

159

Hanging from her sleeves was an assortment of small coral balls with which she played incessantly as she stood in the centre of the stage, a mass of applause all around her. She fiddled with them so much that one by one they fell on to the stage and the next ten minutes were spent treading and kicking away the little objects from under her.

She looked up to the Royal box—and then caused a sensation. "Hiya King," she said—and the celebrity house dissolved. No one knows whether or not the Queen was amused but the King, who loved the music hall, smiled appreciatively. It was, nevertheless, a touchy subject. The British press ignored the greeting at the time. They felt it more seemly simply to report the great success Sophie had been.

Great success? There had never been an evening like it in British theatrical history—and there wouldn't be one again until Danny Kaye had a similar effect on that King's son, George VI, at another Command Performance at the same Palladium Theatre after World War Two.

She sang "Louisville Lou" and the audience clapped enthusiastically. She began "Some of these Days-s-s-s-s", and they were enthralled. By the time she reached "You're gonna miss me honey-y-y" they went wild. She gave her bow and moved off into the wings—as protocol demanded. Except that no one had expected the audience to react as it did. The rule was that the people in the theatre applauded only while the Royal box applauded. This time, they wouldn't stop and just didn't seem to care what the King was doing. Before long, the clapping turned into a standing ovation—again something that had never happened before.

The Royal party, seeing that everybody else wanted more Sophie, started clapping again themselves—while the whole house shouted in chorus: "Sophie! Sophie! Sophie!"

Finally, she had to do what she promised she would not do—she had to go out on to the stage and take another bow. She tried at first to curtsey to the box, but halfway down the big Sophie Tucker frame was not sure it would be able to make it—let alone get up again. As best she could, she straightened herself up, looked once more to the box—and gave the Royal party a smart American soldier's salute.

160

Years later, Sophie was to say: "I'm a full-blooded American, but England is my second home. It took the English to make me a star."

The press were ready with tributes that proved just how big a star they considered her to be. The word spread across the Atlantic—and that was the most gratifying result of all.

In St. Paul, Minn., the *Pioneer Press* declared: "Britons forget decorum and yell for Sophie." And the *Ocala Banker* (Florida) headlined its story: "Hot Mama Pleases King."

At charity bazaars, at the Holborn Empire, at private parties and at the Café de Paris, Sophie was as hot a property as she had ever been in her career—while her own countrymen back home were trying to decide whether or not she was a back number.

As usual, she was adapting her technique, changing her routines to suit the times. Her big hit of the tour was "Lawd You Made The Night Too Long"—into which she interpolated a verse or two of the Jewish devotional song "Eli Eli". This caused a slight stir when people complained of sacrilege. Whether the complaints were genuine or just another Sophie story will never be established for certain.

There are no doubts, however, about an event organised outside the Shepherd's Bush Empire. Twenty or 30 women gathered at the stage door to greet Sophie as she arrived. After she had signed a dozen or so autograph books, two women thrust theirs into her hands at the same time. They started arguing and one snatched a newly signed book from the hands of the other. Sophie tried to intervene and as a result got a black eye for her trouble, intended—so the story ran—for the other woman. It made big stories, with big pictures, in all the national daily press and in the papers in America. But it was all a complete fabrication.

The worst incident of all was still to come.

"Boy Snatched From Car," said the *Daily Herald*. "Miss Sophie Tucker Snatches Child From Under Car," said the *Evening Standard*. "Sophie Tucker Heroine," declared the *Morning Post*. "Miss Sophie Tucker Saves A Boy," reported the *News Chronicle*.

The story was that in High Street, Brentford, a small

161

boy dashed in front of a car and Sophie rushed into the road to pull him back. The child was unhurt, but Sophie's legs were bruised.

"Just a spontaneous action," said Sophie at the time. "I was getting out of my car when I saw the boy run." But it was a spontaneous action thought out very carefully by Sophie's publicist. The boy lived on a barge on the River Thames at Brentford and Sophie was working on a film being made there.

The film had the now unfortunate sounding name "Gay Love" and needed every ounce of publicity it could get. Certainly, Sophie had no noticeable conscience pangs about the affair.

There were also always people who thought that Sophie's predilection for getting in the newspapers could be useful to them. Among these was the first flock of Jewish refugees to reach Britain from Germany. No one then knew of the horrors of Belsen and Auschwitz, but the words "concentration camp" had begun to thrust themselves into most people's vocabularies.

Sophie decided she would write to Hitler to find out what he was up to.

She told him: "For months I have had letters sent to me from German refugees in this country and America imploring me to help them."

The letter went to the Reichstag in Berlin and Sophie added that since she was going to take a little holiday, she would happily spend it in Germany if Hitler would see her there. What Adolf Hitler of all people made of this attempt at intervention by the Yiddisher Mama herself will now never be known. He didn't bother to reply, and as year followed year the murders and the atrocities grew worse.

Before she began that holiday, she renewed her acquaintanceship with the people of Manchester. There, the *Daily Express's* reporter wrote:

"I had tea the other afternoon in a Manchester hotel with Miss Sophie Tucker who is 'Tuckering' at the Manchester Palace this week.

"I call it 'Tuckering' because that is the only adequate word I can think of to describe her amazing performance.

162

"There are no half measures about this woman. Either you adore her show (based largely on the sexual capacity of stout middle-aged women) or you detest it. It is entirely a matter of taste. . . .

"You may walk out on Sophie Tucker in the theatre, but I defy you to meet Sophie Tucker outside the theatre and not be spellbound by her exuberant good spirits and irresistible personality."

Now, she was going to go home to see whether that "irresistible personality" would work with her fellow countrymen.

My People

There were few audiences like the British and Sophie had to wrestle with that fact—before she did, however, she had another chance to break new ground, and there was no doubt whatever that the ground was fertile.

From England she went to Holland, sang "My Yiddisher Mama" there and had a whole new field of admirers ready to worship at the shrine labelled "Sophie Tucker". At one smart restaurant she was disappointed at the lukewarm reception—until she was told it was not considered polite in Holland for ladies to applaud. In Cannes, at the Hotel Martinez, the Riviera audience succeeded in undoing the harm to her prestige that the people of Paris had done a few years earlier. She worked all night, continued her show at the Plantation Café, had breakfast of onion soup and went to bed $1,000 richer.

Back home in the states the only big bookings she could get were in cabaret—which may have been the kind of booking with which she felt more comfortable, but didn't do anything to build up a still sagging ego.

At the Hollywood Café on Broadway, however, Sophie's opening was like the best of old times. *Variety* certainly thought so, and there was no praise she deemed more worthwhile.

They reported on April 10, 1935: "One of those sensational premières that happens every so often occurred at

164

Sophie Tucker's return to Broadway and the Hollywood cabaret restaurant. It was an electric post-midnight. It was a gala occasion in superlative gobs.

"Broad, smart, sophisticated and as daring as 1935 mixed company standards allow, Soph made everything count. Her discourse on post-40 life and love if perhaps too biologically detailed was meant to sound like a lyrical academic discourse on the facts of life."

These were the songs and the stories that got talked about now—the daring risqué tales which tried to reassure ageing matrons that they could get more out of bed than a good night's sleep. Yet, paradoxically, Sophie was a prude. Tell her a dirty story and she would not only fail to laugh, she would scowl. If she were in a bad mood, she would either abruptly change the subject or even show you the door without any undue ceremony.

Her real art, however, was being able to convince people that her stage personality was the real Sophie. The New York *Sunday Mirror* was obviously fully convinced by her performance at the Hollywood restaurant.

"Others come and go by the score," they wrote. "But the incomparable Sophie Tucker goes on for ever. And therein lies the true test of artistry.

"Spend an evening at the Hollywood restaurant where Sophie Tucker is now the attraction and if you are at all responsive, you will come out praising the lady's brilliant capacity to sell a song."

One press report begat another and before long there were queues every night at the Hollywood. It just proved how Sophie still knew her business—by getting her name in the papers whenever she could.

The Yiddish press were very interested in all her doings. She clipped out their reports as she did all the others. Next to one very long piece she scribbled in her scrapbook: "Swell article. Took me a whole hour to read it!"

At a benefit in aid of the Actors Temple, she sang in Yiddish, "Papa goes where Mama Goes". As she said at the time: "Benefits? I've never refused one—particularly benefits for my own people."

Everybody who saw the value of Sophie Tucker backing

their cause was after her, trying to emphasise that commercial undertakings were also worthy of a benefit or two. When Goldblatt Brothers of New York baked their millionth pie, Sophie was the obvious choice to eat it on their behalf for the benefit of the cameras.

She decided it was now time to form an over-40s club for women who had passed that particular milestone. The fact that Sophie was now nearer 50 had nothing to do with it.

She even thought that the time had come to speak out for those under-paid, under-dressed but overworked show girls from the world of burlesque.

What was needed, she said, was a "burlesque code", which would lay down adequate wages and restricted working hours. "We old timers who got our start in the business aren't going to forget it," Sophie declared. As the *New York Post* put it, she was "going to bare the facts of burlesque". She never did, but that didn't matter. The notion had got into the papers.

But if Sophie caught the press with their collective pants down time after time, she was not immune to having her leg pulled unmercifully either. She was playing at the Florida resort of Hollywood when a man phoned her, he said, from the other Hollywood—the one in California.

"I'm doing a coast-to-coast radio hook-up in five minutes," he said to her. "Would you stand by and then on the given signal sing five songs for our listeners?" To Sophie it was not just a tempting request; perhaps here was the green light to that long-awaited radio contract. Who knew how many big Hollywood film producers would be listening, too?

Five minutes later, the call came in and Sophie sang her five songs. When she had finished, the man thanked her. What he didn't reveal was that he was in a suite right along the corridor from her own with a bunch of business cronies who said he wouldn't dare do it. Poor Sophie had sung five songs for a private party and didn't get a penny for it.

While in Florida, Sophie's heart was allowed to rule her head once more. She fell for a story about an old lady in her home town of Hartford who was desperately lonely. Would Sophie kindly "adopt" the woman as her grandmother. Once she realised it would probably get into the papers, she agreed. But the woman told her she was still very lonely. SOPHIE'S ANSWER: she adopted an 80-year-old man as her "grandfather" and arranged a meeting of the two old people.

She arranged for Mrs. Blanche Roper, then 74, and 80-year-old Mr. William Lanier to stay together (with a chaperon and in separate rooms) at her own summer house at Hartford. Nothing came of the "romance", but Sophie was bombarded with requests from other aged prospective grandparents to adopt them, too.

More touchingly, Sophie saved an old friend from a pauper's grave about the same time—and on this occasion, definitely was not worried about the newspapers.

"Princess Rigo", a gypsy performer, died and Sophie found out she had been penniless. So she made the arrangements to have the old woman buried in style. As she said: "Princess Rigo was very kind to me when I started out in show business in 1910. I have never forgotten it. She invited me to her home, the luxury of which astounded me. The first thing which caught my eye was her leopard-skin coat. I decided that the first thing I would have when I earned enough money would be a coat exactly the same. Four years later, I was able to gratify my whim."

It was another way of showing that the people for whom Sophie cared most were her fellow performers. She worked harder for entertainers down on their luck than she would for any close relative—who she might think was taking advantage of her. In May 1935, she received the recognition of the profession for her efforts—although she was not to know then into what trouble she would be led. She was elected honorary President of the American Federation of Actors.

It was about this time that she got her first big radio break—without salary. She hosted a weekly radio programme aimed at "encouraging professional show people who can't get an audition, no less a job."

Despite this, Sophie was getting distinctly worried about the way her career was moving. It was the Big Band age and the thought crossed her mind that she ought perhaps to cash in on the phenomenon while it lasted. She had had her success with the Five Kings of Syncopation, so why not now revert to the old format? The difference was that this time the bands would be really big.

Abe Lastfogel thought otherwise and told her to think again. She did, and decided the time had come to leave the Morris organisation.

Lastfogel gave her his blessing: "Why don't you go ahead?" he suggested. After 26 years under the wing of William Morris and his heirs, she decided to take up the offer made to her some time before by MCA, who were booking the big bands.

They put Sophie out in front of the whole works, brass, woodwind and percussion—and it was a disaster. She couldn't make herself heard over the instrumentation—and her material wasn't made for that ambience.

After one season, she went back to the Morris agency, with no hard feelings on either side.

Through the changes, Ted Shapiro stayed with her— always without a contract. As he told me: "What's the use of a contract? If I wanted to get out of a contract, I could just get out. I could play so badly that she'd be glad to get rid of me. If she wanted to end it, she could have found reasons to do it."

But in that respect Sophie was extremely honourable. Contracts were legal formalities. A handshake or a nod of her now ample chin was sufficient.

She stressed that her new radio services would not be an amateur hour, but that the votes of listeners would decide which of the entertainers appearing on the show merited a booking at the Loews theatre chain.

All that the series really showed was that the big networks had been right. Sophie wasn't really a good radio performer, although she would try again and again to prove that she was.

Variety and the other papers, however, were kind and the show biz bible found yet another new role for Sophie— they nominated her the best-dressed woman of the year. She turned up for the award ceremony in a heavy silver lamé dress with four glass buttons. She also had a velvet scarf.

She cared a great deal for her clothes, but on one

particular occasion in 1936 her efforts at looking well-groomed had an unfortunate sequel. She had come back yet again to the place she believed treated her better than anywhere else and which most appreciated her true worth —London. While posing for photographs something happened that tickled the fancy of the photographers more than it did her. In the words of the New York *World Telegram*, "some inner part of her apparel snapped with a loud report". But, the paper was pleased to report, "no damage appeared to have been done".

She was going to do her usual tour of the night spots—centring this time on Grosvenor House, where she intended to build her act around the favourite song of the new King Edward VIII—"The Man I Love". Sophie herself had decided that no man was worth the agony of loving. She was finally married to show business and there would be no extra-curricular activities, although she saw a lot of Al, paying off a new debt each time but never sleeping with him.

Yet she was still philosophising about love. "Poets say love can't be denied," she told a gaggle of open-mouthed admirers. "Course it can't. Why on earth should it be? It comes when it chooses, goes when it wants to. Nobody can love until they're 40. They get 20 years schoolin' before they realise that love, like anything else worthwhile, is a craft."

Neither was there any recipe for happiness. "There ain't no recipe because either you are happy or you ain't. Anyone with a job, a home, a wife, ought to be happy. If he ain't, he's crazy."

She thought Englishmen were the best dressed in the world—they had their shoulders squared, but never looked square. As for the women, they dressed better all the time.

The general public were certainly happy enough that she was loyal to them.

The *Daily Telegraph* said that Sophie and her American supporting act, Edgar Bergen and Charlie McCarthy, "gal-vanised the crowded restaurant audience into enthus-iasm after midnight". And it went on: "Miss Tucker, who is accompanied by Ted Shapiro, again brings to the stage the vitality, the bubbling good nature and the genius in putting over a number which have made her a kind of American Marie Lloyd." To the British who were still schooled by the music hall, praise could come no higher.

Sophie herself couldn't quite make up her mind how she felt about the BBC. On the ship crossing the Atlantic she had a message offering her £40 to appear on a radio variety show. Sophie cabled back: "No thanks very much. I am worth rather more than that."

"At first, I thought we were going to talk sense together," she said indignantly, her pride in shreds. "But then I found that their price was getting on towards a joke. And I may tell you I do not want to take on something so small that it would make me laugh."

The broadcast went ahead without her. Soon, however, discussions were on for another show—an all-star extravaganza featuring American artists who happened to be in London at the time. It was to go out on December 9. The day after that, Sophie had an event of her own that threatened to make the headlines in the British and the American press. She had organised a concert, also of American artists, only this one would be in memory of King George V. The participants would all be people who had visited Britain during his reign.

The Lord Mayor of London and the Mayor of New York, as well as the United States Ambassador, had all agreed to support the event. As things turned out, the "event of the year" was upstaged by a certain other happening.

Before anything else, though, there was Sophie's commitment to the BBC—for an undisclosed fee.

It was not exactly the most exciting evening's entertainment the BBC had offered, but in a world before tape recording there was little that could be done about it. Right until the moment of air-time, no one knew who would appear. Zazu Pitts said she was so nervous that she would have to work in a studio all by herself—and then finally decided she couldn't face a microphone at all. A singer called Laura la Plante turned up without music—so all she did was introduce the next act. Noah Beery, Douglas Fairbanks, Jnr., Eric Maschwitz and Bebe Daniels and Ben Lyon made up the bill in the end—with Sophie trying to hold the whole thing together for a grateful BBC. She seemed to spend most of the evening apologising for the absences of her fellow countrymen.

The show at the London Coliseum in aid of King George's Fund was hit by factors totally outside the control of anyone—except King Edward VIII and Mrs. Simpson.

Sophie had two music hall appearances to make earlier that evening—firstly at the Chiswick Empire, then at the Metropolitan in London's Edgware Road. From the taxi commuting between the two buildings, she and Ted Shapiro could see a crowd gathering outside a radio shop which was open much later than would ever normally be the case.

"Stop here, driver," Ted ordered, and both he and Sophie got out to hear that a special broadcast was about to be made from the King's favourite home, Fort Belvedere. They stood with the London crowds in the cold, December air and heard the King announce that he was renouncing the throne "for the sake of the woman I love".

Sophie's tears welled in her eyes and flowed down her cheeks. They were still having a disastrous effect on her makeup when she and Ted stepped out on to the stage of the Metropolitan. For probably the first time since her début with the Ziegfeld Follies, she was rooted to the floor of the stage, not knowing what she was going to do next.

Suddenly, however, a little girl called down to her from the balcony: "Carry on Sophie". It snapped her out of that rare mood of silence. She went into "Some Of These Days" and everyone was happy.

The midnight performance at the Coliseum was something else. No one knew whether it was right to sing "The Star Spangled Banner" that evening and if they did, how appropriate it would be to sing "God Save The King" on the night that the king had gone off to France as "Prince Edward". As it turned out, the two anthems were sung and Sophie's concert—for that was what it was—turned out to be one of the most memorable in theatrical history.

Marlene Dietrich and Douglas Fairbanks were on the bill—after having made a trip to Fort Belvedere where they wanted to "beg the King on bended knees" not to abdicate. They had not been allowed past the sentries.

171

There were problems of another sort in the East End music halls. The fascist threat was growing and Sophie's own Jewish people, perhaps still her loyalest audience of all, were showing great anxiety. Sir Oswald Mosley threatened to become the British Hitler and was growing politically fat on a diet of Jew-baiting. Sophie sensed the mood of the folks about whom she sang in one of her hit songs of the year—"My People"— and decided to turn the air of fear and depression into a publicity stunt.

She hired—with great coverage of the result in the British press—a gang of youths to throw stones at her but making very sure they would all miss. She then revealed that she had been attacked by members of the British Union of Fascists.

She went further than that. The fascists, she said, had advised her not to sing "MY People"—which contained the line, "I am proud to be what God made me. . . . We shall survive those who decry my people."

It was a case of there being a good press agent on her books in London, while she saw nothing tasteless about using all his talents. The fact that this put even more fear into the hearts of the Jews of the East End seemed to have escaped her altogether. She even boasted that she intended to go without an escort, despite the risk of having more stones thrown at her.

"I cannot believe that anyone wished me any harm", she declared, straight-faced. She was, however, deleting "MY People" and "My Yiddisher Mama" from her repertoire. "My People," she said, was dedicated to the Jewish people, " a lovely song". And, she added, "I love the East End".

Sophie caused one big surprise during her visit. At the Holborn Empire, she used a microphone. The *Times* was "astonished" that she needed one. "That that voice which has boomed so humanly and kindly to so many audiences should need anything mechanical to encourage it is surprising", said the paper, "but the microphone last night seemed a frail and fugitive instrument which Miss Tucker, with one of her more robust notes, could have whisked away into thin air.

"Miss Tucker belongs to the roaring, glorious, irresponsible twenties and contrives to continue, as those curious years did, the twang and cynicism of the fashion of the time with the deep emotional under-current which inspired it and gave it an importance which those who have only known talking films as their world of entertainment can never understand."

As for her audience, they wanted to hear whatever she said—particularly the women who were fascinated by Sophie Tucker and what she always described as "my perfect complexion". Modesty was never her middle name. "Never mind face lifting", she declared—again forgetting her early "lift". "Never mind beauty treatment when you're over 40 like me, if you want to be beautiful like me use plenty of soap and water on your face like me."

She had done some slimming—and was down from 187 lb to 165. "I was too big a girl for the lovely new dresses and the gorgeous new furs when I was here last. But I just had to wear them. So now I'm a cute little trick weighing only 165 lb." And it was all due to the Sophie Breakfast—coffee and fruit; the Sophie Lunch—salad and meat; the Sophie Dinner—macaroni, bread and vegetables; and the Sophie Supper—"any kind of sweet".

She was so enthusiastic about it all that she was forming another branch of her "Life Begins At 40 Club"—only this time "to take care of young men and women under 40".

The club itself was intended to "keep alive the spirit of achievement, tolerance and understanding and the joy of living that every 40-year-old possesses and to let the youngsters know that they have much to look forward to when they are 40." If Sophie was kidding herself, everyone else seemed to take it very seriously indeed.

Back in America, the people who were interested in such things were wondering how serious Sophie was by her next announcement. She was going back to Hollywood. And this time, it was going to be good-bye to the stage—in all its forms.

Lord, You Made
the Night Too Long

It was a point in Sophie's career when she was grabbing, not so much at straws but at anything that represented security. The woman who needed to be told ten times a day that she was loved by her adoring public, couldn't get used to the idea of being anything but one of the top two or three entertainers of her day—and although London stayed as loyal as ever, she couldn't build her entire career around what still remained a foreign audience.

Her country was America, and America, while not calling her a back number, had placed her in a closely defined niche. She was top for the nightclubs and for the occasional spot on what was left of vaudeville—but radio? Not really. Films? Few had thought of Sophie Tucker since '29 and "Gay Love" had not made anyone noticeably more enthusiastic. Then came a call from MGM. Would she like to make a new picture?

It was a question that the MGM moguls really didn't need to ask. The talk had been around Hollywood for some time that Sophie was looking for something that would re-establish her name in the international sphere and it was not difficult to imagine her reply—give or take a few contract objections that would inevitably be raised simply for pride's sake.

What the Morris agency had been offered on Sophie's

174

part was not a star role, but they were recommending acceptance—in a couple of years even Al Jolson, the man with an ego as big as his talent, would accept third billing in Hollywood films and all Sophie was being advised to do now was set a trend and become a "character".

The publicity office at MGM were busy thinking of Sophie Tucker as "the second Marie Dressler" again, which pleased her no more now than it had before. But the part they offered her was tempting. The star credits went to Robert Taylor, Eleanor Powell, George Murphy and a little girl the studio thought might go places—Judy Garland.

The film was "Broadway Melody of 1938" which Sophie said seemed the most exciting thing she had done for years. She loved the challenge it offered—and was so overcome by having to sing "Some Of These Days" in a scene with Robert Taylor that she forgot the opening line of what was after all, her theme song.

For weeks, she worked with a dialogue coach called Laura Hope Crew, and was so pleased with the way everything went that on the strength of it she bought a new car and rented a 15-room Beverly Hills house complete with the required swimming pool.

After it was all over, Louis B. Mayer called Sophie and told her he thought she looked lovely. So far so good. The word was issued from MGM that Sophie would never go back to the stage and that she was now a film star—period.

As things turned out, "Broadway Melody" is best remembered now for Judy Garland crooning to "Dear Mr. Gable", and in her book Sophie says she thought that she herself "stank"—because all the best scenes were left on the cutting room floor. It is difficult to take too seriously Sophie's reasons for what was undoubtedly a tremendous flop and for a film which confirmed that she was not screen material. In the same chapter in which she discusses "Broadway Melody" she writes of the encouragement given by Al Lackey at the time and how she was desperately trying to keep their marriage going. Her memory was only partly correct. Al was in Hollywood with her as a "friend", but she had after all by then been divorced from him for four years.

She could not even get the name of the film right—

calling it "Broadway Melody of 1937". For that she might almost be forgiven. This latest in a series of what would be 10 films glorifying the street that, in its way, Hollywood was trying to kill, had been started in 1936. It was released in 1937. In "Some Of These Days" Sophie says "Broadway Melody of 1937" was made in 1938—which takes some reckoning!

The critics were hardly ecstatic about the picture, although Sophie herself came out with comparative flying colours. The London *Daily Express* put it on the line: "It all depends on how you feel about Sophie Tucker. Personally, I am her slave. I even went more than once to see 'Honky Tonk', a poorish picture she made years ago.

"So for me, she makes all the difference to this picture. It comes to life so violently when she appears that the lights seem to go out on everybody else.

"When she lifts her hand—you know, the one the handkerchief trails from—tilts back her head and goes into 'Some Of These Days'—well, that's something to go to any picture for."

The *Express* critic was, as he said, a devoted slave. He was however, only partly able to assess the performance of one of the other stars in the film: "Fifteen-year-old Judy Garland (whom Miss Tucker thinks is the new red hot momma) puts over one number brilliantly and struggles through an embarrassing one, addressed by a schoolgirl to a portrait of Clark Gable." Embarrassing it may have been, but it became a classic moment of the cinema and made the tears pour down L. B. Mayer's cheeks as much as they had ever flooded down Sophie's.

Yet despite the flop of "Broadway Melody", MGM went all out to boost their idea of her stepping into Marie Dressler's shoes They said she was going to play the role of Dressler in her life story, to be called "Molly Bless Her" —and to back their hunches sent a note round to all the American papers asking them to return all the stills they had previously been sent showing Sophie in her familiar musical setting.

It is doubtful if any of them did. But there was no doubt Sophie was being wooed to play a really dramatic role and

176

her old image wasn't right for what the studio had in mind. When she heard about the ploy she was furious. "I won't be a second Marie Dressler or a second anything," she declared. The Press were ambivalent about having her play the Dressler part. "Grand idea, maybe," said the London *Daily Express*, "but our Soph has a life story, too."

There were few bright moments in her time at MGM. One of the happiest was when the Howard Brothers, Willie and Eugene, lunched at the studio commissary while Sophie was eating there too. Seeing them, she stepped up to their table and proceeded to take their order. "That's how I started with you fellows, wasn't it?" she said.

As usual, Sophie was fullsome with advice, sometimes —recalling her early days—quite sound advice at that. "Young man," she said to an actor while at MGM, "if you want to be happily married, choose a chorus girl. She has learned that it is cheaper and more enjoyable to cook her own meals at home and she has known so many difficulties that she can sew, balance the home budget and be an excellent companion at the same time."

All a little syrupy and reminiscent of the stories about prostitutes with hearts of gold, but she went on, "She is often unable to tell where the next meal is coming from, so she meets trouble with a smile. She does not grumble and that is something any husband should appreciate."

The trouble Sophie was meeting was her decidedly unhappy state of mind. Her domestic life was now non-existent. She made the odd cabaret appearance while in Hollywood, but nothing to speak of—and apart from the noises being made about her Marie Dressler connection, MGM was decidedly "smalltime" as far as her own progress was concerned. But the studio, which had her for a year's contract, were not giving up. They featured her in third billing after the now sensational box office duo of Mickey Rooney and Judy Garland, in a picture called "Thorough-breds Don't Cry".

Sophie played a boarding house keeper, Judy was her niece and Mickey a young jockey who lived in the house. It was the most serious Sophie role to date and in her tailored costume and small feathered hat she looked enough like an aunt to be convincing. But it was a far cry from the satin and sequins that went with "Some Of These Days" and those who cared about such things got rather worried.

The *Daily Express* said of "Thoroughbreds Don't Cry": "They may not cry, but they would be mortified, I fear, if they knew what was going on behind their well-bred withers in this film. Quite apart from dirty work in the paddock thwarting their natural wish to pass winning posts first there are several reasons here why a thoroughbred might be excused an occasional snuffle:

"Sophie Tucker, the announcement of whose new career in the movies will probably cause the majority of customers to pass the turnstiles, is reduced in her second Hollywood effort to playing stooge to a racehorse and a bunch of 14-year-old children without a single song to put over."

Sophie announced officially that her days of living in a trunk were over and that Beverly Hills had everything she wanted. The people who knew Sophie Tucker thought otherwise and they were right.

With still 12 weeks of her MGM contract to go, she packed up her clothes in that trunk again and took off by train for New Jersey for a 15-week cabaret stint. Al stayed behind—and out of her life for good. She didn't think Louis B. Mayer would sue—because she believed he would be as happy to be released from the burden of having Sophie Tucker on his books as she was to be out of the film business. It was a correct hunch. If thoroughbreds didn't cry, Sophie did—and she was happiest of all doing it in front of a live audience.

Bluebird, Where Are You?

The times were strange. One minute, the world seemed to be on the verge of war, the next it was euphoric. The disgrace of Munich had made the skies blue—for a short time. Then, everything looked black again and Sophie Tucker seemed to be the personification of that public feeling at the end of the 1930s.

Back from Hollywood—where she believed she had sunk to the nadir of her career—she was fêted by New York show business for what she insisted was her 50th birthday.

"All my life I"ve been waiting to be 50," she said without a blush on her plump cheeks. "So I could sit back and pass on a few bits of advice. Personally, I haven't got a lot of advice to give out, though—I'm still using last year's.

She was given a testimonial dinner, complete with a cake and 50 candles. "Blow out the candles not the cake, Soph", said a show business wag, sitting next to her when she began mustering for the task all the strength needed to sing "Some Of These Days" without a microphone.

NBC, denying her a long-term contract all those years, put on a special birthday programme tribute to her—in which Shelton Brooks played "Some Of These Days" and told how he had first sold the number to Sophie.

It was a time for Sophie anniversaries and Sophie celebrations. As far as she was concerned, the best of these was a starring role in her very first legitimate musical comedy—"Leave It To Me", produced by the veteran Vinton Freedley, the man responsible for some of the early Fred and Adele Astaire hits.

At first everything seemed to be going smoothly. The audiences loved Sophie and Sophie herself was in her element. She adored New York and the plush warmth of the Imperial Theatre was so much more her scene than chromium-plated Hollywood.

The critics could only find fault with the billing—which read: "William Gaxton and Victor Moore in
    Leave It To Me
    With Sophie Tucker and Tamara".

Said *Night Life* magazine: "This is all wrong, Mr. Freedley. A performer of Miss Tucker's topnotch position deserves better than co-featuring with Tamara, who is a newcomer with a rather slight voice and little else." A judgment confirmed by history.

What he did not say was that "Leave It To Me" also introduced a young lady called Mary Martin, who sang a song called "My Heart Belongs To Daddy." As for Sophie, her heart once more belonged to Broadway. And Broadway responded. In June 1939, to mark her 30th anniversary in the theatre, there were more celebrations—including a buffet luncheon on the stage of the Imperial.

Everything seemed wonderful again for the career of Sophie Tucker. After so many downs, she was on an upswing again. Not only was she a hit in "Leave It To Me", Sophie Tucker, with Ted Shapiro at the Piano, doubled at a night club called the Versailles. At the same time, she finally had a 26-week contract for a commercial radio show for Roy Tann cigars, which were owned by George Washington Hill, who also made Lucky Strike cigarettes.

That, too, was a great success—both with the listeners and with Mr. George Washington Hill—an elderly man who used to love to sit in the control room and hear Sophie sing her songs, particularly the old ones.

The only dark cloud on the horizon was represented by Sophie's son Bert, who still had not been able to make the grade that his mother considered suited her station in life.

She and Lillian still did not get along and the young Tuckers were usually in financial need, without very much help from Sophie. For a time, Bert had a job in the Morris agency—working in the mailing department.

As usual Sophie was not showing very much concern for her family. She would bark her orders at her brother Phil, who was still her manager, and keep her sister Annie, who had a back complaint and ran a clothing shop, like a dog on a lead.

It was the same old Sophie, the star who was busy again and recognised for her worth. Not really a comeback, because she had not been away, it was more of a recognition; as far as she was concerned, a recognition that had begun to fade.

It was the time of the New York World's Fair and America's biggest city was in its glory. The theatres were full, queues lined up outside the cinemas and Sophie was just one of a dozen top entertainers having people eating out of the palms of their hands at night clubs.

But suddenly, something happened to change all that. For a woman like Sophie who ate, drank and slept publicity almost as much as she worshipped the sound of applause, she was about to head a show that was going to get her name and her pictures in newspapers all over the world. Only this time she did not like it at all.

As President of the American Federation of Actors, Sophie had taken her job seriously. She was not exactly most people's idea of a militant trade union leader, but she spoke out as frequently for the rights of the vaudeville and musical comedy performer as she had about the advantages of marrying a poor, overworked, underpaid chorus girl.

Not only were those who worked, worked too hard, she believed, but there were too few benefits for those who were unemployed. She insisted that a fund be set up to pay unemployment benefit. And that was the start of the trouble.

The *Hollywood Reporter* had been hinting about misuse of funds for weeks when, finally, accountants went over the books of the organisation in a blaze of publicity which suggested that the New York District Attorney had called for the documents. It never got as far as legal action but a

181

stormy meeting of the Association brought Sophie to more tears.

The meeting was called to discuss the problem, with a bespectacled Sophie taking the chair and explaining reasonably why she did not want to question the integrity of her officials.

But as she spoke, she was immersed in a flow of invective from the general body of the hall. The 750 people present at a New York hotel booed and howled—while Ernie Mack, known as "The Man With A Thousand Faces", started a punch up with a Texan blonde beauty appearing at the World's Fair called Helen Johnson.

Sophie ranted and raved, attempted to call the meeting to order with her gavel and in the end, just sat down and buried her face in her hands. Everybody present seemed to think she had been crying, but Sophie denied it.

"I was so hot the perspiration was rolling down my face," she said after the shindig. "I had been on my feet more than an hour when up jumps an enterprising photographer and takes a picture of me. Sophie Tucker is no cry baby."

And she emphasised: "There's a lot of trouble coming to anyone who spreads any more of these underhand stories. There's no money missing and there's a nice libel suit in store for anyone who suggests there is. I've been playing a show on Broadway for nine months and we are going to take it out on the road soon. I'm all booked up until spring and then maybe I'll do another trip to England."

If Sophie pretended not to be worried, her friends were. Eddie Cantor, for one, begged her to resign. "You have been misled in this present controversy," he wrote to her, "and I plead with you to resign as quickly as possible or you too will innocently involve yourself."

Sophie did not bother to write back to him. Instead, she phoned him up and said: "Eddie my boy, even a murderer is entitled to a trial. Eddie, you have found us guilty without hearing our evidence."

Cantor had by now resigned from the union but Sophie told him: "Eddie, I suggest you withdraw your resignation until this investigation is completed."

Eddie replied with a telegram to Sophie: YOUR BIGNESS OF HEART BLINDS YOU TO THE FACT THAT THERE IS A GROSS MISMANAGEMENT OF THE AMERICAN FEDERATION OF ACTORS.

To that Sophie replied that Cantor should send his own accountants to look at the AFA's books.

Following this, Actors Equity urged Sophie to resign. Meanwhile, she talked of amalgamating her group with the stagehands' union.

Equity issued a statement, without naming Sophie, but the implication was clear:

"The treasonable and disgraceful act of certain performers in delivering their brethren to the stage hands will receive our immediate attention. As for any actor who participates in this betrayal of his fellow actors, we will take immediate action against him and his kind."

The association's magazine accused certain people of "treason" too and demanded that they appear before Equity's council to answer the charges.

Equity was the governing body of all the theatrical unions. Sophie refused to appear—because, she said, she had no confidence in the body. She was backing to the hilt Ralph Whitehead, the Executive Secretary of AFA, who had been virtually accused of having his hands in the till.

Sophie was not mentioned by name in the Equity magazine either. It said: "It takes a somewhat bigger person to admit a mistake than it does to make a stand and maintain it in the face of right and reason. And the more generous and sincere such a person is, the harder it is to admit having been deluded and misled.

"But the issues now facing the actors of the entire entertainment world are too grave and the alternatives too serious for any such person to be allowed to stand on his dignity or to dignify his stand on personal grounds. That is why Equity has moved to institute disciplinary proceedings and why it must follow them to any lengths which may be necessary."

Sophie was placed on temporary suspension. It meant that she was banned from a theatrical appearance of any kind until she faced a hearing of Equity's (also known as the

Four A's—the Associated Actors and Artists of America) charges.

In particular, this meant that "Leave It To Me" which had closed for the summer, could not reopen.

The 4 A's were particularly angry when Sophie finally officially announced she would affiliate the AFA with the International Alliance of Theatrical Stage Employees—known as the "Stagehands' Union". She felt that it would bring all the benefits Equity had, in her eyes, failed to produce.

Sophie was philosophical about this: "From past performances, we are not in the least surprised at the vindictive attitude of the Four A's," she declared. "If, as reports have it, they have really suspended me from membership, I'm afraid they're letting themselves in for more than they bargained for.

"Our first consideration is the interests of our general membership and we are being extremely careful that no act on our part will result in putting the actor in the middle."

Allegations continued to fly and the fight became more and more bitter. But she said that nothing would change her or her attitude.

She was, however, particularly upset by a blistering attack from Ruth Richmond, Executive Secretary of Chorus Equity, who said that chorus girls everywhere would blame Sophie if the industry came to a halt because of the dispute.

This time, there were real tears in her eyes. "I love the chorus girls and wouldn't hurt them at all," she declared to waiting newsmen. "Put that in black type boys. Put that in black type."

The only person who seemed to benefit was George E. Browne, President of the Stagehand's Union, who personally issued Sophie with a charter and said he was anxious to "broaden our jurisdiction for the purposes of protecting our organisation so that all actors in this country will obtain the protection and improved working and living standards."

Battle was waged between Sophie and her Association on one side and that other daughter of Hartford, Connecticut, Katharine Hepburn. Miss Hepburn was now Chairman of the 4 A's, who were keeping "Leave It To Me" firmly closed. Kate, who was working in a Broadway play, was a little worried about the decision of the American Federation of Labour—the AFL—to arbitrate.

"Any attempt by the AFL to disregard the claims of Equity will be a breach of faith," she declared.

Sophie's answer was to say: "Don't worry. Sophie Tucker will always make a living."

James Cagney and Miriam Hopkins were already aligned with La Hepburn and a plane load of other stars were coming from Hollywood for what looked like another punch up. Franchot Tone, Olivia de Havilland, Wayne Morris, Edward Arnold and Mischa Auer were among them.

"I've been up against big billing before," said Sophie. "I'll simply have to give the best show of my life, I guess. Believe me, we vaudevillians were darn glad to have stagehands say a pleasant good-day and wish us luck before we went on. No one else ever did." And that was why she pressed ahead with her amalgamation plans.

The big fight opened in Atlantic City and Sophie went down for the count. The AFL withdrew its charter from the AFA and told Sophie and her members to break away from the Stagehands' Union.

The stagehands promptly talked about a strike that would paralyse the whole of show business, but in the end decided not to do so. As for Sophie, she joined a new union—the American Guild of Variety Artists—and the curtain finally went up on the reopened "Leave It To Me". The Sophie show went on.

Leave It To Me

"Leave It To Me" did well and Sophie did well with it. But the war with the unions was not over and was still having its repercussions.

Writs flew here and there—with Sophie being sued for libel by the Four A's, and Ralph Whitehead suing Four A's officials for what he also alleged to be defamation. In June 1940, however, as if to symbolise the new decade, both parties dropped their actions and promised peace and goodwill to man. Meanwhile, France was being swallowed by Germany and less than 18 months later Japan would attack Pearl Harbour.

Sophie herself had settled back into her role as America's favourite night club entertainer—and was making enough money at it to stop worrying about the parade passing her by in other directions. Just about this time, Noël Coward—the darling of an entirely different kind of night club crowd—found himself in trouble. He had billed Sophie as one of the principal acts at a benefit cabaret. The only thing was he had neglected to tell her about it. So in his own hand, he wrote:

"Dear Sophie, I want to explain something to you that may come to your attention which can be classed as an unfortunate mistake, but which I trust is not a very serious one.

"Jack Wilson is running a cabaret at the Allied ball tomorrow night in New York and as I was coming over, I agreed by cable with him to take on the job of being master of ceremonies. The other thing I said in the cable was that I was particularly anxious that you of all people should be asked to appear in the cabaret.

"He cabled back how delighted he was, but suggested that I ask you personally on arrival as he had only just met you and I knew you so much better.

"This, we agreed to arrange and your name was put down on a list of half a dozen artists including Bea Lillie, Gertrude Lawrence and others who agreed to appear. The programme went to press and your name appears there as being one of the artists. . . . When I arrived, I found that you had gone to Chicago and reluctantly abandoned the idea of my favourite entertainer being on the list."

It is safe to assume that neither Mr. Coward nor Sophie were heartbroken over the mistake, but it gives an interesting insight into the value she represented in cabaret circles.

A year later, in Hollywood, columnist Sydney Skolsky saw her and wrote: "Sophie Tucker wowed them at Ciro's on Sunday night. Her friends gave her a great ovation."

Noël Coward, had he been there, would probably have been among those friends. But he would hardly have bothered to join Sophie in the venture on which she embarked in the autumn of 1941. She agreed to star in—and jointly produce it with him—George Jessel's musical show, "High Kickers", which was a spoof on what was, in truth, really the spoof of all show business, burlesque—the "old burlecue" which Sophie had experienced at first hand all those years before.

If anyone had any reservations about the wisdom of this move, the fact that the ungainly Sophie Tucker was expected to do a striptease in the show should have confirmed those doubts. But do it, she did—or at least, she attempted to do it.

With another lady called Lois January, Sophie took private lessons in the art of garment removal—from strippers who were working for the Gaiety Burlesque show. The pair of them watched the strippers and the strippers watched them as they rather desperately tried to deceive the eye with

187

the quickness of the hand—the hands in question holding big ostrich fans which were supposed to hide the fact that Sophie, at least, was wearing something looking suspiciously like woollen long-john underwear beneath the feathers.

Their teacher was not particularly impressed. "You gals could never work at Minsky's," she told them—and decided that there were easier ways of making a living than working in this kind of education.

The show was the talking point of Broadway—but not because of the performance. Show biz gossip columnist Louis Sobel wrote: "So many people have a piece of George Jessel's forthcoming 'High Kickers' that when he was asked why he didn't dismiss an always-late showgirl, he said: 'I couldn't. She's a partner.' "

Mr. Sobel had also heard a thing or two about the striptease in the show. "This department fears the worst," he said. "Any day now, there will be an announcement that Greta Garbo or Norma Shearer is sacrificing her all from head to foot, above and underneath—for the sake of art."

When it came to the opening, Sophie herself decided to sacrifice whatever possible in the cause of publicity. She had dreams of glory, of celebrities lining up for the first night. One of these she believed might even now have the impact that he had had at the Kit Cat Club in London. But by return, came a telegram in reply to her offer of free seats: DUKE AND DUCHESS OF WINDSOR ARE VERY SORRY THEY CANNOT ATTEND OPENING OF HIGH KICKERS ON FRIDAY NIGHT AS THEY HAVE A PREVIOUS ENGAGEMENT.

Another telegram read: CHARLES AND PAT BOYER SEND LOVE AND BEST WISHES.

The book of the show was by Jessel himself, assisted by Bert Kalmar and Harry Ruby. When it opened for a pre-Broadway showing at Philadelphia, the *Inquirer* noted:

"Burlesque has an acute attack of nostalgia in George Jessel's 'High Kickers' at the Forest. But it survives with the sentiment and the soot included in the symptoms—and so do the audience. Sophie does her striptease and it is an appalling spectacle that would be cheesecake for any snooping surrealist. A timely attack of nostalgia saves the day and show when she sings 'Some of These Days'."

Considering all, the show had a fairly respectable run on Broadway, aided considerably by the fact that it was war-time and people were grabbing every opportunity that presented itself to escape from reality. And seeing Sophie do a striptease was that all right. The theatre management even thought it worthwhile organising two shows on Sunday.

That, of course, was just another publicity stunt—a good story to boost falling takings. What Jessel and Sophie thought would be funny—her striptease—turned out to be just grotesque.

But her audiences were still devoted to her. One evening in August 1941 she had gone to keep a date at Covington, Kentucky, suffering from a distinctly uncomfortable bout of laryngitis. "Man, tonight I wouldn't sing for the Pope," she declared. "I'll appear on stage, but I won't sing." By the time that a police motor cycle escort conducted her car into the Devou Park stadium, 32,000 people were waiting for her—joining in community singing until she arrived.

But once the crowd had got into the second chorus of "Some Of These Days", Sophie just could not avoid the temptation of joining in. "I can't disappoint these suckers," she said and sang along with them.

With the outbreak of war, Sophie immediately saw an opportunity to relive her undoubted glories of 1917-18. She would do everything for the Servicemen—and even in some misguided moment started sending them photographs of herself. How she imagined these would stand up to the competition offered by Betty Grable and Lana Turner isn't on record. But she announced she would go wherever the soldiers wanted her—and, if necessary, was ready to organise another smokes fund.

She also wanted to go abroad and help cheer the fighting men near the front line. But this was stopped before it got started. Abe Lastfogel, who in addition to running the Morris agency was now in charge of the USO—the United Services Organisation which was running the troop shows —told her to forget it. He was not so much concerned with her safety—although this was inevitably always a factor with entertainers, and Sophie couldn't run so well now that she was in her 50s—but her reputation.

"I don't want to take any chances, Soph," he told her. "Just in case in one of these camps, there may be some chaplain or other who would object to your songs. The men would love 'em. But I would hate to have the chaplain object to your material and force the government to cancel you. That would be a bitter blow and the papers would say the Government forced Sophie Tucker to cancel because they object to your material."

All Sophie could say was: "You're the boss", and agree.

As it was, Sophie was bitterly disappointed—as much as anything else, because she was being denied the most exciting audience then available in the world, an audience crying out to be entertained and the one that was giving new youth to all the big performers of her generation.

She did, however, make one long tour of camps in the States—with very careful attention paid to her material. And there was always a required visit to the nearest camp or military hospital whenever she did a civilian cabaret engagement. There was never any question that when she played in Chicago or Boston, she would go to a local army hospital too.

The fan mail continued to pour in as well. Including one, on notepaper embossed with the name "Corporal R. L. Greenspan, 36914301, United States Army".

It read: "Dear Aunt Soph. Yesterday I reached the ripe old age of 19. I'm getting to be an antique. Thanks for the candy, I must say it's the kishka's neck. Love Ronnie."

At that time, she was supplementing her cabaret income by playing in vaudeville theatres and cinemas. Ted Shapiro says of that time: "She never lost her touch or her drawing powers." A number of shows in which she performed were with Joe E. Lewis and Harry Richman. Later, she toured with Ted Lewis and George Jessel.

She did a number of recordings, too. Her special songs went very well, but we all make mistakes and Sophie's principal one at this time was to record pop songs of the age. They were not her, and the results were almost disastrous.

Sophie was as subject to the shortages and problems of

war as anyone else. On one trip from Los Angeles to Chicago—where she was to open at the Chez Paree night spot—the problem was a shortage of railway compartments.

She usually travelled with a maid in their own drawing room, while Ted Shapiro had a much smaller compartment. On this occasion, there was no reservation to be had. Sophie knew the President of the Union Pacific Railroad—but even he could not immediately help.

All the trains were taken by the Army, and a call from the prestigious Beverly Wilshire Hotel, where Sophie and her party were staying, asking for the usual accommodation, had no more effect than would one from a resident of the local YMCA. Finally, the President of the line called up to say: "If you wait in the lobby of your hotel, we'll try to get back to you in an hour."

It was now 4 o'clock on a Friday afternoon and the train was leaving for Chicago at 9. So Sophie, her maid, Ted and an assorted collection of suitcases sat in the lobby of the Beverly Wilshire watching the world go by. It was the cheapest way of seeing Sophie Tucker in a generation.

As they waited, an attractive blonde matron called Mrs. Rose struck up a conversation with Sophie. "I've got to get to Chicago," she said. "So have I," said Sophie. "Wait here, I'll get you on the train."

An hour later, the President of the railroad was true to his promise. He had managed to book two compartments for Sophie Tucker and companion. Fine—or, at least, it would have been fine had the attractive blonde, Mrs. Rose, not arrived on the scene. Ted says today that for a moment his mind began to boggle. "I had visions of this very attractive lady sharing one compartment with me and Sophie and her maid Emma sleeping in the other one." But Sophie had other ideas. "Emma, you and Mrs. Rose share one compartment. Teddy, you don't mind sleeping in the upper berth. . . .?" It was a question for which there was no answer. His ideas came to naught and another of those embarrassing nights was in front of him. He still regarded Sophie as a mother figure and she certainly had no compromising thoughts about him. But embarrassing . . . it was going to be that, all right.

191

Ted Shapiro, with more than 20 years working with Sophie behind him, ought to have known better. He should have thought a little and reasoned that nothing about Sophie Tucker could be predictable. He certainly could not have imagined the way this particular trip would work out.

They got into the train at about 6 o'clock, ample time in normal circumstances in which they could all get comfortable before the start of the journey three hours later. They had two nights and a day to look forward to.

As soon as their baggage was settled, their seats checked, and they had all decided they were as comfortable as the circumstances would allow, they stretched their legs and Sophie made a suggestion to her piano player: "Teddy, let's play some gin."

She fancied herself a master at the game—mistress would not have been a suitable title for Sophie Tucker in any circumstances—but experience should have taught her that Ted was better. The game began—and lasted all that first night. They stopped for breakfast—by which time, Sophie was doing better than Ted expected and was ahead.

They carried on again and stopped next at lunchtime. Then they played some more until dinner. The game went on and on, adjourning only for meals and for calls of nature, throughout the whole 60-hour journey.

When the train finally pulled into Chicago station, at 6 o'clock on Sunday evening, Shapiro was in the lead. In fact, as he says, "I was so ahead of her, it wasn't funny." But as the train chugged into the station, Sophie was on a triple blitz. Then as the engine and its coaches shuddered to a halt Ted called "Gin"—wiping out all the previous three games.

Sophie was livid. She looked at Ted, with—as he puts it—"real venom in her voice". "You're just dirty," she said. "What do you mean?" he asked—with an admittedly happy glint in his eyes. "You're just nasty and dirty," she replied. "You always go for gin!" Which of course was not a particularly unusual thing for a gin rummy player to do. As he told her she usually tried that herself. "Yes," she replied, "but when I go for gin, you always undercut me." Then, came the spite. She told him: "You're going to wait a long time for your money."

He did. She lost $400 on that trip and he waited a year to get it.

They had never really played for high stakes together, not since Sophie began losing fortunes at poker in her early days "with the boys". She and Ted started playing for a cent a point—but he won so consistently that in one evening's session he could come away with a promise of $100, for which he would always have to wait. One night, after losing another $100, she told him: "You're only going to get $10. I've decided we've only been playing for a tenth of a penny a point."

Sophie fought for every game as though it were a Broadway audience needing to warm up. But, says Ted, "she was not too good on her arithmetic. When she kept score, there were always a few mistakes." She played cards to pass away the time. It was the one way in which she could most comfortably feel occupied. She would also read—and her local bookseller had a standing order to send her all the latest best-sellers. She enjoyed reading— she even more enjoyed talking about what she had read. She hoped it would impress her friends.

As the war drew to its close, Sophie was completing her own first excursion into the world of literature—the highly imaginative, ghosted autobiography "Some Of These Days". She had been working on it since returning from Hollywood at the end of her MGM contract—often doing the best work at 3 o'clock in the morning in her hotel rooms. An accomplished writer was given the task of assembling Sophie's scribbles on headed hotel notepaper and inter-viewing the people who could best fill the gaps in the Tucker memory. The trouble was, Sophie was not all that helpful in supplying these names. She told her to see her brothers Moe and Phil, her sister Annie and a woman in Philadelphia to whom Sophie over the years had sent her cast-off clothes. Anyone who might say an unkind word about her was forbidden territory. Ted Shapiro, for one, was not inter-viewed—although he had said he would be happy to do so if Sophie wished it.

The position of Sophie's brothers at the time was a strange one—as indeed was the continuing situation of Bert and Lil, who would send her birthday, Mother's Day, Christmas and Jewish New Year cards all of which would find their way into her scrapbooks, but get seemingly little in return.

Often, Moe and Phil would be treated as mere servants. Phil would act the business manager and offer advice, to which she always listened. Then she would tell him brusquely: "Oh, you don't know what you're talking about—just shut up."

Phil did not like the idea of Sophie spending a lot of money. He would say: "Why spend so much on a suite, surely a nice bedroom would be enough?" Sometimes, she would agree, sometimes she would decide that since the suite was her home and she had plenty of money, she had every right to enjoy it. On one occasion, he tried to persuade her to get rid of Ted because he said he was too expensive. That suggestion received one of her more choice responses.

If you wanted to get on the right side of Sophie, you flattered her. If you didn't, she would tell *you* how good she was—or how nice she looked. "Isn't my hair lovely?" was a typical question to a visitor who had been slow in making the observation herself. She was known to say: "You know, I have the clearest and softest skin of anyone I've ever met." And she had. She always kept her hair immaculate and her gowns were superb. She was not necessarily quite so fussy about her personal habits. When Ted Shapiro's wife Susie called to see Sophie at her Park Avenue apartment one day she was shocked to see newspapers on the floor. As she bent to pick them up, she noticed that Sophie had been spitting on them.

The war brought out the toughness in Sophie's character. She worked in Hollywood again—making a couple of potboiling pictures that were really filmed vaudeville shows—made more stage and cinema appearances on the West Coast and toured the camps and hospitals in the area. She worked because she did not know any other way to spend her time.

If there were charities that wanted her help, she was only too willing to oblige. For years, she had been a pillar of the Jewish Theatrical League. In 1945, she was also made an honorary member of the Catholic Actors Guild, after having made a contribution of $5,713 to their welfare fund.

The Jewish Theatrical League had its own Actors Temple. On Yom Kippur, the rabbi would make his appeal for charity from the pulpit and give the performers top billing in response to their donations. When he got to Sophie who had just offered $1,000 he would announce: "Sophie Tucker, our darling Sophie, now appearing at . . . Sophela, where are you playing this week, darling . . . the Palace? Good . . . Sophie Tucker $2,000." He always got his money.

Her charity work never meant her neglecting her own nest egg. When she and her pianist didn't go by train, Ted would often drive Sophie from one engagement to the next. They were at Bingham, New York, in mid winter, with Sophie slumped in the front seat next to Ted, a fur coat over her ears, as they stopped at a set of traffic lights. A little gruff voice made itself heard from within the mountain of fur. "I own that," said Sophie in barely discernible tones. "Own what?" asked Ted. "That." She pointed to an impressive building, one of a portfolio of valuable pieces of real estate that she had been gradually acquiring.

This ever-growing collection of business investments was largely the result of yet another piece of advice from "the boss" William Morris. "Buy dirt, Soph," he had told her. "You'll never lose your money if you buy dirt." When she played a town and saw a tempting investment in the shape of a building she would take it and pay off the bill every week.

By those late war years, she also had a cinema in the Bronx and a chunk of stock in the 20th Century Film Corporation. She owned, too, a large shareholding in a sewing machine company. Years later, Ted asked her: "How much are you worth? I've heard you have $10 million and even $20 million." All she would tell him was: "Well, maybe."

I'm Nobody's Fool

The year 1945 was doubly notable for Sophie. It saw the end of World War Two and the publication of "Some Of These Days". Whatever concessions it may have made to her own deliberately faulty memory, the book undoubtedly helped a great many people—every penny she might have made in royalties went to charity.

Night after night in draughty theatre lobbies and in the overheated foyers of hotels, she would sit, sweat mounting droplets on her forehead, selling books and then autographing them. She would do it after matinées and at the end of gruelling early morning floor shows. The value of publicity was still an important consideration but now it was all aimed at her one consuming desire: to sell books that would raise money for other people.

If she heard she had lost 10 or 15 customers who might have bought books but couldn't breast their way through the crowds, it seemed to be a tragedy as big as if she had just heard a vaudeville booking had been cancelled. Her friends would tell her sometimes: "What difference if you don't go out there in the cold tonight and sell a few books?" The reply would always be the same: "I've got to go." It became almost an obsession.

The Morris agency would look after the financial arrangements. They would count the money collected, book it into their ledgers and then arrange to distribute it to one of the causes Sophie had specified.

In 1948, Sophie came back to her most loyal audience of all—in London. It was a London still creaking under the strain of post-war austerity with some foods still rationed. Sophie, as keen as ever to embroider her facts to the point of unrecognisability, pointed to a pile of food she had brought over with her on the Queen Elizabeth and said they were American steaks.

Since no one in England had seen a decent piece of meat for nine years, the reporters were prepared to take her word—without worrying too much about how the steaks could survive the week-long journey and the taking in and out of practically non-existent deep freezes.

If she didn't bring meat with her to London, she certainly brought a lot of other foodstuffs—and as usual the necessary staple of any American visitor's diet at the time, coffee. Ted Shapiro had various groceries shipped over for himself too, as a result of which his rented house at Chester Mews—it belonged to R. A. Butler, later Tory Deputy Prime Minister—was a popular venue every night for his friends.

Sophie was in town for two reasons—to star at the Casino Theatre and to sell the British edition of "Some Of These Days".

She arrived with 28 dresses, 20 new songs and 182 lb. of weight. "And I'm as tough as ever," she told reporters. "What's the secret? Doing what the doctor tells you. I've cut out smoking and drinking. All I have left is gin rummy—they can't take that away from me."

When she booked into the Savoy Hotel, there was a letter awaiting her from Queen Elizabeth (now the Queen Mother) welcoming back the woman she had first known as the "Jazz Queen".

That, at least, was the story that Sophie put out. In actual fact—and in fairness it only partly diminishes the impact of the tale—Sophie had written to Buckingham Palace informing the Queen of her impending trip to London. A message was indeed waiting for her at the Savoy—one that said: "Her Majesty expresses her gratitude for her attention being called to the presence in this country of Miss Sophie Tucker whom Her Majesty well remembers meeting and conveys Her Majesty's greetings and her best wishes for a happy and successful visit to this country."

By return, Sophie sent the Queen a copy of her book with others addressed to the King, Queen Mary, Princess Elizabeth (now the queen) and to Princess Margaret. They were delivered to Buckingham Palace by special messenger.

British proceeds of her book—it had already raised $245,000 for American charities—were going to the Save The Children Fund. Because of that, and partly because he was an old fan, the Lord Mayor of London, Sir Frederick Wells, gave a civic reception at the Mansion House in her honour—something that had almost never happened before for a show business figure, let alone an American entertainer.

As she was waiting outside the Mansion House for a cab—the Lord Mayor had not thought of sending a car for her—the driver of a No. 6 bus called out: "Hi-ya Soph—where do you want to go?" She told him the Savoy. "Hop in," he said. "We pass the door." She did hop in—for her first ever ride on London Transport.

If nothing else, the world in 1948 taught her to worry slightly about the value of money—and the sense, or possibly lack of it, of investing in insurance. Ever since her mother had drained Mr. Abuza's trouser pockets and put ten cents of her ill-gotten gains into an insurance policy fund, Sophie had been following her example. In more recent years, she had inserted an accident clause in the policy and her ten cents a week had increased to an annual figure that now amounted to thousands of dollars.

Just before she was due to leave for London, she had fallen over and broken a bone in a foot. "Aha," she said to Annie, "this is where they pay out." The claim form went off to the insurance company and the firm sent a representative to meet her. "Yes," he agreed, "we'll pay out—at $30 a week."

"How much?" Sophie almost exploded. "I get $3,000 a week and that's what I'm going to miss by not showing up, so you'd better send me that."

198

But, as they usually do, the insurance company won. It seems that in all the years that Sophie had been increasing her premiums she had ignored one little detail. She had forgotten to alter the name of her profession on the policy. In 1948, and approaching half a century as a top-line entertainer, she was still classified as a "bartender or waitress". And the most that "bartenders or waitresses" could expect to get when they had accidents, the insurance company ruled, was $30 a week.

She rightly decided that she should invest her money elsewhere.

In 1948, one of those investments was an hotel in Miami Beach—the Robert E. Lee for which she paid $55,000. And in this case, it seemed that her heart had finally softened. She announced that it was a 15th wedding anniversary present for Bert and Lil. Bert, she declared, would be the man in charge. What she did not reveal was the extent to which she would be watching the books.

While in London—a city that had recently been taken by storm by Danny Kaye—she went to the cinema and in the lobby was surrounded by a crowd of admiring youngsters, none of whom could ever have seen her live or really known any of her primitive films. Said the *Evening Standard's* "Londoner's Diary", "That's fame—and that's personality."

She had to content herself with the love of her audiences —and of her profession. In London, the theatrical order, the Lady Ratlings, made her their Dame Ratling. To anyone with literary pretensions, the honour accorded her by Foyle's, the big London bookshop, was just as welcome. They gave one of their celebrated luncheons to mark the publication of "Some Of These Days".

The lunch became a typical opportunity for a typical Sophie performance. Of course, there was a piano on hand and, of course, she sang "Some Of These Days".

It was as good a way as any of plugging the book's title. C. B. Cochran, the top impresario who acted as toastmaster for the afternoon, seemed to enjoy the commercial immensely.

London, Sophie declared, had not changed. Neither had the taste of the Lord Chamberlain, the State-appointed censor of all theatrical performances. In those days, every script had to be submitted to the Lord Chamberlain's office, and that went for every song sheet, too. He took one look at the music planned for Sophie's Casino performances and decided that changes were indeed necessary. She was planning to be too risqué by half—although Sophie herself had declared that any dirty jokes were in the mind of the listener, or words to that effect. "If you see anything naughty in them, that's your fault," she said.

But one day, impresario Bernard Delfont, her agent Harry Foster and her old journalist friend Hannen Swaffer sat down with her to tone down the material.

"Inhibition Poppa" had Delfont's eyes "popping out of his head", said Swaffer. Sophie had to agree to make enough changes to totally emasculate the number—if that is not too inappropriate a phrase—and finally to abandon it. "In America, any woman goes to a psychiatrist," she said, as if making the first trickle in what was soon to become a flood in that direction. "People talk openly of repressions and sex complexes. But I know I can't sing that here."

Also out were "Love Is My One Bad Habit" and "Vitamins, Hormones and Pills". But she managed to get by with "Never Let The Same Dog Bite You Twice" and "I'm Having More Fun Since I'm 50"—which came as many years after her half-century as "Life Begins At 40" had followed her fourth decade. She was now admitting to 60.

The risqué songs still gave a totally inaccurate impression of Sophie's attitude to sex jokes. If people told her a dirty story, she would—just as she had years before—either tell them to keep quiet or ostentatiously vanish. She had a similar attitude to drunks. If when signing books, customers would swamp her with alcoholic fumes, she would get up and walk away. She did, however, occasionally play "drunk" herself for the sake of keeping a party going, slurring her words with the best of them. But when an important telephone call came or there was some other urgent message for her, she could immediately become as sober as a judge.

The Casino audience responded to her perfectly. The emotion got to her, too. She sang a number about being glad

200

to be back in London—and forgot the words. "Let's start again," she said—and the people out front gave her a huge round of applause. She sang "My Yiddisher Mama" and the proverbial pin drop turned into a stampede of shouts and applause from a frenzied mob of devoted slaves.

In the *Daily Mail*, Cecil Wilson reported: "She came back larger, louder and more loveable than ever, and won the reception her artistry deserved, leaving the audience hoarse with cheering, herself in tears and the stage looking like the Chelsea Flower Show."

In the more staid *Daily Telegraph*, the reviewer wrote: "As always, Miss Tucker displayed the strongest of personalities, the most individual of techniques. And few artists, it must be admitted, could have held an audience spellbound as she did with a lengthy song in Yiddish.

"The microphone was used though I suppose to diminish, rather than amplify those famous stentorian tones."

The *Sunday Times* noted: "She can make a song like 'Don't Let The Same Dog Bite You Twice' sound as honest and as healthy as if it really were about animals and not about men."

She repeated her American practice of autographing books in the Casino foyer after each show. One night, there was a familiar face in the queue of people milling around her—Lady Edwina Mountbatten. Sophie asked why she was waiting in line. "It's good enough for the others, and it's good enough for me," she replied.

In London, she did her required number of charity performances—including one for 200 children from the Jewish orphanage at Norwood. Later, she sang for the crippled ex-Servicemen at their home at Roehampton.

Her trip was so successful that she phoned the Morris agency in New York and asked them to try to cancel her American plans for early August. She wanted to do a tour of the provinces after impresario Harold Fielding had made her an offer of £10,000.

At the Houses of Parliament she was entertained by MPs—including Mrs. Leah Manning, the weighty Member for Epping who was known as the Sophie Tucker of

201

Westminster. "You stick to politics", the real Sophie told her. "I'll stick to parlour tricks."

She had supper with ballet star Anton Dolin—who complained that he was running out of a certain staple necessity, "I use two or three pairs of tights at every performance and I wash them myself," he said. Sophie presented the dancer with a bar of soap to take home with him.

There had been talk of her provincial tour being of the Moss Empire theatre chain—which also controlled the London Palladium. But it never happened. They were so upset that she had worked at the rival Casino that the tour was cancelled.

The party circuit was a pale imitation of its pre-war self, but one was held in her honour at the Albany Club and she sang there—with help from Hoagy Carmichael and Bud Flanagan.

There was something about this Sophie Tucker that made her different from the entertainer she had been previously. In her early days she was craving stardom. Her prayer: "Please let me be a headliner", had been among the most sincere ever offered to heaven and it had been answered with bonuses. Now, there was no need for it any more. She was still tops in her field, but she no longer tried to go beyond that.

Her friend and contemporary Al Jolson was in the midst of the most sensational comeback of all time and had been voted America's top vocalist but Sophie couldn't aim in that direction. She was fortunate, however, to be still recognised as the tops in cabaret—even though the kids who now bought Jolson records by the million would no more dream of buying a Tucker disc than one by, say, John McCormack.

But cabaret was a whole different ballgame. In November 1948, *Variety* could report that her first week at New York's Latin Quarter night spot grossed $51,000—$5,000 more than her stint there the previous year.

Early in 1949, Sophie made a very unusual opening— for her at least. Perhaps bitten by the literary bug that struck with the success of "Some Of These Days", she decided it was time to pay her very first visit to the New York Public

202

Library—and, while there, hand them her entire collection of some 2,000 scrapbooks. She would go on collecting everything that arrived with her name on it—newspaper clippings and Christmas cards—and sticking each of them into her scrapbooks, but as one book was finished, so it would now be sent off to the library. It had first asked her about doing this back in 1944, but it had taken five years to get her to make up her mind and finally agree.

It was a day of long and rather boring speeches—by the director of the library, the deputy director and the heads of all the departments.

Sophie looked the most bored of all. When it came to her turn to hand over the books—there were so many of them they had to be delivered in a convoy of small vans—all she could say was: "Here are the books—kid." Then she explained her desire to stay up to date. "I'm wearing bobby sox—because I don't want anyone to call me an old timer." But she did add: "Yep I'm laughing, but really I'm sad." She was parting with part of her life—in a way, the most important part. Almost everything she had done before had been aimed at finding a place in one of those books.

A few days later she went down to Miami Beach to celebrate what she said was her 62nd birthday with Bert and Lil at the Robert E. Lee. The town's then big show business community turned out in strength—Joe E. Lewis, Dean Martin and Jerry Lewis, Bill "Bojangles" Robinson, Frances Langford and Harry Richman among them. The Mayor of the town was there, too.

Sophie, later that week, opened a four-week cabaret spot at the Beach—but not at the Robert E. Lee. She worked at the rival Beachcomber. Perhaps that was the writing on the wall for Bert and his business venture. When she realised that the hotel was not making any money, she sold it and Bert looked for another job.

There were people who said that Sophie's mean streak showed itself in public, too—although that was very rare. It was not so rare, however, for her to find herself in trouble with her trade union. It happened again in November 1949 when the American Guild of Variety Artists put her on "trial" and fined her $100 for "soliciting performers" to give

203

free performances at her opening night at Ciro's nightclub. It was something she had been doing all her professional life—getting the celebrities who turned up to see her to sing for their suppers; most of them loved the chance of showing how talented they were, but for once the union stepped in and said: "No".

She still loved her associations with the big stars. When Al Jolson returned from entertaining the troops in Korea in 1950 two weeks before his death, she sent a "welcome home" bouquet to his wife Erle. When Erle replied with a visiting card, the card went in her scrapbook. Then Sophie sent *her* a note—thanking her for thanking Sophie for sending the flowers. It was still the best way she knew of keeping friends.

Yet when she sang a song called "How Do We Old Gals Do It?" it was still a question worth asking—and few did know what drove this incredible and now elderly woman. No one could guess how much she still craved affection, yet found it so difficult to return.

As the years went on, the risqué material grew more questionable, and although people like George Burns still said she had a gift for joking about her age—while former stars like Blossom Seeley pretended that the years had forgotten how to go by—some questioned the taste of her singing "You'd better make it legal, Mr. Segal".

There was still no doubt that she was a phenomenon. In October 1950, the Hollywood *Reporter* noted: "Sophie Tucker is absolutely murdering them at Latin Quarter in Manhattan where she opened a few nights ago and celebrated her 45th year in show biz."

Talk was she was going into television—but the Morris agency vetoed any idea of her settling for the $10,000 she had been offered by one of the networks. A reporter who saw her at the Latin Quarter pleaded with Sophie to go on to the small screen. "You can't Tucker out, Tucker," he wrote. On stage, she talked, wiped more tears from her eyes and thanked Ted Shapiro for making her career possible for her.

It was a notable year. For the first time, she visited Israel, calling at the kibbutzim that were not merely an experiment in living, but the lifeblood of the then two-year-old country. "I'll be fulfilling one of my longfelt ambitions," she said before flying off to the country with Ted. "I've always been a Zionist. I guess my mother's zeal for the Holy Land was instilled in me."

When she first saw the sun shining on the sprouting towns of settlements, she burst into tears.

Back home, she was elected a life member of the Friars Club—with lots of jokes from the other Friars about the cheques they had received made out to Al Lackey which had been endorsed over in payment for gambling debts.

One fellow Friar apologised for not being there—Belle Baker, another "big talent" performer of Sophie's generation who had never had her international reputation. For years, there was talk of a feud between them, but Sophie always denied it.

Big portions of her money still went on her clothes. For her Latin Quarter opening in 1951, she spent $25,000 on a new wardrobe. "Now instead of calling me Red Hot Mama, they will call me Hot Rod Soph," she joked. But she was quite serious when she added: "Of course, I'm still vain and of course, I still knock myself out. I'm still a fuss about my work. I've been a performer for a lot of years."

Finally, she made her TV debut—with Jimmy Durante, in a show called the "All Star Revue". She said afterwards: "I knew everybody was looking at me. There's nothing like that feeling."

She got the same feeling when she went back to Britain in 1952. She weighed in at 16 stone—and with an offer to make a film in the country for £30,000. The offer was turned down with thanks. She really had decided now to stick to her own brand of show biz. But her performance at the London Palladium was broadcast on radio by the BBC and most of the listeners still thought she was exciting.

She came over on the Queen Elizabeth. "It still needs a big boat to carry me," she joked and explained how proud she was of her newest acquisition, a chain of clothing stores all over the States called "From Tots to Teens".

But London was still the place that showed her its heart most warmly. When the first-night curtain came down at the Palladium, she said she had just received the biggest ovation in 49 years' entertaining. "Their applause just dried me up with emotion," she said.

The *Daily Mail's* Cecil Wilson reported: "She rode the stage like a blonde and pink battleship studded with diamonds. She played on the house like an orchestra. She could command tears with a sigh, laughter with a wink. . . . She is, in short, a tremendous artist and that applies to more than mere girth."

Perhaps the *Daily Herald* summed it up: "American stars who come over here can, after all, be divided into two classes—Sophie Tucker and others."

While in town she doubled at the Bagatelle restuarant. Variety recorded "Soph's socko opening" there.

As for "Soph" herself, she was still offering homilies of advice, still trying to make the best of the calendar. "Life," she declared, "begins at 60."

When They Get Too Wild For Everyone Else

The coming of the 1950s had an intriguing effect on the position of Sophie Tucker, entertainer. Suddenly, she was not just a brash professional or even—in her own field—a super star. She was an elder stateswoman. Younger entertainers would come to her for advice—and as she frequently admitted herself, she could be brutal.

She would generalise about the new generation of performers—some of whom today are now easing themselves into the respectable establishment role that she occupied then—and be ruthless. "The kids in show business lack something we all had—the combination of humility and push . . . the feeling of humbleness and the push to do the things that have to be done, to learn by hard, hard grinding work the things that get you up on top and keep you there. But if you go out and ask 100 of those kids what Aunt Sophie is talking about, only one of 'em will know."

That one was a girl Sophie had met at Miami Beach, a youngster she had described as a "Scarlet O'Hara type". The girl had asked Sophie to see her new stage show and since the young lady's father owned the hotel where Miss Tucker worked, she agreed. The girl's name was outside the theatre in letters that were five feet high and a press agent had gone to work on her.

The girl's name was Janis Paige. Sophie told her she

didn't approve of the build up. "I worked hard, terribly hard, for years and years before I saw my name up in lights. I fought my way up from the 10-cent theatres to the 25-cent theatres, to the 50-cent theatres and finally to the top. But my name never got put up in lights by any press agent. The public put Tucker up there."

She was even more brutal when she talked about the girl's act. "Your gowns are ugly, your beauty is hidden under layers of awful make-up. How do you people dare to appear before the public with so little? Where do you get that much nerve?"

A year later, Janis Paige bumped into Sophie again—at her dressmaker's, where the latest $1,500 Tucker creation was being fitted. "Aunt Sophie," she said, "I understand what you meant in Miami. I've started over again and I'm going to work and work until I make it the right way."

Sophie was particularly impressed by Janis's decision to leave her husband back in Florida while she went on the road. "Taking your husband along with you on the road is no good," said the old-timer. "You got no time for worries when you're working." That at least had been a lesson well-learned.

Her worries, if she gave much thought to them, were still centred around Bert and Lil who lived in their small apartment, while Sophie had installed herself in luxury in Park Avenue. She had finally decided not to live out of suitcases and took to the flat all the accumulated treasures and junk that she had collected over nearly 50 years of travelling from one hotel to the next and had kept in storage. The scrapbooks may have been in the New York public library, but her address book—now with some 5,000 names in it—stayed with her. Every one of those 5,000 people always received a Christmas card from her.

She insisted that she knew them all personally and could remember how she met each one. Like Lou Goldblatt of Riverside Drive—"took me to the Embassy Club for dinner in 1948"; Mrs. I. Phillips of 891 Park Avenue, "sent me a contribution for the Sophie Tucker playground at Surfern, New York. . . ."

When Ted Shapiro married his wife Susie, Sophie took

charge of her bridal outfit. She insisted that she had to have the best handbag and the best shoes to go with the ensemble even though Susie hesitated about spending the money. Sophie met the bill.

A little later on, Susie agreed to help Sophie out of a problem. She bought dozens of high-quality sweaters which Sophie wanted to send off as presents. They were delivered to Park Avenue—but each of the packages looked distinctly squashed. Sophie was furious. She rang through to Ted and gave him a piece of her so angry mind. When Susie came on the phone, she proceeded to shout and rave in the vilest terms. Mrs. Shapiro told her firstly that she was sorry they had arrived that way and secondly not to take it out on Ted. Sophie continued to rant and finally put the phone down —while Susie demanded an apology. Apologising was the most difficult thing Sophie could be asked to do. Days later, however, she did so in as roundabout a way as she knew.

She was happiest in her role as adviser to the young, and if she was wrong, she neither wanted anyone to know about it or to admit it herself. As far as she was concerned, grey hairs had to be removed by tweezers, schoolgirl complexions were contained in tubes in the bathroom and you remained young by stopping at 39—"for 40 years". As to the stars of the future, she could see only one—Judy Garland.

Sophie nurtured a dream about Judy—the girl she had first seen on the set of "Broadway Melody". She wanted her to play the main part in a film to be called the Sophie Tucker Story. When that failed to get off the ground, she gave her full-hearted support to Betty Hutton taking the role and for a long time, the idea was talked about and almost reached contract stage. The main stumbling block was that Betty —then a big star with a reputation for making a production number out of a request for a cup of coffee —wanted her husband to direct the picture and no studio would agree.

All the time the project was being mooted, she studied Sophie at work, had meeting after meeting with her and posed for lots of newspaper pictures.

Sophie also went to see Betty at work—at the Curran in

San Francisco. It was not an auspicious start to their relationship. The place was half empty and those people who had paid to go were only lukewarm. Betty asked Sophie what she thought of her performance. "Not much," she told her. "You can't take this flop. You show it in your work. It isn't right. It isn't right sloughing off your audience. Why didn't you accept the applause you got?"

She was fortunate to get another chance—at the Sands in Las Vegas. This time she was tremendous. As an observer said at the time, "she out-Tuckered Tucker". Abe Lastfogel told Sophie: "You made a great star out of Betty Hutton. Everything you said sank in."

As Sophie said around about this time: "All youngsters today know is: 'Give me a break'. All right—so I answer their letters all the same way. I tell them: 'We troupers when we started out, never asked anybody for help. We found our breaks for ourselves. Our school of touring was hustle for yourselves.'"

Sophie was also working in San Francisco when Betty Hutton was at the Curran. She was playing at the swank Fairmont Hotel's Venetian Room.

On one of the city's top radio programmes a commentator said: "I don't know how many times I have seen a singer step into the spotlight in the Venetian Room, resplendent in the latest hairdo and fashionable gown, raise her arms in welcome and then attempt to charm her audience with her songs. But I do know this—I saw and heard the best of them last night. . . . Yes, Sophie Tucker, the last of the red hot mamas is back in town and next to her, the rest of them pale away to nothingness."

Dwight Newton wrote in the San Francisco *Examiner*: "Sophie Tucker's patter routines at the Fairmont are not for television. Blue? Phew. But when she sings the old songs, she's the most exciting personality since Jolson left us."

Indeed, it was this comparison with Jolson that struck home with Sophie—and which made her more determined that ever to get her filmed life story off the ground. "The Jolson Story" had been so sensational that there was a sequel called "Jolson Sings Again" and even a third picture was talked about; only his death put a stop to that.

To her, the idea of a film represented not only the best chance of publicity in a generation, but also a memorial. "It won't be a sugar-coated fable," she insisted. "I want an honest story that tells everything about me."

But it was not to be. She had to content herself with those amazing cabaret critiques. As the *Examiner* reported ecstatically: "She sings the familiar voice to a hushed audience. And then the roof falls in as she hits the chorus line—'Summm of theez daaze—you're gonnna miss me honeeee!' The greatest. Amen!"

In San Francisco she took up again with a woman who had first got on to her Christmas card list 40 years before —on an early vaudeville tour—the Chinese-American doctor, Margaret Chung, who was known by all the locals as "Mom Chung". "My doctors insist I work only two hours a day and keep regular hours," said "Mom". "But they's be crazy if they think I can keep regular hours with Sophie Tucker in town." So she moved into Sophie's suite at the Fairmont.

Sophie herself was limiting her working hours now for the first time in 60 years. "I've slowed down completely. I can only do 35 weeks of shows now—20 years ago, I could do 40 or 45 weeks. I'm a tired child."

In one show, Ted called to her: "Don't you think you've reached the stage where you should act your age?" She answered him with a new Jack Yellen song: "How Can I Grow Old When My Boy Friends Are Keeping Me Young?"

She still refused to apologise for her songs. "They're educational. They have a message—'make him say please and make him say thanks'. I don't try at any time to be offensive. The women take the hint, too. After the show they tell me, they're going to make their husbands say 'please'. One of my husbands—my second, I think—said I was the most unsophisticated sophisticated girl in show business."

Ed Sullivan ranked her as "the greatest of our femme pop singers ever to appear on any stage".

The tributes were coming in all the time.

The Mayor of San Francisco, Elmer E. Robinson, presented her with a gold-seal commendation, saying that "San Francisco, a high-spirited warm-hearted city, hails and

211

salutes Sophie Tucker, a high-spirited and warm-hearted lady who is America's first lady of show business. For 50 years, Sophie Tucker's radiant personality has won her a special place in the affections of the American people. May she enjoy many more years of bringing happiness to others; may that happiness return to her 100-fold and may she always feel, wherever she may be, that San Francisco is truly her home."

A similar citation came from Mayor Vincent R. Impelliteri in New York—to mark her 50th anniversary in show business. But the big event of the year was a dinner at the Waldorf Astoria in October 1953 to commemorate that golden jubilee. It was sponsored by the Jewish Theatrical League and the big guns of show business came out to fire off salvoes in her honour. Said Sophie herself: "It's a funny thing but I can't think of anything but my golden jubilee. It just keeps click, click, clicking through my head . . . jubilee . . . jubilee . . . jubilee. . . . I'm older than hell, but I've never felt better." She composed a poem for the occasion:

> "Success, is it really fame and gold?
> You won't know the answer till you're old
> And look down the road where the years have fled
> Then up the little stretch that lies ahead. . . .
> Not with gold and with glory will my trunk be packed
> When the Big Booker Up Yonder closes my act
> All I'll take with me then will be the souvenirs
> Of the real gold in my golden 59 years."

In the end, some 1,500 guests paid a total of nearly $70,000 to pay her homage at the dinner. Sophie herself turned up in a 24-carat gold gown and a $9,000 white mink. Her jewels were priceless.

At another luncheon organised by the Friars, Frank Sinatra, Milton Berle and George Jessel were on the platform.

The jubilee was recognised as an important event in show biz history. Mercury Records brought out an album called "Sophie Tucker—50 Glorious Years". It was another excuse for Sophie to sit out in hotel lobbies and give the proceeds to charity. She sent one copy each to President

Eisenhower and the Queen—both of which were accepted with thanks.

Sophie took to recording remarkably easily—considering that a live audience was so important to her. In the early years, she would interject her typical comments to Ted at the piano. For instance, "He's Tall Dark and Handsome" began with the words "Teddy, I'm so excited and I'm just as nervous as I can be" to which he replied, on disc, "Well so many things keep happening to you, who'd be surprised?" Later on, she would spend the boring moments waiting for the orchestrations to be organised and the engineers to be quite ready like the old lady she was—calmly doing her knitting. And perhaps mentally clocking up the cash she was going to be able to give to her good causes.

As always, it was the charities nearest home that were the most important to her. The San Francisco Chapter of Hadassah—the American women's Zionist organisation —declared her an "Imma, a mother of Israel" in response to a generous donation. And as the years went on, her associations with Israel grew closer.

She established Sophie Tucker youth centres in the country and seeing them gave her a lump in her throat the like of which she had not experienced since the first time the name Sophie Tucker went up in lights.

She loved seeing the smart Israeli soldiers—who in her honour exhibited as much spit and polish as probably at any time in the state's existence; spick and span are not usually the adjectives accorded to this force. As soon as she saw the guard of honour laid on for her visit she did what she could do best—burst into tears.

From the Dan Hotel in Tel Aviv, Sophie and her faithful Ted at her side were driven on the first evening of Passover to a secret destination—with the blinds of the VIP car tightly drawn. She was not allowed to know where she was heading. It turned out to be an Army camp where a military seder service—the ceremonial enacted since the time the Children of Israel were released from bondage in Egypt—was about to start. Chief Rabbi Isaac Herzog was there to conduct the prayers and General Moshe Dayan was sitting at the top table next to the then Minister of Labour,

Golda Meir. Near the end of the ceremonial, the Chief Rabbi and a group of religious soldiers began dancing— enjoying all the levity that the requisite four glasses of wine drunk during the evening allowed. Dr. Herzog was finding it very difficult to keep his yamalkah on his head.

Sophie and Golda sat and talked, reminiscing like two Yiddisher Mamas—both of whom were later to consider how much more time they should have spent with their children—about Milwaukee in the days when the Israeli cabinet minister lived there. After the service, Sophie entertained—singing one chorus of "Yiddisher Mama" after the other.

Back in America, she continued to philosophise: "From birth to 18 a girl needs good parents. From 18 to 35, she needs good looks. From 35 to 55, good personality. From 55 on, she needs good cash. I'm saving my money."

For a time, it looked as though the "Big Booker Up Yonder" was finally going to close the Tucker act. In Winnipeg in 1955 she caught flu, was taken to hospital and for two weeks was reported to be gravely ill. But she pulled through and announced she was going to make yet another world tour.

In 1957, London papers were reporting that she "still has punch"—and she went on to prove it with a tour of the country.

Of her opening at the Café de Paris, the *Evening Standard's* respected critic Milton Shulman said: "Sophie Tucker manipulates her 70-odd years as if they were a set of questionable statistics . . . a bubbling mound of pastel pink and sequins, she attacks her audience like a bulldozer gone berserk. Her pudgy arms beat the air, her raucous voice pins your ears back and her body quivers like a minor earth quake."

That minor earthquake had just played herself in the Frank Sinatra film "The Joker's Wild"—the story of Joe E. Lewis—and had also played a dramatic role in the CBS Radio Workshop series.

"Youngsters today," she said, "head for the bar and get drunk. They haven't learned to like to be around people. When I finish my act, I'm out front saying hello to

214

everybody, greeting them all, letting them know I love them."

In London, she was showing her favourite audience —the fast-diminishing Jewish population of the East End—how much she still loved them.

She went to the place known as the "Yiddisher pub" and ate blintzes and drank beer there, while everyone cheered and called "le chaim". At Blooms' kosher restaurant, she ate lockshen soup, salt beef and latkes—and said how much it reminded her of Abuzas' place. The restaurant sent a constant stream of salt beef sandwiches to her hotel and was so thrilled at having her with them that her face appeared on the front of their brochures for the next five years. She nudged her sister Annie, "You know when people stop remembering me, I don't think I shall want to live any longer."

She doubled at the Dominion Theatre—and that was my own introduction to the live Sophie, so very different from anything else on a stage and still so magnetic.

Sophie had begun to mellow over the years. During this Dominion tour, a young comedian, desperate to make a name for himself, was on just before the first-half curtain. He was given 14 minutes to do his stuff—anything over that would have to come off of the star's time, Sophie's time.

On this occasion, the youngster did 22 minutes. He came off stage into the wings and into a huge row with the management. Cyril Berlin, the Fosters agency man in charge of booking the entire show, was livid. When he saw Sophie, he didn't know how to apologise enough—after all, it meant that the great star's own carefully planned routine would have to be trimmed by eight minutes.

All she said was: "I don't mind—the responsibility is yours. You tell that boy . . . but don't tell him from me. I'm not paying him. Tell him if it ever happens again. . . ." Berlin says today: "She understood that this was his big opportunity and doubtless thought, 'there but for the grace of God. . . .' She could see the reason for it. There was no mercy there because she warned what would happen if he did it again, but there was understanding."

Of all the big American acts who came to London

Sophie was one of the easiest to "service". She rarely queried amounts on bills presented to her; never demanded hospitality—the many friends she had in London were always around to make her feel at home.

Off stage as she waited to go on for a performance, she was plainly strung up. Once the curtain had gone up on her, it was as though she were simply having a meal. In a way, she was. She couldn't have lived without the sound of the audience clapping and cheering.

As usual, the pièce de résistance was left till last—"Yiddisher Mama". Over the years she had learned she couldn't sing it at any other spot on the bill—"otherwise it would kill me".

While in London, she sang at the annual reunion of the 14th army, the British troops who had fought in the Burma Campaign. There were no more than a handful of Jewish veterans in the crowd, yet when she called for requests, it was "Yiddisher Mama" that bellowed out loudest from the centre of the Royal Albert Hall.

She would talk about London incessantly, even back in the United States. Once in New York she was having dinner with Jimmy Durante and extolling the wonders of a British audience. "You know, Soph," said Durante, "Maybe I'd like to play in London again." "Good," said Sophie, "I'll talk to Val Parnell at the Palladium and get you a wonderful bill booked."

"The Schnozzel" was visibly excited. "I'll go in November," he said. "You'll do no such thing," she countered. Londoners don't like going to the theatre in November when it's cold and foggy. Go in the spring." Once more Sophie the generous performer offering the very best advice to a respected colleague.

Back in the States she played Las Vegas again and ended up in the company of an ice pack. She bumped into a piano while doing her act at El Rancho and a small blood clot formed in her leg. "It's just hardening of the arteries," she explained. "You can't stop in this business—or you are through." She was not going to admit that she was through, although her legs were beginning to plague her and the extreme weight which she still persisted in joking about was

216

causing more and more problems. She still went to the Actors Temple for the High Holyday services but walking up the stairs to the ladies gallery became more of a chore each year.

Deep down, she would have liked more than anything to see the Sophie Tucker Story go into production. Someone joked, "She ought to make the Betty Hutton Story herself."

When in London, Variety Club Tent 25 presented her with a gold heart award at a lunch in her honour. She promised them that film or no film she would send them a three-figure cheque for the organisation's boys' club every month for the rest of her life. By that time, she estimated, she had given $2,500,000 to charity.

In May 1959, she scored another sensation at the London Palladium and appeared on TV, too, "knocking the pop singers for six", said the *Daily Express*. She was making more and more money yet she was now beginning to count the dollars as well as the years—and now there was more sadness creeping into her life than she had known for a long time. Her brother Phil had died and her sister Annie followed him. Annie died as they spent Yom Kippur together, fasting as usual. It was a bitter blow, so bitter, in fact, that she cancelled her next engagement and refused to rehearse.

Her experiences with television were not of the happiest either. "The trouble with TV," she said, "is that it gives too much for nothing. You can't give the people too much for nothing. It makes them disrespectful to the artist, makes everybody a critic."

What inspired that comment was that in California, a 10 year-old kid had gone up to Sophie and told her she had seen her on the screen in the Jerry Lewis programme. "How was I?" she asked. "You stank," said the girl.

With Your Life, You Can Do What You Will

Sophie began the 1960s with a new motto: "Retire—that's a dirty word". And she did all she could to prove it—even though her double chin sagged and wobbled as she spoke, her legs became more and more tired and her voice was just a loud foghorn.

I interviewed Sophie on her visit to London in 1962. When she told the young porter at the reception desk of her hotel to send me up, he replied: "Yes, sir."

The years did not stop her being outrageous. In New York in November 1960, she turned up for a cabaret engagement wearing tight sequinned pants and a 10-gallon hat.

When she appeared at the London Palladium in 1962 for the Royal Variety Performance, she was more restrained. She described the ovation she received that night as the greatest of her career. "I've worked 50 years for this—and I reckon I've earned this night," she said. The Queen told her: "I was thrilled by your performance", and Prince Philip added: "You were wonderful." Bernard Delfont said: "Sophie made this show. I've never heard anyone get a reception like that on this kind of occasion before." She was in London to appear at the Talk of the Town night-spot—after which she said she was off to Cape Canaveral to train with the spacemen! "The only trouble is I don't think

218

they've got a rocket powerful enough to lift me off the ground."

In the end, she confined her training to watching other contemporaries at work. She and Maurice Chevalier appeared together on the Ed Sullivan TV show, performing the "I Remember It Well" number from "Gigi". Chevalier would walk to his hotel from Sophie's Park Avenue apartment—as much to reminisce about the past with Ted Shapiro who accompanied him on the journey as to plan the future.

Chevalier was to tell me of her: "She was always so good, a little bit fat, but very attractive. She had that wonderful connection with an audience. . . ."

It was probably this idolising of Sophie by her fellow entertainers that kept her going—even though Paul McCartney referred to her as "that great American group". Her feelings about the Beatles are not on record.

On and off, people were still talking about a film of Sophie's life, but although that didn't come to fruition, a Broadway show called "Sophie" which was based on her early life opened in May 1962. It starred a brash youngster called Libi Steiger. Alas for Miss Steiger—and for the memorial the real Sophie craved—the show was a disaster.

She really worried about her weight now and went on a whole succession of diets—but nothing would take off the pounds. She loved late snacks but then suddenly tried to cut them out and eat nothing but greens and salads. When she was on one of those "kicks", it was up to Ted Shapiro, faithful as ever, to see that the food was always there—and to make sure that she ate it. "Many times," Ted recalls, "she'd say 'Oh, I can't eat this grass' and I'd have to coax her into eating it."

To her public she had to appear to be nothing but the same old Soph, yet in 1963, even she couldn't avoid being pushed into an airplane on a wheelchair. "Just feeling a bit tired," she explained.

In many ways, she was like a child. She would spend hours combing the hair of Susie and Ted Shapiro's children, showering on them the sort of affection she had always denied Bert. Somehow she was like a grandmother to them—free of the responsibilities and conscience of parenthood.

In 1965 Sophie was back in London for yet another important show—a memorial concert for Jack Hylton the impresario. During the trip, Ted bought a Wedgwood figure of a bird of which he was very proud. He showed it to Sophie, who immediately went into a sulk.

Ted was so perturbed by this that he asked her maid why she was acting so strange. "Don't you know?" she asked. "She wanted that bird. She really felt that you ought to give it to her." Shapiro did—and Sophie's sulk ended. If he or anyone else had cause to phone Sophie and thank her for some act of generosity she would usually put the telephone down on them in the middle of the call. She could accept thanks no more gracefully than she could ever apologise. She was always afraid that the people who fawned over her so lavishly were the rest of the time talking about her behind her back.

The critics were still talking about her kindly—both to her face and behind her back.

She was still very much in harness. In October 1965, she opened for yet another season at the New York Latin Quarter. But she was on stage for only two minutes when she complained of feeling nauseous and, as gently as she could, apologised and hobbled towards her dressing room. It was the first time in her entire career that she had done that. Her doctor suggested that she rest for at least two days, but the next night she insisted on going back to work.

The doctor had said he was sure it was just a stomach upset. "You're as strong as an ox," he said—and she really thought she was.

A few nights later, she insisted on appearing at a benefit concert organised at the Latin Quarter by Ted Lewis. She went on—and again she felt sick and had to leave the stage only minutes after starting her act. The song was, "With Your Life You Can Do What You Will". She completed the song, but her doctor took one look at the pallor of her cheeks and insisted she go to hospital.

Ted Lewis told the audience: "She'll be back."

The next day, X-rays were taken and the worst was

known. Sophie Tucker had terminal lung cancer. Years of very heavy smoking had taken their toll. No one told her the truth. Doctors said it was intestinal flu, but she was confined to a wheelchair and the pounds started dripping away from her as she went from one X-ray and cobalt treatment to the next.

Ted Shapiro went to see her. "Tell you what, Teddy" she said. "I'm going to be here in the hospital for a while and I'll have to rest before I go back to work. Instead of hanging round here, go home to Miami and your family. As soon as I get better I'll call you and we can start again."

The call never came. In January, she celebrated her 79th birthday, sitting in a wheelchair. The huge hulk that had been Sophie Tucker had wasted into a little wizened old lady. She was home again on Park Avenue, being looked after by a nurse.

In February 1966, Sophie Tucker called out: "Where's Teddy, my son?" In a sad sort of way it was the stamp of approval on the piano player who always regarded Sophie as a mother figure. But he was not there to hear her. Immediately after these last words Sophie went into a coma.

Shortly afterwards, on February 10, she died. The curtain had finally come down on the woman who always said: "I've got to carry on. I'm the last of the red hot mamas."

The obituaries proved one thing: she was still a headliner.